The Cost of Doing Politics

Using quantitative and qualitative evidence, Sumner shows how consumer boycotts can work to dissuade companies from donating money to politicians, but may also encourage companies to attempt influence by largely invisible means. Boycotts do not work as many people expect – by threatening sales. Instead, Sumner shows how boycotts are less a statement of consumer behaviour than a way for people to signal their political inclinations, and they primarily hurt companies by tarnishing their reputation. Political influence is about building relationships, which means that companies have many more options for influence than just PAC contributions and formal lobbying. With these options available, companies can decide how to influence politics when they need to, and the tarnish of boycotts to a company's image can push some businesses to pursue options that are less noticeable to the public.

Jane L. Sumner is an Assistant Professor of Political Science at the University of Minnesota, Twin Cities. Her research has been published in the *Journal of Politics, Political Analysis, Political Science Research and Methods*, amongst other publications.

Business and Public Policy

Series Editor

ASEEM PRAKASH, University of Washington

Series Board

Sarah Brooks, Ohio State University
David Coen, University College London
Nathan Jensen, University of Texas, Austin
Christophe Knill, Ludwig-Maximilians-University, Munich
David Konisky, Indiana University
David Levi Faur, Hebrew University, Jerusalem
Layna Mosley, University of North Carolina, Chapel Hill
Abraham Newman, Georgetown University
Leonard Seabrooke, Copenhagen Business School
Mike Vandenberg, Vanderbilt University
Edward Walker, University of California, Los Angeles
Henry Yeung, Singapore National University

This series aims to play a pioneering role in shaping the emerging field of business and public policy. *Business and Public Policy* focuses on two central questions. First, how does public policy influence business strategy, operations, organization, and governance, and with what consequences for both business and society? Second, how do businesses themselves influence policy institutions, policy processes, and other policy actors and with what outcomes?

Other books in the series

KATHRYN HOCHSTETLER *Political Economies of Energy Transition: Wind and Solar Power in Brazil and South Africa*
PAASHA MAHDAVI *Power Grab: Political Survival Through Extractive Resource Nationalization*
STEFAN RENCKENS *Private Governance and Public Authority: Regulating Sustainability in a Global Economy*
SARAH BAUERLE DANZMAN *Merging Interests: When Domestic Firms Shape FDI Policy*
LILIANA B. ANDONOVA *Governance Entrepreneurs: International Organizations and the Rise of Global Public-Private Partnerships*
NATHAN M. JENSEN AND EDMUND J. MALESKY *Incentives to Pander: How Politicians Use Corporate Welfare for Political Gain*
RICHARD W. CARNEY *Authoritarian Capitalism Sovereign Wealth Funds and State-Owned Enterprises in East Asia and Beyond*
TIMOTHY WERNER *Public Forces and Private Politics in American Big Business*

(continued after index)

The Cost of Doing Politics

How Partisanship and Public Opinion Shape Corporate Influence

JANE L. SUMNER
University of Minnesota

Shaftesbury Road, Cambridge CB2 8EA, United Kingdom

One Liberty Plaza, 20th Floor, New York, NY 10006, USA

477 Williamstown Road, Port Melbourne, VIC 3207, Australia

314–321, 3rd Floor, Plot 3, Splendor Forum, Jasola District Centre, New Delhi – 110025, India

103 Penang Road, #05–06/07, Visioncrest Commercial, Singapore 238467

Cambridge University Press is part of Cambridge University Press & Assessment, a department of the University of Cambridge.

We share the University's mission to contribute to society through the pursuit of education, learning and research at the highest international levels of excellence.

www.cambridge.org
Information on this title: www.cambridge.org/9781009124584

DOI: 10.1017/9781009128568

© Jane L. Sumner 2022

This publication is in copyright. Subject to statutory exception and to the provisions of relevant collective licensing agreements, no reproduction of any part may take place without the written permission of Cambridge University Press & Assessment.

First published 2022
First paperback edition 2024

A catalogue record for this publication is available from the British Library

ISBN   978-1-009-12325-9   Hardback
ISBN   978-1-009-12458-4   Paperback

Cambridge University Press & Assessment has no responsibility for the persistence or accuracy of URLs for external or third-party internet websites referred to in this publication and does not guarantee that any content on such websites is, or will remain, accurate or appropriate.

This book is dedicated to the memory of my grandmother, Sandra Lawrence. She would not have accepted it any other way.

Contents

List of Figures	*page* x
List of Tables	xi
Acknowledgements	xiii

1	Introduction	1
	1.1 Introduction	1
	1.2 What We Know About Political Influence	3
	1.3 Who Seeks Political Influence and Does It Matter?	9
	1.4 Political Influence Is Everywhere	12
	1.5 Contributions	16
	1.6 A Note on Terminology	17
	1.7 Overview of Book	18
2	Where Does Political Influence Come From?	22
	2.1 Introduction	22
	2.2 Why Companies Seek to Influence Politics At All	25
	2.3 The Nature of Political Influence	31
	2.4 Common Problems and Solutions	38
	2.4.1 Information Problems	38
	2.4.2 Financial Problems	41
	2.4.3 Performance Problems	44
	2.5 Conclusion	49
3	How Does Public Opinion Shape Corporate Political Advocacy?	51
	3.1 Introduction	51
	3.2 How to Use Voice	53
	3.2.1 Evading Activist Attention	74
	3.2.1.1 Hidden Advocacy	75
	3.2.1.2 Distanced Advocacy	77
	3.2.2 Defusing the Public Response	79

viii   *Contents*

	3.2.2.1 Creative Advocacy		79
	3.2.2.2 Careful Advocacy		81
3.3	Conclusion		82

4   Why Does the Public Care About Corporate Political
    Influence?   84
    4.1 Introduction   84
    4.2 The Claim   86
    4.3 Why and How It Might Be Wrong   90
    4.4 Sources of Evidence   93
         4.4.1 Evidence from Survey   93
         4.4.2 Evidence from Social Media   94
    4.5 Why Do People Respond Negatively to Corporate
         Advocacy?   96
         4.5.1 Test A: Reaction to Real-Life Information   98
         4.5.2 Test B: Reaction to Fictional Situations   111
    4.6 Are Boycott Tweets Political Signaling?   118
         4.6.1 Do People Share Political Boycott Tweets
                More Frequently?   120
         4.6.2 Does the Language of Boycott Tweets
                Suggest Partisan Signaling?   123
    4.7 Conclusion   128

5   Why Do Companies Care About Public Opinion?   130
    5.1 Introduction   130
    5.2 The Claim   132
    5.3 Why and How It Might Be Wrong   135
    5.4 Sources of Evidence   137
         5.4.1 Evidence from 10-Ks   137
         5.4.2 Evidence from Interviews   139
    5.5 Which Companies Fear Public Backlash?   141
    5.6 Do Companies Connect Political Advocacy with
         Public Backlash?   154
    5.7 Conclusion   159

6   Do Companies Try to Avoid Public Backlash?   162
    6.1 Introduction   162
    6.2 The Claim   163
    6.3 Why and How This Might Be Wrong   167
    6.4 Sources of Evidence   169

	6.4.1 Evidence from Federal Lobbying and Campaign Contributions	170
	6.4.2 Evidence from Interviews	172
6.5	Are Some Companies Less Likely to Lobby in Their Own Name?	173
6.6	What Do Companies Do to Influence Politics?	182
	6.6.1 Evading Attention	184
	6.6.1.1 Hidden Advocacy	184
	6.6.1.2 Distanced Advocacy	185
	6.6.2 Defusing the Public Response	188
6.7	Conclusion	190
7	So What and Now What? Summaries and Concluding Thoughts	192
7.1	Summary of Book	192
7.2	Big Takeaways	196
7.3	Areas for Future Research	202
Appendix A: Interview Methods		206
Appendix B: Chapter 4 Study Methodology and Full Results		211
Appendix C: Chapter 5 Robustness Checks		224
Appendix D: Chapter 6 Robustness Checks		227
References		230
Index		238

Figures

3.1	The causal chain that links a company's political advocacy efforts with damage to its reputation	*page* 55
4.1	Approval of Walmart PAC's political donation	99
4.2	Approval of Walmart PAC's political donation by recipient	100
4.3	Approval of Walmart PAC's political donation by recipient and partisanship of survey-taker	103
4.4	Reported change in Walmart shopping frequency as a result of knowing about political donation, broken down by treatment	105
4.5	Reported changes in Walmart shopping behavior in response to the PAC information, broken down by treatment, party, and survey-taker's Walmart shopping frequency	108
5.1	The percentage of 10-Ks in each year citing as a concern sales/revenue, reputation/brand, social media, protest, and boycott	148
6.1	The percent of companies in the sample that filed at least one federal lobbying report in each year between 1999 and 2020	175
6.2	The percent of companies in the sample that donated at least once through a PAC to a candidate for federal office in their own name for every election year between 2004 and 2020	176
6.3	Participating in lobbying or campaign contributions by company size, 2018	178
6.4	Participating in lobbying or campaign contributions by gender of top manager, 2018	180

x

Tables

4.1	Results of ordered logistic regressions predicting a survey-taker's approval of Walmart on a five-point scale	*page* 101
4.2	Results of an ordered logistic model predicting professed changes in consumer behavior by party	107
4.3	Results of an ordered logistic model predicting professed changes in consumer behavior by shopping frequency	110
4.4	Results of ordered logistic regressions predicting respondent approval based on company's actions	114
4.5	Results of ordered logistic regressions predicting respondent approval based on company's actions among people who support the policy	116
4.6	Results of ordered logistic regressions predicting respondent approval based on company's actions among members of party that supports the policy	117
4.7	Regression results predicting retweets as a function of partisan tweet content	122
4.8	The results of a logistic regression predicting the presence of common insult words (idiot, stupid, dumb, and imbecile) as a function of partisanship	127
5.1	Top five industries in the data and representative companies from that industry	143
5.2	Results of a logistic regression predicting each of the three sets of terms – boycott, social media, and reputation/brand damage – in the 10-Ks as a function of company attributes plus sector random effects	150
5.3	Logistic regression that models having at least one sentence linking social media with brand or reputation damage. Model contains sectoral random effects	153

6.1	Logistic regressions predicting filing at least one lobbying report or donating to at least one campaign through a PAC in the company name in 2018	183
B1	Full results of ordered logistic regressions predicting a survey-taker's approval of Walmart on a five-point scale	214
B2	Full results of an ordered logistic model predicting professed changes in consumer behavior by party	216
B3	Full results of an ordered logistic model predicting professed changes in consumer behavior by shopping frequency	218
B4	Full results of models predicting the effect of a company's actions on respondent approval	219
B5	Full results of models predicting the effect of a company's actions on respondent approval among people who support the policy	221
B6	Full results of model predicting the effect of a company's actions on respondent approval among people in party that opposes policy	222
C1	Logistic regressions predicting the occurrence of topics in the 10-Ks as a function of company attributes. Omitted category for operating revenue is 0–10th percentile	225
D1	Logistic regressions predicting lobbying or contributions through PACs as a function of company size	228
D2	Logistic regressions predicting lobbying or contributions through PACs as a function of company size and CEO gender	229

Acknowledgements

I always enjoy reading the acknowledgements section of books because of the glimpse they provide into the journey of the book itself. Although this book has only one author, there are many people without whom it never could have been written. As such, I could write an acknowledgments section that might double the length of this book. Since I don't want to make this book much longer, I will attempt to be brief, so please know this list is not exhaustive.

First, no one outside my immediate family has listened to me and provided as much reassurance throughout this process as Emma Claire Foley, Emily Farris, and Ellen Key. Emma Claire has been listening to me agonize over every aspect of this book daily since before it even really existed. Emily and Ellen have been tireless cheerleaders, keeping my spirits up and believing in me when I did not believe in myself. All three have patiently talked me through difficult times with this book, during times when it's very possible I would have just short-circuited and given up. I'm sorry. Thank you. I can't wait to tell you all about my ideas for my next book.

Jennifer Gandhi was my dissertation adviser and is still my friend. I would have dropped out of grad school had it not been for her. Jen taught me most of what I know about thinking through difficult problems and being careful and thoughtful in my research. She has given me so much time, attention, and detailed feedback, and she's who I try to be as I make my way through academia. This book could not have happened without her training, support, and mentorship.

I would never have gone to grad school at all – let alone completed it – without the mentorship and encouragement of Andrew Kerner, Leanne Powner, Hans Noel, Jenna Bednar, Rob Franzese, and John Jackson. Andrew deserves particular mention for graciously giving me more time, energy, and attention than I warranted at that time, and, perhaps unintentionally, making me believe I had a future when I did

xiii

xiv *Acknowledgements*

not believe I did. Leanne Powner responded to a pivotal sobbing phone call my third year of college and provided guidance that shaped the rest of my career. Thank you all for providing support and mentorship to a directionless, underperforming undergrad.

Josef Woldense is better than anyone I have ever met at seeing the big picture. More than once he helped me see the forest when I couldn't stop scrutinizing the patterns on the tree bark. Mirya Holman is just plainly a gift to humanity and academia and I'm glad to know her. She's given me more advice, feedback, accountability, and opportunities than I can even begin to list or process. Mirya and Tiffany Barnes both were instrumental in helping me figure how to even write a book in the first place. Tiffany very patiently talked me through several aspects of writing and publishing a book on several occasions. Mark Bell was always my go-to person for logistical questions about writing a book. He saved me countless hours of googling to figure out how to, for instance, make my citations actually show up. You should read all their books too.

In my time at the University of Minnesota, I've benefited enormously from very supportive colleagues. Nisha Fazal and Helen Kinsella have been extremely supportive mentors, always checking in on me, answering all my questions, and providing endless support. Paul Goren, Chris Federico, Joe Soss, James Hollyer, David Samuels, Andy Karch, Cosette Creamer, Tim Johnson, Nancy Luxon, Kathryn Pearson, Amy O'Connor, and Gurneeta Vasudeva Singh have all, at various points in this process, provided comments, advice, feedback, or support that made this book possible.

We also have an outstanding staff in the political science department, who do all the hard work that makes the department function. Without Alexis Cuttance, Lydia Bolder, Jessie Eastman, Kyle Edwards, Kersten Falvey, Sara Flannery, Becky Mooney, and Carrie Vorpahl, nothing at all would work and this book would not have happened. Tia Phan, apart from just generally being delightful, made all the arrangements for my book conference, and then handled all the week- and day-of drama when all the flights and arrangements were thrown into question due to a snowstorm.

On a related note, I thank Nate Jensen, Sonal Pandya, and Rachel Wellhausen for braving Minnesota in February, dealing with the delayed and canceled flights due to the snow storm, and giving their time and energy to helping reorient and refocus the first full draft of

Acknowledgements   xv

the book. John Freeman did not have to deal with the canceled flights, but he was instrumental in not only providing detailed feedback but also serving to synthesize and organize all the feedback and help plan on next steps. Carly Potz-Nielsen sat through the entire book conference and took detailed notes so that I did not have to. The book in front of you is very different from the one you all provided feedback on, and that is largely due to the people who helped out at the book conference, so thank you all.

I have cultivated a large and wonderful professional network, who have all provided help in various ways throughout this process. In particular, I'd like to thank Sarah Bauerle Danzman, Rebecca Kreitzer, Melanee Thomas, Amanda Bittner, Grace Deason, Julia Azari, Erin Tolley, Erin Heidt-Forsythe, Erin Cassese, Jennie Sweet-Cushman, Melody Crowder-Meyer, Jamil Scott, Ray Block, Monica Schneider, Grace Deason, and, I'm sure, countless others I will kick myself for accidentally omitting. Whether through reading drafts, providing professional advice, or just listening when I needed some to listen, you've all been outstandingly helpful.

I've worked with many brilliant and wonderful students at UMN. If this book sometimes reads like I'm trying to teach research design, it's because that's how I spend most of my time. Writing instructions and explanations, and answering questions, for my undergrads shaped how I wrote this book, and I'm grateful for them and for that. I've also worked with an amazing group of undergraduate research assistants while working on this book. You may not all see your fingerprints here, but even if not, you helped me with foundational elements. Sometimes (many times) you helped me figure out I was wrong and made me change course. Thank you to Amari Bauer, Dasom Ham, Lydia McComas, Mahima Gupta, Sheradyn Romo, Savannah Wery, and Zi Xue.

Between the time I started writing this book and when I submitted the manuscript, I had two babies. All my gratitude goes to Dr. Rebecca Petersen, Brittany White, Angie Reed, Byrd Shuler, all the doctors and nurses in Labor and Delivery at HCMC, and everyone at the Women's Health and Pediatrics clinics at Hennepin County Medical Center, for getting me and the kids through two pregnancies, one rough delivery, and all the issues that pop up with infants and young children. Along similar lines, I'd like to thank Camille Carlson for helping untangle my brain. Everyone should be lucky enough to be in therapy, especially if they're writing a book.

For similar reasons, this book literally could not have been written without the amazing teachers, directors, and staff at my kids' daycare. Without them, I wouldn't have had the time or the peace of mind of knowing my kids were in such capable and caring hands that enabled me to write this book. Thank you for giving such outstanding care to my children.

I also owe a big thank you to Kathleen Eischeid, my high school creative writing teacher, whose voice I periodically heard in my head when I was writing this. I've tried to retain the voice she helped me develop. I leave it to the reader to decide whether that's a good thing.

Solcana Fitness in Minneapolis has been fundamental to my physical and mental health while working on this book. Thanks to Hannah Wydeven, Morgen Larsen, KK Korbitz, Jerik Hendrickson, Garrett Hoffman, Garrett Ferderber, Jeff Lockhart, and other coaches and fellow athletes for helping me get strong without getting injured and giving me a break and physical outlet while I otherwise existed purely in my own head. I am pretty sure that taking an hour break most weekdays to lift heavy things was a crucial component to getting this all done.

I also want to thank a handful of my friends who've really been enormously helpful during this process: Lynzie Johnson, for always telling me my writing needs more sharks and ninjas; Ariel Trangle, Shira Rosenberg, and Zach Zeid for checking in on me regularly; Corinna Turbes for listening, reading, and letting me bounce ideas off her; Justin Esarey for being Justin Esarey; and Bethany Morrison, Rebecca Hartsough, and Ryan Tans for getting me through grad school.

Thank you to my parents, Peggie and Daniel Lawrence, and my sister, Stephanie Erickson, for always being there and never asking me how the book was going.

My husband, Ed, is the best person I have ever known. Thank you for being.

And finally, thank you to my kids, Lawrence and Cassandra, who have given me perspective, love, and many hours awake in the middle of the night to think.

1 | Introduction

1.1 Introduction

Mary got an email calling her a c*nt.

She got off easy. There were a few other emails calling her names, and a couple of people who delivered their curses in person. Maybe a few people stopped coming in. She engaged some others in productive conversation. There weren't organized boycotts or protests. Her business didn't suffer.

Weighing in on political matters – "doing politics" – can be costly for companies. Mary[1], who owned a restaurant in Minneapolis, says it's just in her personality to stand up against something she thinks is wrong. Minneapolis' proposed minimum wage increase, which would have gradually increased the hourly wage of the lowest-paid worker for private companies to $15, was one of those things. It ignored a lot of nuances, she thought, that weren't immediately obvious to people who were not in her position. It didn't take into account that her employees got health insurance, for instance. Buoyed by the strength of her convictions, she publicly took a stance against the minimum wage bill.

Even though I'm neither using her real name nor naming her business, people who follow Twin Cities politics might be able to guess who Mary is anyway, because Mary may be the only representative of a company who publicly opposed the minimum wage increase.

In part this is because the policies were fairly popular, as municipal minimum wage increases tend to be in large, progressive cities, especially in recent years. Minimum wage increases are often viewed by their supporters as a moral issue, framed around the problems faced by low-wage laborers, citing the difficulty these workers have with affording an apartment or supporting a family. Yet the minimum

---

[1] Not her real name.

wage is also an economic issue, and one which poses problems for companies. Minimum wage increases hurt companies by increasing their labor costs.

The consequences of minimum wage increases don't hurt all companies uniformly. Some companies rely more heavily on low-wage labor than others. These companies are spread across industries and economic activity, but one thing that unifies many of them is their thin profit margins. In other words, they don't sell their product or service for much more money than it costs to make it. To make any profit at all, they try to keep the production costs low. Restaurants like Mary's are a good example: the food they sell is inexpensive, so if they don't keep their costs low – by buying ingredients in bulk, for instance, or not paying high wages – there's no point in operating because they'd be losing money. Yet this problem isn't limited to restaurants. Although the majority of workers who make the federal minimum wage (or less) are employed in the leisure and hospitality industries, mostly in restaurants and other food service jobs, almost all industries employ people who are paid at or below the minimum wage (U.S. Bureau of Labor Statistics 2019).

Yet, despite this, Mary was still one of the very few company representatives who voiced concerns about the minimum wage laws. According to a journalist who covered both cities' efforts, by the time St. Paul began considering their own minimum wage ordinance, the organizers of the opposition couldn't come up with any business owners for them to talk to at all.

Why?

It certainly wasn't that they didn't care or that they necessarily supported the ordinances. Minimum wage is a policy of considerable importance to a great many companies. And indeed, carve outs were discussed to accommodate some of these industries. There was discussion, for instance, about exempting franchises of large companies on the grounds that they are more like small companies. There were heated discussions about how to treat tipped workers. Yet many companies were still facing significant cost increases. Instead of speaking out, many individual companies chose to work through industry groups or through the Chamber of Commerce.

But again, why?

A lobbyist I spoke with about this told me that working together is more efficient and that, as she put it, companies don't like it being about them if it's not about them. She meant that they prefer to pool

1.2 *What We Know About Political Influence* 3

resources and present a united opposition. This puts the focus firmly on the policies and their consequences for business more broadly. Standing up individually against a policy instead places the focus on the characteristics of individual businesses. But there is another truth in her words. Companies don't want it to be about them because, when the conversation is about them, there can be consequences. Standing up for themselves can hurt their business because people increasingly mobilize against companies whose political actions they don't like. Mary's business didn't suffer any consequences for her political actions, but it could have, and most companies are more risk-averse than Mary.

In this book, I ask the question of how public opinion – how the fear of a public backlash – shapes how companies engage in politics. If people call for a boycott against companies who take political stances they oppose, a hallmark of so-called "cancel culture,"[2] does this change how companies behave? In this book, I argue that it does, and specifically that negative public opinion shapes how companies engage in the political system. The core argument I make is that these organized boycotts, especially those that catch fire on social media, mostly function to hurt companies by dragging their reputations through the mud and harming their brands. Yet these boycotts do not actually stop companies from doing politics. Why? Because they don't address the core issue. Companies try to influence policy because policies affect them and, like anyone, they try to agitate against policies that hurt them and for policies that help them. Fear of public backlash doesn't stop those policies from being threats to businesses, and so fear of backlash doesn't stop the influence-seeking. What it does, instead, is change its shape. I argue that fear of public backlash prompts companies to approach their political advocacy strategically, taking steps to either hide it from public view or make it more palatable to a discerning political audience.

1.2 What We Know About Political Influence

To answer the question of how political influence changes in response to public opinion requires understanding the underpinnings of political influence – how does it work and where does it come from?

---

[2] See Bromwich, Jonah Engel. "Everyone is Canceled." June 28, 2018. New York Times. www.nytimes.com/2018/06/28/style/is-it-canceled.html.

4   *Introduction*

Research on political influence has primarily focused on two strategies: lobbying and campaign donations. Both of these are thought to be very powerful ways that interest groups of all stripes recruit and retain politicians to support their policies. Yet there is some intellectual and public disagreement about exactly how and why these two methods work.

According to de Figueiredo and Richter (2014), lobbying is a "transfer of information in private meetings and venues between interest groups and politicians, their staffs, and agents." Lobbyists – agents who are paid by interest groups to lobby on their behalf – cultivate personal and professional connections with politicians and their staffs and then use these connections, in addition to expert knowledge, to advocate on behalf of their clients (Bertrand, Bombardini, and Trebbi 2014). Campaign contributions, similarly, are another common tool of political influence-seeking in the United States. Companies, their political action committees (PACs), and their owners can all donate money to candidates for political office, political parties, and issue organizations (Powell and Grimmer 2016). Within the literature, lobbying and campaign contributions – sometimes lumped together, sometimes considered separately – have been variously viewed as functioning as a form of exchange, as a method of persuasion, and, as Hall and Deardorff (2006) term it, "a legislative subsidy."

Influence-seeking as a form of exchange seems to fit best with how the general public understands both lobbying and campaign contributions, as a quid pro quo (or, more colloquially, as a form of vote-buying or bribery). The core idea is that lobbyists or other agents acting on behalf of interest groups trade something of value that they have – money, information, promises – for something that the legislator has, such as a vote or access. This way of conceiving of influence more generally is often the basis for the distaste many people feel for influence-seeking, because it seems so unfair. If this story is accurate, votes (or access) should often just accrue to whatever interest group (or person) has the most money – effectively setting up a plutocracy, or rule by the rich – and that person or entity is seldom going to be the average citizen.[3]

---

[3] This understanding also tends to conflate lobbying and campaign contributions. Lobbying, in some circumstances, does not, and in fact cannot, involve the exchange of money or goods. A state government lobbyist I spoke to pushed

1.2 What We Know About Political Influence

The problem with the theory of influence-seeking as a form of exchange is that it doesn't really make sense theoretically and there is very little evidence to support it. Theoretically, the exchange theory suffers from a fatal commitment problem. That is, when a politician accepts a campaign contribution, there is nothing committing the politician to take the company's side. If politicians vote the "wrong" way, the company has no recourse except to not support them in the future. For example, in the months leading up to the congressional vote on the 2010 Affordable Care Act, health insurance companies, which opposed the bill, donated $44,595,421 to congresspeople, about 56 percent of which went to Republicans and 44 percent to Democrats.[4] Even so, the bill ended up passing. The companies that donated the money couldn't do anything to the politicians who received their money and voted for the bill anyway. Several studies have aimed to resolve this problem, arguing variously that contributors can give what amounts to a deposit before the vote and a reward afterward (Stratmann 1998, p. 88) or that long-term reputational concerns keep the politician from breaking their "promise" (Snyder 1992, p. 18).

In addition to its theoretical problems, there is also little evidence to support the exchange theory. In other words, it simply can't make sense of many of the patterns we observe between lobbying/campaign contributions and voting patterns or patterns of access to lawmakers. For instance, there is ample evidence that interest groups most often target their lobbying resources toward those who already agree with them and are likely to vote the "right way" anyway. According to the theory of exchange, this would be a poor use of resources – why target your ideological allies instead of buying off people at the margins or on the opposing side? Why "buy" politicians who don't need to be "bought"? Further, as Hall and Deardorff (2006) point out, this theory cannot really explain why some groups, such as certain nonprofits and think tanks (such as the Cato Institute or the Heritage Foundation), manage to obtain access and influence far in

---

back against the popular perception that they were just buying gifts for politicians – "I can't even buy anyone a cup of coffee," they said.

[4] "Insurance: Top Contributors to Federal Candidates, Parties, and Outside Groups: 2010." Open Secrets. www.opensecrets.org/industries/contrib.php?ind=F09&Bkdn=DemRep&cycle=2010.

excess of the resources they have to trade. Yet the theory of lobbying as a form of exchange isn't entirely without empirical support. A clever study by Kalla and Broockman (2016) that aimed to tease out the causal relationship between campaign contributions and access to lawmakers did find evidence that groups that *identify themselves* as campaign donors had more luck scheduling meetings with politicians, giving them an opportunity (at a minimum) to have their voices heard. In other words, although there's no evidence of vote-buying as such, it may be the case that lobbying and campaign contributions can be used in exchange for access.

Ansolabehere, de Figueiredo, and Snyder (2003) explicitly push back against the theory of exchange, arguing instead that campaign contributions are not intended to influence politics at all but are instead a "consumption good." A consumption good is something that people buy because they enjoy or value it, and they buy more of it as their income increases. It's not purchased with any particular intent or as part of an exchange – it's more like buying an expensive car.[5] Part of their rationale is the evidence that most campaign contributions – at least at the time of their writing, which was before *Citizens United* v. *FEC* changed the laws surrounding campaign contributions by interest groups – came from individuals and were in small amounts. They also point out that politicians can very easily raise funds from individual donors, which gives donors who are expecting some kind of quid pro quo a lot less power than they think.

Lobbying as a form of persuasion is what many people think lobbying *ought* to be. Lobbyists have information and specialized knowledge, and they try to use that information to persuade lawmakers to vote in a way favored by the interest group they represent. Lobbyists can convey factual information about the issues at hand to lawmakers and their staff, and also, and perhaps more importantly, information about how taking a position on the issue will affect the politician politically (de Figueiredo and Richter 2014). Where legislators lack a dedicated professional staff, lobbyists can be crucial for

---

[5] Notably, they compare campaign contributions with charitable contributions as a way of arguing that campaign contributions are a consumption good, as do Milyo, Primo, and Groseclose (2000). They don't consider, as I discuss in Chapter 2, that charitable contributions may also be tools of political persuasion.

1.2 What We Know About Political Influence

transmitting information to the legislators and, indeed, can play an important role in crafting legislation. The lobbyists and politicians I spoke to emphasized this point: not every lawmaker, regardless of staff size, can be an expert in every issue, especially when the issues they are voting on are nuanced and fairly specialized. Even lawmakers who educate themselves on the issues at hand may miss unintended consequences. This is especially severe when, as one lobbyist I interviewed put it, the issues at hand pit moral imperatives against economics, as in the minimum wage example. Policymakers may be persuaded by their constituents about the moral dimensions of an issue but not consider the potential economic downsides. A lobbyist who is informed about the issue – and who is of course not objective because they're being paid to make a particular point – can fill in these gaps in the lawmaker's knowledge. In other words, an increased minimum wage or paid parental leave are persuasive on moral grounds – many people believe that a minimum wage job should allow someone to live a decent life and that parents of newborns deserve time off to take care of and bond with their baby[6] – but there are both obvious and less obvious economic consequences to both. The minimum wage has often been linked, theoretically and in the public imagination, with decreased scheduled hours and layoffs. In extreme cases, such a policy may cause a company to relocate or shut down entirely, which could result in the arguably worse outcome of no income as compared with a lower income. Parental leave policies can hamstring certain types of companies because they can't find or afford short-term replacements for their workers. Lobbyists can provide information about these unintended consequences and then leave it up to the policymakers to decide.

Lobbying as a "legislative subsidy," in contrast, is closest to how the lobbyists I interviewed understand what they do. Hall and Deardorff (2006) argue, in their influential article, that direct lobbying is a way to "subsidize" lawmakers who already support the cause. In other words, lobbying saves ideological allies scarce money and time by providing information and, in effect acting as additional staff members. This allows lawmakers to learn about the issue without dedicating as much of their time or staff time to it as they'd

---

[6] And not make anyone else the victim of their sleep deprivation.

have to in the absence of lobbyists. The lawmaker can then use the time they have saved to learn about and work on other issues while still being able to be influential on the issue the lobbyist is helping with. Hall and Deardorff give the example of providing content for a speech – this allows the lawmaker to have influence by giving a speech without investing the time or resources to develop expertise and to give other speeches on other issues with the time it frees up. In some circumstances, especially in state legislatures where legislators have little to no staff support, lobbyists and special interest groups can write some or all of a bill that the legislator will propose (Hertel-Fernandez 2019).

Yet the language the government affairs professionals and elected officials I spoke to used most often reflected that they view political influence-seeking primarily as relationship formation and maintenance. Of course, these relationships are not formed and maintained for their own purposes. By forming and maintaining good relationships with policymakers and trying to assure the victory of additional sympathetic policymakers using campaign contributions, companies can try to secure a sympathetic audience when they have political or policy concerns. A lawmaker or staffer with whom a lobbyist has a good relationship is more likely to make time to listen to them, more likely to think they're being honest and forthright, and more likely to listen to their concerns. At certain points, this may look like persuasion or exchange, but that's only sometimes, and it's part of a broader story. In many ways, this is similar to the logic of the legislative subsidy except it's broader. It's not just that lobbyists are freeing up time and resources for lawmakers – they're taking all the necessary steps to build a solid relationship based on familiarity, appreciation, and trust. As a few of the state lobbyists I spoke to emphasized, honesty and trust are the only currency they have, so they have to be careful to respect and maintain it.

A crucial way that lobbying as relationship differs from lobbying as legislative subsidy is that it implies a much wider range of ways for a company to actually obtain influence. First, interest groups that want to cultivate influence can use another party's existing relationships instead of cultivating their own. This is the logic behind hiring contract lobbyists – people who, among other things, professionally cultivate relationships with policymakers and other important people. Yet such relationships aren't limited to contract lobbyists. If the point is relationships – and not necessarily money, knowledge, skill, content,

1.3 Who Seeks Political Influence and Does It Matter?

or other things – then any third party with an existing relationship is fair game.

Second, understanding lobbying as relationship opens up a variety of options that interest groups and their proxies can use to build and maintain these relationships on their own. These can include philanthropy, as Bertrand et al. (2018) discuss, or anything else that gets (and keeps) a company or its agents in the lawmaker's good graces. What this looks like in practice depends on what the lawmaker values and needs. Politicians need many things – money, information, and to do their jobs well (or to be perceived as such) – and interest groups can build and maintain relationships by attending to these needs.

Yet why, when, and how do companies choose different strategies – what circumstances and which lawmakers call for a PAC donation and which call for enlisting a contract lobbyist? In what situations does a company work through its interest group and when does it attach its name to its influence-seeking? When does a company have its employees clean up a public park and when does the company employ its in-house lobbying team? The answer to these questions are poorly understood because our conventional understanding of influence-seeking is narrow. Milyo, Primo, and Groseclose (2000) acknowledge that the focus on PACs is overblown – "essentially an exercise in 'looking under the lamppost'" – and that extends to lobbying as well. Yet our understanding of campaign contributions and lobbying is almost tautological: we know a lot about PACs and lobbying because they are tracked, and we track them because we think they're important, but we know little to nothing about the other forms influence-seeking can take because they aren't tracked, and they aren't tracked because they don't fit into a narrow conception of influence-seeking. One of the contributions of this book is to reconceive of corporate influence-seeking in a way that helps to logically establish the forms it most commonly takes (Chapter 2). Another is to build on this conceptualization of the influence-seeking arsenal and develop (Chapter 3) and test (Chapters 4–6) a theory of why, under different circumstances, companies choose to deploy different parts of those arsenals.

1.3 Who Seeks Political Influence and Does It Matter?

All this discussion of influence-seeking raises another important question: Who seeks political influence? What is an "organized interest"?

Since most of the research in this area is interested in the effects of lobbying or campaign contributions, all types of organized interests are typically considered one and the same. Walker (1983) defines an interest group loosely as a voluntary association with open membership that is concerned with "some aspects of public policy at the national level."[7] An interest group is just a group of people that have some "special interest," a set of interests coupled with a related thing they want accomplished, in common. Although special interests are often demonized, nearly everything you do or enjoy is attached to its own set of "special interests," as one lobbyist I spoke to reminded me. Do you want nice trails so you can hike, bike, walk, or run? That's a special interest. Do you enjoy playing video games or listening to music? Special interest. Do you like puppies, apples, or clean air? All special interests. An interest group is just a group that forms to advocate lawmakers on behalf of people who share their set of interests.

Yet, even given this explanation, there are good reasons to think that companies might be different from other interest groups in ways that are theoretically important. Of course, in many of the ways stated earlier, they're exactly the same: just like an environmental group, a group of cyclists, or any individual, companies seek to influence policies that are important to them, and they have the same tools at their disposal as many other groups. Indeed, for the purposes of most of the research on political influence, it makes sense to group companies or "business interests" in with other special interest groups since they're primarily interested in the effects of the lobbying or the PAC, not who or what it's on behalf of. Kalla and Broockman (2016) address the distinction between businesses and other interest groups specifically by pointing out that, although their experiment focused on a grassroots, liberal interest group, they would expect that informing a legislator about a contribution from a corporate executive or other wealthy group should have an even stronger effect, but not one that is theoretically distinct. According to them and many others, if businesses are distinct from other interest groups, it's because they have more resources.[8]

---

[7] Of course, interest groups also develop out of shared interest in public policy at the state or local level.

[8] Milyo, Primo, and Groseclose (2000) make a similar point: they focus on corporate PAC contributions as a way of pushing against the argument that PAC contributions matter a lot and are or should be "an important component of corporate business strategies," but they don't argue that they are theoretically different than other groups (p. 85).

1.3 Who Seeks Political Influence and Does It Matter? 11

Another common reason why businesses are sometimes separated from other interest groups is because businesses have a distinct and unique set of political interests. For instance, following the vast literature on the determinants of tariffs and other forms of trade protection, several articles and books have focused on corporate political influence over that trade protection. Grossman and Helpman (1992) focus on the ability of companies to "buy" trade protection as a function of characteristics of both the company and the lawmaker(s) in question, which has been followed by several other articles and books, both by the authors and others, building on the theory and aiming to test it empirically (see, e.g., Gawande and Bandyopadhyay 2000). Bauer, Pool, and Dexter (1972), similarly, focus on businesses because their interest is in influencing trade policy.

Businesses are different from other interest groups not only in terms of their resources or their policy interests, however – they are also distinct because companies do not exist primarily to further a policy objective, and this gives us insight into how they may choose their strategies. They are thus very different from, for instance, the National Rifle Association (NRA), NARAL Pro-Choice America, or other prominent interest groups that are primarily interested in furthering policy objectives for social and ideological reasons. The NRA, for instance, while also focusing on firearms education, conceives of itself as a "civil rights organization" and centers all of its activities on promoting and protecting the use of firearms. NARAL, similarly, focuses on promoting and protecting policies that protect women's health and right to abortions. Companies, on the other hand, sometimes *form* interest groups – to use Walker's definition – that are voluntary and have relatively open membership in order to advocate on behalf of a group of companies, and these industry groups do have a lot in common with other interest groups. Companies themselves, however, are very distinct from other interest groups in that they pursue a set of policies not for their own sake but in the pursuit of profits or continuation of the firm. Put more succinctly, companies exist to sell things. They don't exist primarily to pursue an agenda.

Yet, as I argue in Chapter 3, this distinction gives us a lot of insight into why companies seek influence in the ways they do. The reason is that many people get upset when companies lobby and donate money to candidates. As the most commonly recognized, commonly studied, and commonly demonized manifestations of influence-seeking, some

12 *Introduction*

people hate companies donating money or lobbying because it seems undemocratic. There's something about companies, or any "special interest," being able to marshal its resources to secure influence and access in excess of what any average voter or group of voters might hope to achieve. Other people may not exactly hate companies lobbying or donating money in principle, but they do get upset when they disagree with the stance the company is pushing. This happens a lot because the interests of companies often conflict with the interests of everyday people, especially (but not only) when the people in question are progressive. Many people like the idea of minimum wage, paid parental leave, strict protections of air and water quality, and similar policies that protect society from companies. Many companies, understandably given their interests, are less in favor of such policies.

The reason this matters is that the very same company that doesn't want to be required to pay its lowest-paid workers a higher minimum wage or give its employees time off for the birth of a child may also need to sell things to people who love those policies. If its consumers find out the company has been fighting those policies, they may get angry enough to change their consumption – meaning they may organize a boycott or just individually stop buying the company's product or start buying from its competitors. This puts the company in a strategically difficult place: Should it exercise its influence to try to quash the policy and risk a backlash from angry political consumers, or should it just let the policy go – find some way to deal with it – and not risk the boycott?

In this book, I argue that companies in that position may be able to both fight for their policy priorities and minimize the probability of consumer backlash by crafting a strategy that distances the company's name and brand from its political activities and/or by pursuing more popular (and less commonly recognized) forms of political influence. Specifically, certain types of companies – which I explain in more detail in Chapter 3 – should be far more likely than other companies to engage in politics in a way that keeps their own name out of it and far more likely to use strategies like philanthropy and community development to influence politics.

1.4 Political Influence Is Everywhere

Although most of the research on political influence has focused on the federal level, political influence-seeking is by no means confined to

1.4 Political Influence Is Everywhere

the halls of Congress. Companies seek influence everywhere policies are passed that might negatively affect them, and this includes at the state, county, and municipality (city) level. In fact, there are reasons to believe political influence-seeking may be growing at the local government level. This is because local governments are increasingly becoming policy laboratories whose goal is to remedy larger environmental and social problems. Local governments can also be more nimble than higher-level governments and especially faster at considering and passing policy than the often deadlocked federal government. Adding to this the fact that big city governments tend to be progressive and more likely to pass ordinances at odds with corporate interests creates a relatively new arena for companies to fight for influence. Thus, there are myriad other reasons why studying local governments is important and interesting in this context.

First, cities are normatively important because local governments are fundamentally important to the daily lives of the people who live within them and can be, at least in theory, more responsive to individual concerns. Local governments are responsible for many of the public services that shape our daily experiences. Whether the streets or sidewalks are cleared of snow and debris is shaped by local politics and government. Whether people have clean water to drink is driven by local politics and government. Whether the parks are clean and maintained, whether the roads are safe, whether there is good public transportation, whether public safety is functional and protective of all people – all of these (and more!) are determined by local government and politics. Yet, when many people think of "politics," "government," or "corporate political influence," at least anecdotally, it brings to mind the federal or perhaps state government. This is the case even though local government is closer to people, may affect more of their day-to-day living experiences, and, at least theoretically, should not be at all immune to corporate political influence. Local government is also the level of government that, at least in principle, individual people have the most ability to change. My first political experiences were with my local school board when I was in high school, and I was fascinated to find that, unlike Congress, which was abstract and far away, one sufficiently motivated sixteen-year-old could actually have an impact on an election in a city of 60,000 people, even if she couldn't vote. Thus, cities are normatively important because they have such a great impact on people's day-to-day lives, but there are still many things we don't know about the politics of local governments.

Yet, even though local governments might theoretically be more accountable to their constituents than other levels of government strictly by virtue of proximity, corporate political influence is actually very prevalent at the local level. Clarence Stone's (1989) *Regime Politics*, for instance, emphasizes the role that Coca-Cola has played in Atlanta politics. Every major city has one or two companies at least that are especially prominent and politically powerful at any given time. Even – or especially – in smaller cities and towns, companies can have enormous influence over what happens. A former government affairs employee that I interviewed emphasized that his firm had many operations in very small towns, where the company's influence over politics was nearly absolute. As the largest employer, it was always in the government's best interest to keep them happy, and the company could easily reward the mayor for her efforts by inviting her to company events before elections, giving her a free platform to reach most of her voters. At the same time, we don't really understand the contours of political influence over local governments in the same way that we understand and have researched corporate political influence over Congress or even state government. It's hard to even answer the descriptive question of "who has political influence over local policy?" let alone to ask more theoretical questions about why companies seek political influence or what shapes that influence, even though these questions are also enormously normatively important.

Beyond the normative and the substantive, local governments are also theoretically interesting when it comes to understanding political influence because the options and choices that companies have for influencing politics at the local level are slightly different (although not entirely distinct) from the options and choices they have at the state or federal levels. There are a few reasons for this. First, companies have a credible exit threat when dealing with cities that becomes rapidly less credible as the geopolitical area increases in size. In my conversations with people about this project, I've encountered skepticism that companies would even bother trying to influence local politics since they can just move to the next city or county to avoid the policies they don't like. And indeed, there's a body of literature – most famously, Paul Pierson's *City Limits* – that makes the point that cities just don't make policies that are unfriendly to businesses because companies can so easily move. This raises the puzzle of why companies would, or would have to, try to influence local politics at all since the exit threat

1.4 Political Influence Is Everywhere

should be enough to stop the city from even trying, and if it doesn't, why not just leave? In Chapter 3, I argue that the threat of exit is vastly overstated – a point I back up with interviews with corporate accountants – but it remains the case that the exit threat, at least, does exist in a way that is mostly unique to cities because the larger the geographic area of the political unit, the less credible the exit threat is. Moving from city to city or county to county strikes most people as plausible in a way that a company moving from state to state or leaving a country simply doesn't. This credible exit threat gives companies a different set of options to dealing with policy, which makes the choice of how to deal with local government policy somewhat theoretically distinct from how they'd deal with state or federal policy.

Second, local governments and the politicians that operate within them are different from politicians at the state or federal level in several ways that are important for understanding how a company would cultivate political influence everywhere. Local politics tends to move faster and be less held up by gridlock and bureaucracy than policy-making at higher levels of government. Local politicians, meaning city or county councils and mayors or county executives, may be newer, less professionalized, and less tied in with party networks. They are also likely to have smaller staffs or no staff at all. Some mayors and city councils operate on a volunteer basis or are paid very little, and many hold their position on top of their actual jobs.[9] The issues that are electorally important in cities are also different from those at the state and federal level. At the local level, there is evidence that people care a lot about quality-of-life issues, such as potholes, crime, and the quality of the public schools (see, e.g., Burnett and Kogan 2016). In Minneapolis, where I live, people care a lot about the unhoused populations, the quality of the parks, and public transit. We also fight over the names of bodies of water.[10] Policing is a big issue in cities in a way it may not be at the state or federal level (Cohen et al. 2019; Eckhouse 2019). All of these different issues mean that politicians care about ensuring different things for their constituents when they're running for election or reelection, and, as I discuss in

---

[9] This is also true of some state legislatures.

[10] Shockman, Elizabeth. "Calhoun or Bde Maka Ska? Lake Name in Limbo." April 30, 2019. MPRnews. www.mprnews.org/story/2019/04/30/calhoun-or-bde-maka-ska-lake-name-in-limbo.

16   *Introduction*

Chapter 2, this means that companies face a different landscape when trying to form and maintain good relationships with local politicians because local politicians have concerns that are systematically different from state and federal politicians (although, to be clear, many – like the need to fundraise to run a campaign – are shared).

One reason why political influence at the local government is so poorly documented and understood, despite its importance both theoretically and to every individual's daily life, is that local government is incredibly difficult to study (Sumner, Farris, and Holman 2019). There are almost 100,000 local governments in the United States, compared with fifty state legislatures or governors and one Congress and president. Collecting data on all of them, or even a significant percentage of them, is daunting. In this book, I draw on local governments to understand the nature of political influence and to develop my theory, and I include interviews with current and former city and county elected officials, but I was unable to actually perform any empirical tests within cities or counties. The lack of data on lobbying and campaign contributions at the local level – which exists for some cities and counties but not very many and is so different across those cities and counties as to make comparisons functionally impossible – is a real stumbling block in efforts to understand corporate political influence. Although it would be a huge undertaking, future researchers would do a great service by collecting and standardizing these data, and local politicians and government employees with an interest in transparent government could do a great service by publishing data in a standardized format. In the absence of that, however, many of my empirical tests focus on the federal government.

1.5 Contributions

This book makes two primary contributions to political science research. The first is the one that's been discussed the most so far in this chapter – I explain why companies are different than interest groups, I reconceptualize political influence-seeking in a way that makes clear the nearly infinite possibilities for influencing politics, and I argue that companies that are vulnerable to boycott are more likely to use strategies that distance their brand from any potentially unpopular political move.

The second contribution addresses periodic criticism of another literature. There is, especially in recent years, a large and growing body

1.6 A Note on Terminology

of research that asks how people feel about a variety of economic phenomena driven by corporations: trade, globalization, investment, and offshoring (see, e.g., Owen and Johnston 2017; Feng, Kerner, and Sumner 2019; Kerner and Sumner 2019). This literature has grown out of and expanded economic theories of preference formation – in other words, theories that explain why some people should like trade and others shouldn't. It faces periodic criticism that, it doesn't matter how people feel about trade, globalization, investment, and offshoring because those are low-salience issues and public opinion about them is not politically relevant (Guisinger 2009). There are good reasons to believe that's true. This book contributes to that literature by arguing that it may not matter in terms of how people vote or who gets elected, but there is evidence that companies actually do (or can) care about how people feel about their actions, in particular if it can lead to negative publicity or a potential boycott.

1.6 A Note on Terminology

Political influence, influencing politics, political influence-seeking, and political advocacy are closely related terms that are sometimes used interchangeably but are nonetheless different. Since I will use all of these in this book, it behooves me to be clear about what I mean when I use them, what they have in common, and what is different.

"Political influence" is a state of being and is a matter of degree. A company that has political influence or is said to be politically influential is one that has the ear of politicians, policymakers, and others in positions of power and therefore has the ability to be heard by them and the potential to sway political and policy outcomes. By virtue of their size and the political importance of the economy and jobs, many companies might be considered to have political influence, although some companies certainly have more than others. Political influence can be geographically constrained – meaning a company may have significant political influence in one area but not in others – and it may also be contextual in other ways. A company that has political influence in certain situations may not have as much political influence, or any at all, in other situations.

"Influencing politics" is a verb. It is what companies that aim to shape politics and policy hope to do. Companies that have political influence influence politics. Companies that do not have much political influence also try to influence politics. Any time a company makes

18   *Introduction*

a concerted effort to change something about a political or policy outcome, it is trying to influence politics.

Finally, "political advocacy" and "political influence-seeking" are two more terms that I use interchangeably. I use them both because they were used roughly interchangeably by the people I interviewed for this book. These are the actual actions companies take to try to influence politics. If political influence is what connects the company's actions to outcomes, political advocacy and political influence-seeking is that set of actions. Influencing politics – and having political influence – is the goal, and political advocacy and influence-seeking are the things companies actually do to get there. Conventionally, corporate political advocacy and influence-seeking are typically discussed in terms of campaign contributions and lobbying, but, as I discuss in this book, corporate advocacy and influence-seeking are truly the full set of actions a company can take to build and maintain relationships with politicians and other important people such that a company can build political influence and, ultimately, influence politics.

1.7 Overview of Book

In Chapter 2, I ask why companies perceive a need to influence politics, what political influence is, and what actions companies can take to obtain it. I start the chapter by addressing the question of why companies would try to influence politics at all. I draw on interviews with lobbyists, legislative employees, in-house government affairs professionals, and state and local (city and county) elected officials to explain why political influence-seeking can be best understood as relationship formation and maintenance. I explain in more detail what exactly that means and what it looks like in practice. Understanding political influence as being about relationships opens up a wide range of options for companies or interest groups seeking political influence. For one, it suggests they can use relationships cultivated by other people – contract lobbyists, but also third parties – as a way to seek influence. It also lends itself to different forms of political influence-seeking and corporate advocacy than the conventionally accepted lobbying and campaign contributions because companies can form and maintain relationships with politicians by targeting their interventions to the particular needs and interests of specific politicians. I argue that problem-solving is one way companies can form

1.7 Overview of Book

relationships, and I discuss common problems elected officials face: the need for money, the need for information, and the need to do their jobs well (or to be perceived as such). I focus my exploration in this chapter on city and county elected officials because doing so provides insight into the job performance metric that helps to better understand state and federal officials as well. I conclude this chapter by discussing which influence-seeking strategies this implies, other than the strategies commonly studied, and discuss how this lends itself to questioning why companies choose different strategies.

Chapter 3 addresses an inherent tension in corporate advocacy and influence-seeking. That is, companies often perceive a need to advocate for their interests, and yet advocating for their interests in the political arena can trigger a substantial public backlash. As the case of Goya Foods, whose CEO made favorable comments about Donald Trump, or Land O' Lakes, which donated money to the Iowa Republican Steve King, or Olive Garden, which was *mistakenly* identified as having donated to Donald Trump, all demonstrate, a company taking a political stance for any reason can lead to an uproar as people call for boycott of the company's products. In Chapter 3, I explain how the fear of that backlash shapes the ways companies engage in the political system. Specifically, I outline a probabilistic chain of events that can lead from a company engaging in advocacy to being noticed and criticized by activists, to that criticism spurring a larger public response, to eventual damage to a company's brand and reputation. Certain attributes of companies and advocacy strategies increase (or decrease) the probability of each of these events happening, which means that (a) some companies are inherently more vulnerable than others and (b) companies can take intentional steps to reduce these probabilities in order to engage in advocacy while reducing the probability of damage. This chapter produces a set of expectations I test in the remainder of the book – that public backlash to corporate advocacy is a form of political speech and signaling rather than a statement about consumer behavior; that companies fear this backlash and "boycotts" primarily because of fear of brand damage, not necessarily sales; and that companies engage in particular strategies to either hide their political advocacy or defuse the public anger over it. Those expectations provide the outline for the rest of the book.

In Chapter 4, I focus specifically on the public opinion aspects of the theory. The core argument about public opinion in this book is that, when people talk about boycotting a company, they are not really talking about their consumer intentions and behavior. Rather, calls for and supporting boycotts, especially in online formats, function in large part as a way for people to signal their partisanship to their social networks. In other words, someone tweeting or retweeting about boycotting Goya Foods in the summer 2020, after its CEO made favorable comments about Donald Trump, is not providing reliable information about which brand of chickpeas they are buying; they are instead telling the people around them that they disapprove of Trump and also reaffirming to themselves as to where they stand politically. In this way, disapproval of corporate advocacy in public serves dual functions of reaffirming someone's individual partisan identity and also signaling loyalty to an in-group by disapproving of an out-group. To that end, in this chapter I ask two questions: Why do people respond negatively to corporate advocacy? And are boycott tweets political signaling? I use two sources of evidence in this chapter: a survey with two embedded experiments and social media (Twitter) data on boycotts. The survey and experimental data use the individual as the unit of analysis to test whether disapproval of a company's political activities is primarily partisan. The Twitter data focuses on what aspects of a tweet make it more likely to gain traction and be retweeted. In both tests, I find strong evidence that partisanship is a strong predictor of disapproving of a company's political advocacy, as well as taking a public stance against it.

Chapter 5 takes up the issue from the company's perspective and asks whether companies are aware that consumers might boycott (or claim to boycott) in response to their political activities and whether the types of companies that have those fears line up with the theory. Specifically, the theory suggests that larger companies, companies led by women, and companies with valuable brands ought to be the most highly scrutinized by activists and therefore the most likely to have their activity detected and scrutinized by activists and that larger companies and companies with valuable brands also ought to be most vulnerable to the type of brand damage this sort of backlash can cause. Evidence for this chapter comes from two sources: corporate reports and interviews. Specifically, I use 10-Ks, reports that publicly traded companies file with the Securities and Exchange Commission (SEC) and which are intended to provide stockholders and potential investors with relevant information about the company. Although women CEOs are rare, I find evidence that companies led by women

1.7 Overview of Book

are more likely to cite concerns about the kinds of issues that a public backlash can cause, as are larger companies. Further, I find evidence that suggests that companies are particularly worried about this with reference to brand and reputation damage rather than revenue. I supplement this with evidence from interviews with people with first-hand experience of corporate decision-making and find that companies are quite concerned about the risk of boycott and understand the threat inherent in their political influence-seeking.

Finally, in Chapter 6, I test whether these concerns about public backlash actually translate into changes in corporate political behavior. The theory suggests that companies that are worried their political advocacy might get them into hot water with the public and thereby imperil their reputation and brand ought to take one of two broad strategies: either hide their political behavior (by keeping it off the record or working through third parties to distance the activity from their name) or take steps to make the activity more palatable to the public (by using strategies that might not parse as political advocacy or influence-seeking or by carefully targeting less partisan candidates or issues). I test this using two sources of evidence. The first is data on federal campaign contributions and lobbying, which allows me to test whether companies that theoretically ought to be concerned about public backlash are actually *less* likely to engage in the kind of explicit, trackable political influence strategies that might get them in trouble. The evidence suggests that both campaign contributions through PACs that share the company's name and direct lobbying at the federal level are relatively rare, even among companies with the most resources to do it, that companies led by women are less likely to engage in both, and that companies that cite concerns about social media and reputation damage in their 10-Ks are less likely to engage. Having demonstrated that these companies are less likely to do these things raises the question of what, if anything, they are doing instead, which I address using interviews. I find strong evidence that companies take concerted steps to both hide their political advocacy and somewhat weaker evidence that they try to make it more palatable.

In the concluding chapter, Chapter 7, I focus on synthesizing the findings from the book and addressing some lingering normative questions. Specifically, I ask what this means for boycotts, whether forcing political activity underground is really preferable to having it more out in the open, and what this means for if and how corporate influence can be tamed.

2 | *Where Does Political Influence Come From?*

2.1 Introduction

"The 265 members of Congress who sold you out to ISPs, and how much it cost to buy them" That was a headline in *The Verge*, a technology website run by Vox Media, in the aftermath of a 2017 Congressional decision to overturn an Obama-era rule restricting what internet service providers (ISPs) can do with their customers' data. As the title says, the article lists 265 Senators and House Representatives who voted to overturn the rule and how much money they had received from the telecommunications industry and its employees. "They betrayed you for chump change," read the subtitle.[1]

This language – politicians bought, votes sold – is commonly deployed in discussions of vote outcomes in which corporate or other organized interest groups have a pronounced and visible stake in that outcome. The implication is that, in the absence of the influence of organized interests, the outcome would have been different, and the language strongly implies a quid pro quo. Organized interests pay and politicians respond by supporting those interests.

In most cases, this is an oversimplification of the process through which organized interests influence politics.[2] Political influence isn't really about writing checks or lobbying – or, rather, it's not *just* about writing checks or lobbying. It's about building and maintaining relationships. Sometimes this requires writing checks and lobbying, but political influence, at its core, is about building up enough goodwill

---

[1] Sottek, T. C. "The 265 Members of Congress Who Sold You Out to ISPs, and How Much It Cost to Buy Them." March 29, 2017. The Verge. www.theverge.com/2017/3/29/15100620/congress-fcc-isp-web-browsing-privacy-fire-sale.

[2] Certainly, this oversimplification is often a rhetorical device and a way that people express frustration, not a clear expression of their understanding of political influence.

2.1 Introduction

with people in power that they want to listen when you have a concern, take you seriously, and perhaps take up your cause. This is true whether you're a Fortune 100 company or a small nonprofit,[3] and it's true whether you're looking to cultivate influence at the national, state, or local level. Influence is about relationships, regardless of who you're seeking to influence and why.

Most of the existing research on political influence has focused on two very prevalent tools: donating money to candidates for political office and lobbying lawmakers. With these as a starting point, much of the research on political influence has asked two very important questions: How they work to influence politics and whether they actually work at all. These are very important questions because they get at the core of representative democracy. If we want a representative democracy to function, it's crucial to understand whose interests representatives truly have in mind and why.

In this chapter, I ask different questions: What is political influence and how can a company (or anyone else) get it? If political influence is really about relationships, as I argue in this chapter, it implies a much wider range of possible strategies than lobbying and campaign contributions. Organized interests can, for instance, either cultivate their own relationships with people in power or co-opt someone else's existing relationships. If they opt to build their own relationships, then the question is how to do that. I argue that organized interests have to understand what the politicians in question want and need and then attend to those wants and needs. Campaign contributions and lobbying are especially prominent tools for seeking influence because they address two critical needs that unite most politicians: the need for money to run campaigns and the need for information. Yet politicians also need to do their jobs and to be perceived as doing their jobs well. This opens up additional needs and wants that companies can address.

---

[3] What I write in this chapter applies equally well to individuals, even though I situate it in the context of organized interests because I am ultimately interested in how corporations approach influence-seeking. Although many of the conventional options for influence-seeking require someone to have access to significant financial resources, and I assume for the sake of focusing on companies that those resources exist, the principles here can be applied to anyone seeking political influence without a lot of money: If you can find a need and help solve it, it should, in principle, help you obtain influence. This is probably easier said than done.

To discuss how politicians' wants and needs translate into influence strategies, I depart from the traditional sole focus on the US national government and instead, in this chapter, I use multiple levels of government as a way of thinking through the portfolio of wants and needs that politicians can have. The vast majority of research on political influence has focused on influence over the federal government and specifically over Congress. This focus makes sense because Congress is a very powerful and high-profile governmental entity, and it makes important decisions that affect the entire country. This is a shortcoming, however, because the United States, as a federal and multilevel structure, has many levels of government below the federal government – typically state, county, and municipal (city) – and those levels include a multitude of elected and appointed officials, all of whom make important decisions that can be influenced by organized interests. Political influence and political advocacy are important wherever politics is the process through which policy arises. In other words, everywhere. This means it's important to not dismiss the role of sub-national politicians when we think about influence but also that we might be able to learn things about political influence at all levels by considering politicians at different levels of politics. Just as it's likely we can learn about political influence over city council members by studying Congress, it's equally likely that the experiences of city council members might help us better understand members of Congress.[4]

In the following sections, I first address the question of why companies would need to seek influence at all. Then I review existing theories of political influence and explain why relationship formation and maintenance is a more encompassing explanation for understanding political influence across levels of government. I argue that interest groups that want to build their own relationships, rather than use the preexisting relationships of third parties, do so by focusing on the needs and wants of politicians. I then expand upon my discussion

---

[4] In this book, the majority of the quantitative evidence comes from the federal level because of data availability and quality, not interest or scope. Specifically, this is because state- and city-level data are often not very good, they are seldom comparable across units or even within one unit across time, and sometimes they don't exist at all. It is my great hope that this book spurs additional data collection and study of the breadth and character of corporate political influence at lower levels of government within the United States and also outside of the United States.

2.2 Why Companies Seek to Influence Politics At All

of the three major problems that politicians face – information problems, funding problems, and job performance problems – and how each of these problems maps onto tools that interest groups can use to influence politics. This suggests that interest groups actually have a large and customizable arsenal of influence-seeking tools to choose from, which leads to the question I ask in the next chapter: How do companies choose?

2.2 Why Companies Seek to Influence Politics At All

Why do companies try to seek influence? The answer to this may seem obvious: Companies try to influence politics in order to sculpt a political landscape that favors them. "Companies," however, are not a monolith, and many companies in the corporate world share few common interests. Some companies have an interest in lower corporate tax rates, whereas other companies recognize their reliance upon taxpayer-funded public services and view lower overall tax revenues as a threat to the quality of the services they depend on (Jensen 2006), or they may even support the development of a welfare state for their own purposes (Mares 2003). Some companies favor reducing government regulation. Other companies favor *greater* regulations as they serve as a barrier to entry for competing firms. In some cases, interests are shared in common across industries. Research on tariffs and trade competition, for instance, has frequently focused on the industry as the unit of analysis (see, e.g., Busch and Reinhardt 2000; Hiscox 2002). Yet sometimes there are cross-cutting cleavages within industries, such that those interests – and what would constitute a favorable political landscape – lead companies to advocate largely on their own (Kim 2017a). Regardless, it is clear that companies advocate for their interests to shape the landscape to benefit themselves.

On the other hand, there are good theoretical reasons to believe that companies should not need to try to influence politics because the political landscape should favor them naturally. One set of theories that supports this idea is the family of theories that posits that right-wing parties represent capital, whereas left-wing parties represent labor, which suggests that companies, in their role as "capital," should naturally have representation without substantial effort (e.g., Hiscox 2002).

A second theoretical framework is Albert O. Hirschman's influential exit, voice, and loyalty framework (Hirschman 1972), which stipulates that anyone faced with a difficult situation – for instance, policy proposals they don't like – has two options: they can use exit or voice. "Voice" means that they try to change the situation – by complaining, exerting influence, or mobilizing – whereas "exit" means they simply leave, removing themselves from the difficult situation while allowing the problems to persist. The deciding factor in whether people use exit or voice is, as the title suggests, their loyalty. A loyal actor will stick around and try to use voice to change the situation. A disloyal actor will leave.

This framework has been applied to different types of actors in different types of difficult situations, and it applies equally well to companies faced with government policies they don't like. In the context of companies, however, it does not make a lot of sense to think about "loyalty." To claim that any company is loyal to a particular jurisdiction flies in the face of mounting evidence that companies, provided they are not state-owned, are, in fact, effectively stateless and loyal to no particular government (Rothkopf 2012). Yet that lack of loyalty implies that companies should always leave. Instead, we do frequently see companies trying to change their political landscape.

Instead of loyalty, the key consideration for companies is mobility. "Mobility" refers to how easily and inexpensively a company can move. Although companies are seldom loyal to a place, they are sometimes "stuck," meaning that moving would be expensive, difficult, or unappealing, rendering them relatively immobile. A company that can't easily or inexpensively move somewhere else is effectively forced to be loyal to the place in some sense: because exit is a less appealing (or perhaps impossible) option, they are often forced to use voice. Companies that are more mobile can leave and therefore may choose to exit instead of trying to remedy the situation.

Different literatures situate companies at different ends of the mobility/loyalty spectrum, implying very different things about how often we should expect to see companies seeking to influence politics. On one hand, the literature on the "obsolescing bargain"[5] and political risk in international political economy places companies squarely on the "very immobile" side (Vernon 1971). This literature stipulates

---

[5] In this context, "obsolescing bargain" refers to a contract specified at the outset that changes, or becomes obsolete, as the balance of power shifts from being in favor of the company pre-investment to being in favor of the state post-investment.

2.2 Why Companies Seek to Influence Politics At All

that companies are only relatively mobile up until they've decided where to invest. Once the company has invested, however – once it's put down roots by investing in plant, property, and equipment (PPE); hiring and training employees; and establishing supply chains – the company becomes immobile. It's this dynamic that gives governments power over companies because the governments have reason to believe that the company will put up with a lot of "post hoc contract renegotiation" – meaning changes from what the company thought it was getting into when it invested – before it's actually worth the pain and expense of moving (Kerner and Lawrence 2014). This framework predicts that companies ought to try to influence politics (or use voice) when faced with policies they don't like because they're probably not going to be able to leave, and so they need to work within the system to improve their own situation.

On the other hand, there's a body of literature in urban politics and economics that argues that companies, as "capital," are actually incredibly mobile and that this mobility gives them a lot of power over their political landscape. These arguments draw on the Tiebout model of sorting (Tiebout 1956). The Tiebout model, applied to this context, argues that companies will naturally "sort" by moving to places where the policies are favorable to them. To assure that companies don't depart for greener pastures, governments need to maintain a business-friendly political atmosphere. If all governments agree on wanting to stop companies from moving away, the model predicts that they should all adopt business-friendly policies and not pursue policies that might cause companies to want to leave. Paul E. Peterson's *City Limits* (Peterson 1981) is one of the most prominent advocates of this model as it applies to companies in American cities, arguing that municipal governments are largely hamstrung by competition with other municipalities and the threat of capital exit.[6] The logical extension of this literature is that companies should never need to try to influence politics because being considered simultaneously valuable and a credible flight risk should be influential enough to ensure they're seldom in a situation that would require it. In other words, their interests are taken into consideration naturally, without the necessity of advocacy.

---

[6] Einstein and Kogan (2016) provide a good overview of this and point out that the empirical evidence is mixed.

One of the key reasons why these theoretical frameworks come to such different conclusions about the mobility of companies is that they are considering different types of political jurisdictions.[7] Applications of the obsolescing bargain framework – for instance, Raymond Vernon's *Sovereignty at Bay* (Vernon 1971) and Nathan Jensen's *Multinational Corporations and the Modern Nation-State* (Jensen 2006) – focus on companies that are choosing which country to invest in. The Tiebout model and Peterson's book, on the other hand, focus on within-country competition, either between states or between municipalities. This accounts for much of the difference in predictions because mobility can differ substantially depending on the distance and cost of the move. For most companies, for much of history, the choice to move from one country to another was expensive, as well as logistically and legally difficult.[8]

Leaving a city for the suburbs or even one state for another state, by contrast, is a lot easier and less far-fetched of an idea. If a city enacts a policy a company doesn't like, it isn't hard to imagine that a company might move a few miles to a neighboring city. In other words, companies are relatively mobile within countries – especially when the move itself is a short distance – but relatively immobile from country to country. Yet, increasingly, companies are less tethered to any individual country (Rothkopf 2012), with corporations moving their headquarters across national borders fairly frequently (Birkinshaw et al. 2006; Baaij et al. 2015). This suggests a degree of corporate mobility and fluidity that is at odds with the idea of

---

[7] A second reason is the implicit assumption that companies share interests, which, as I discussed previously, is not always true. Most of this literature focuses on taxation and redistribution, where that assumption is a reasonable one. It is less applicable when thinking about other policies that may divide the corporate community or even individual industries.

[8] To be clear, companies absolutely do leave one country for another, but not easily. For instance, many companies have moved production facilities from wealthier countries with more expensive workers to poorer countries with less expensive workers, a phenomenon known as "offshoring" that's driven by much lower expected labor costs over time, making up for the actual cost of relocation. (For more on offshoring, see, e.g., Owen 2017; Owen and Johnston 2017; Kerner, Sumner, and Richter 2020.) Other companies leave in response to political factors but often only when the situation is dramatic. Several multinational corporations fled Venezuela under the Maduro regime in response to capital controls, government seizures of assets, and other very extreme political actions.

2.2 Why Companies Seek to Influence Politics At All

the "stuck" company, which suggests that political influence-seeking should be rare, since, as Peterson argues, the mobility of companies should act as a check on the city government's behavior without the companies needing to actually use voice at all.

This, however, is where "why do companies try to influence politics?" actually becomes a puzzle. If companies can so easily move – whether from city to suburb, from state to state, or from country to country, crossing borders to take advantage of advantageous policies and avoid damaging policies – then this mobility should act as a check on government policy. Of course, it is certainly likely that some policies are never proposed because of the fear of corporate flight, yet politicians still often propose policies that companies oppose, and companies often try to influence politics at all levels of government. Why is that? The short answer is that mobility is complicated. The longer answer is that, even with the existing theoretical framework being broadly correct, it's also true that companies and industries differ in their mobility and that operations within companies can differ in their mobility as well.

Part of the disconnect between theory and reality is that companies and capital are, in some cases, used almost interchangeably. In some cases, this makes sense. One of the key ways that companies (and wealthy individuals) differ from the rest of the population is that they are capital-rich. Yet this conceptualization is a problem for two reasons. The first reason is that, although companies often have a lot of capital, they are not *just* capital. Companies are a combination of capital, labor, land, complex supply chains, consumers, institutional knowledge, intellectual property, brands, and other tangible and intangible assets, all of which are important to the company's operations. Even if a company's capital is especially mobile, the rest of it may not be. Labor, land, supply chains, and consumers may be particularly immobile. If moving any of these assets is difficult or impossible, companies may not be able to move, or they may be unwilling to move. This implies that companies that are especially dependent upon relatively immobile factors should be more apt to try to do politics and less likely to leave to avoid adverse policy.

The second reason is that not all capital is equally mobile. Fully liquid capital – for instance, the money that accountants and financial analysts keep track of and direct for payroll, purchasing, and the like – mostly doesn't actually exist in any physical location. It exists on the internet, in bank accounts, and in spreadsheets, and therefore "moving" the money between countries, operations, or cities seldom requires any currency actually moving.[9] Relatively illiquid capital, such as highly specific machinery (sometimes called "fixed capital"), on the other hand, is harder to move.[10] Unlike money in a spreadsheet, illiquid capital exists in physical space and can be difficult or expensive to move. A company may not be able to sell (or "liquidate") certain assets if they are, for instance, highly specific to the company. This suggests that companies that are more dependent upon illiquid capital than liquid capital are less mobile and therefore should be more likely to use voice than exit.

The corporate financial professionals I spoke with for this book[11] echoed these points and identified, individually and collectively, long lists of considerations that might stop their companies from moving even a short distance, such as to a neighboring suburb, in response to an adverse policy. In sum, they agree, moving in response to a government policy is a complicated question, and they'd have to ascertain that the cost of a move wouldn't be worse than the negative impacts of the policy. A financial professional from a small insurance company cited the possibility that employees wouldn't want to move and that goods and services might be more expensive at a new location.[12] Someone from a large manufacturing company was also concerned about labor (especially trading a mature workforce for a less experienced one) and added other considerations: the disruption in supply chains, changes in freight costs to move products in and out of the factory, tax implications, the costs of terminating the lease for a factory, and even the possibility that it might be bad for public relations.[13] It is typically possible, another corporate financial analyst in the manufacturing sector pointed out, to offset increased costs imposed by unfavorable policies by moving other levers: increasing

---

[9] Anonymous corporate financial professional interview #8.

[10] See Kerner (2014) and Kerner and Lawrence (2014).

[11] I conducted an anonymous survey of corporate financial professionals using snowball sampling in the spring of 2019. However, this sampling strategy did not result in enough observations to analyze quantitatively, and therefore I treat the survey responses like interviews.

[12] Anonymous corporate financial professional interview #2.

[13] Anonymous corporate financial professional interview #3.

2.3 The Nature of Political Influence

prices or renegotiating with suppliers, for instance.[14] A fourth put it bluntly: "Based on the high financial and non-financial costs to relocate, it would take major changes, such as devastation of our physical area, to get us to relocate or close."[15]

In summary, companies that can't easily take their workers, their land, their customers, or their carefully calibrated supply chains with them are really not that mobile at all. Instead of moving, they're likely to stay and try to change policy. And because they may not even be able to credibly threaten to move in response to adverse policy, the looming threat of their leaving is likely not credible enough to stop cities from making policies they don't like. This suggests that many, perhaps most, companies instead must decide how to influence politics and policy – how to use voice – because exit is not really a viable option.

2.3 The Nature of Political Influence

How does a company, or any other organization, cultivate political influence? Research on political influence has primarily focused on two strategies: lobbying and campaign donations. De Figueiredo and Richter (2014) define lobbying as a "transfer of information in private meetings and venues between interest groups and politicians, their staffs, and agents." Lobbyists, whether they work for the company or organization ("in-house") or for a lobbying firm or law firm ("contract lobbyists"), play an important role in the legislative process because they are more knowledgeable about their issues than the legislators in question are. Simply because legislators and their staffs cannot be experts on everything and pick up on every nuance of an issue, lobbyists serve as specialized supplements. They cultivate personal and professional connections with politicians and their staffs, and these relationships allow them to transmit information and advocate for positions when they need to (Bertrand, Bombardini, and Trebbi 2014).

Campaign contributions, the other focal point strategy, are very much what they sound like: financial gifts made to a politician's election or reelection campaign by or on behalf of an interested party. The

---

[14] Anonymous corporate financial professional interview #1.
[15] Anonymous corporate financial professional interview #4.

specifics of how campaign contributions work – who or what entity can make them, who or what entity can receive them, what they can be used for, what limits are set upon them, and so forth – have changed over time and vary by election type and jurisdiction. The language and rules most people are familiar with, including political action committees (PACs) and super-PACs, and the limits (or lack of limits) imposed on each, refer to rules set by the Federal Election Commission (FEC), which regulates federal elections. The terminology, language, and rules are different at the state and local levels and are set by each state (or sometimes municipality) independently. At the federal level, for instance, companies and other interest groups can donate on their own or by sponsoring and collecting money through a PAC (Powell and Grimmer 2016). This money can be donated to a candidate directly, or it can be used on their behalf for electoral purposes – for instance, by sponsoring advertisements to support their candidacy or oppose their opponents' candidacies. In addition, executives of companies can donate as individuals, and companies can enlist their employees to donate and support causes (Hertel-Fernandez 2018). Although important for legal scholars and practitioners and for the functioning of our electoral system, these variations are less important for understanding political influence-seeking itself. Suffice it to say for our purposes, companies can try to influence politics by donating money to (or for use on behalf of) politicians.

There are a few reasons why those two strategies have dominated both the conversation and research about political influence. The first reason is that, at least at the federal level, the data are easy to obtain, which makes them relatively easy to study (issues of establishing causality aside). Both strategies are tracked fairly extensively. As Milyo, Primo, and Groseclose (2000) put it so well, "The inordinate attention given to PAC contributions is essentially an exercise in 'looking under the lamppost'; data on contributions are readily available and PACs are easily linked to their corporate or industry sponsors. It is therefore a straightforward endeavor to explore statistical relationships between corporate or industry PAC contributions and the committee assignments or roll call votes of legislators." In other words, we study campaign contributions (and lobbying) because we can study them.

The second reason is that both campaign contributions and lobbying are forms of political influence-seeking that are transparent in their purposes. An interest group is unlikely to donate money to a politician

2.3 The Nature of Political Influence

or lobby for or against a proposal for reasons other than trying to influence politics or policy. That means that it's unlikely that analyzing either contributions or lobbying raises the risk of accidentally picking up on some alternative aim of the action. Compare this with philanthropy. Bertrand et al. (2018) call charitable giving "tax-exempt lobbying" and demonstrate that 7.1 percent of US corporate charitable giving is driven by political motives, which dwarfs both annual PAC contributions and federal lobbying expenditures.[16] Yet, although philanthropy can be used for seeking political influence, it isn't exclusively used for seeking political influence – again, they conclude that only 7.1 percent of corporate charitable giving is for political motives – which distorts both discussion and analysis. This makes it hard to truly label philanthropy as political influence-seeking because most of it isn't.

The third reason has to do with theory: how we think political influence-seeking even works. The way we understand how political influence-seeking works – who wants it, from whom, who gets it, why, and to what ends – fundamentally shapes what we think it will look like in practice and, therefore, what we talk about (and track and measure) when we talk about political influence-seeking. In other words, how we think it works naturally lends itself to certain forms of conceptualization and measurement. There are three especially prominent ways of understanding political influence, which, in turn, make it clearer why campaign contributions and lobbying have dominated our discussion.

The first, influence as a form of exchange, is the closest to how most non-researchers seem to think about political influence: as a quid pro quo, where interest groups give something of value to a politician in exchange for the politician's vote. The *Urban Dictionary* definition of lobbying – an imperfect but instructive view of public opinion – reflects this. The top definition of lobbying on *Urban Dictionary* since March 2015 has been "the legal form of bribing the government."[17] This is a fairly simple and straightforward way to think about influence-seeking, and it's intuitive: if you want someone

---

[16] Their sample is limited to large companies, those in the S&P 500 and Fortune 500, and only those that have grant-giving foundations, because philanthropy is not tracked as well or as effectively as either campaign contributions or lobbying. This means this is likely an underestimate.

[17] www.urbandictionary.com/define.php?term=Lobbying.

to do something, you give them something of value and they do it for you. It is reflected in every discussion of a vote in which an organization or person is accused of "buying" the vote. If this is how someone understands political influence-seeking, then the key strategy of interest is campaign donations, along with an inaccurate understanding of lobbying. (A state lobbyist I spoke to told me that she often speaks to groups of students about her job and is asked about writing checks and giving gifts, to which she responds that she's not even legally able to buy anyone a cup of coffee, let alone anything of greater value.)

There are both theoretical and empirical reasons why this understanding of influence-seeking is flawed. Theoretically, there is a commitment problem: Once the influence-seeker has given the money (or other thing of value) to the politician, there's nothing forcing, or even constraining, the politician to adopt their stance. Although a few mechanisms have been proposed to overcome this commitment problem, ranging from the role of reputation (a politician doesn't want to be seen as not honoring their commitments) to the role of repeat play (a politician doesn't want to not get money from the group in the future). Yet none of those really overcomes the theoretical problem. In part, this is because politicians are often being lobbied by multiple sides and receiving campaign donations from many people, so this is a commitment problem repeated many times over. If one group gives a politician money to do something and another group gives them money not to do something, the politician can't honor both. Even if the commitment problem remedies are right, the politician is in a position where they have to disappoint someone. Either way, they will be sullying their reputation and endangering their future contributions.

Empirically, there just isn't a lot of evidence to support this understanding of influence-seeking. The patterns in the data don't really match up with what we would expect to see if this were truly how the world worked. For instance, interest groups usually lobby their allies – politicians they can expect to vote the way they want them to simply for ideological reasons. Understanding influence-seeking as a form of exchange can't really make sense of this unless you suspect that interest groups don't know who their allies are. Otherwise, it seems irrational to "buy off" politicians who agree with you and not those at the margins or on the opposing side. Why "buy" politicians who don't

2.3 The Nature of Political Influence

need to be "bought"? Further, as Hall and Deardorff (2006) point out, this theory cannot really explain why some groups, like certain non-profits and think tanks (such as the Cato Institute or the Heritage Foundation), manage to obtain access and influence far in excess of the resources they have to trade. It also implies we should see a lot more money in politics than we actually do (Milyo, Primo, and Grose-close 2000; Ansolabehere, de Figueiredo, and Snyder 2003). Kalla and Broockman (2016) do find evidence that groups that identify them-selves as donors are more likely to be able to schedule meetings, suggestive of something of a quid pro quo as far as access is con-cerned, but falling far short of someone being "bought." In summary, if political influence-seeking is understood as exchange, then it makes sense to focus on campaign contributions, but there's not a great deal of evidence that this is how the world works.

A second common way of understanding political influence-seeking is as a form of persuasion. In this understanding, companies (or their agents) seek influence by providing politicians with information and trying to use this to convince the politician that their side is the right side. This conceptualization of influence-seeking is less problematic than viewing it solely as a form of exchange, and there is some truth in it. Lobbyists have the ability to develop specialized knowledge on the topics they work on. Politicians, on the other hand, typically cannot do this for every issue. Lawmakers without professional staff or with minimal professional staff and part-time lawmakers are even less able to become experts on everything than legislators with more time and research resources. A lobbyist who is informed about an issue can fill in these gaps in the lawmakers' knowledge. This makes lobbyists a very efficient way to transmit information, and the side effect is that, because the source of information is not unbiased, the lobbyist also has the opportunity to persuade.

Influence-seeking as persuasion also has the benefit of being able to make sense of some of the observed data. At minimum, it makes it clear why nonprofits and think tanks have as much influence and access as they do, even though they aren't exactly writing the big checks. It still doesn't really explain why most groups lobby their ideological allies, although this finding is less confusing given this understanding of influence. One might expect more persuasion of those who might really be close to undecided and less of deep ideolog-ical allies. In any case, there is more evidence for this understanding even though it too is incomplete. Like the exchange theory, the persuasion theory also helps explain the shallow pool of strategies, since, if influence-seeking is about persuasion, then it is mostly about lobbying.

A third and very influential model of influence-seeking is as "legislative subsidy," which is formally modeled in Hall and Deardorff (2006). By legislative subsidy, Hall and Deardorff mean that lobbyists – or, really, any influence-seeker – get influence by saving lawmakers their scarce resources (money and time) by doing research for them, providing them with information and content for ads and speeches, and basically acting as "adjunct" staff members. In this conception, influence-seeking serves an important function for lawmakers, who want to be influential on issues but lack the unlimited time, staff, resources, and knowledge to be influential on as many issues as they'd ideally like to be. By "subsidizing" the lawmakers, influence-seekers permit lawmakers to have influence on more issues by reducing this burden and by providing knowledge, resources, and even, in some circumstances, staff. This frees up time and resources for lawmakers to dedicate to other issues. When multiple influence-seekers are taken into account, it explains why lawmakers with fixed time and resources can become influential on so many issues simultaneously. This lends itself to a broader arsenal of potential strategies because influence-seekers can act on the lawmaker's "budget line" in various ways, such as by providing money, other resources, knowledge, or even staff, but it still lends itself most clearly to lobbying and campaign contributions.

Yet almost one hundred percent of the government affairs professionals (whether in-house, contract lobbyists, or PAC employees) and legislative staff that I spoke to emphasized that they viewed influence-seeking as the act of forming and maintaining relationships. Interest groups and their agents form relationships with lawmakers, their staff, and other potentially influential people. These relationships grant access, facilitate listening and information transmission, and allow for the influence-seeker to be taken seriously. These relationships can act like a legislative subsidy or like persuasion, but they don't have to.

Interest groups can choose to build their own relationships from scratch, or they can make use of preexisting relationships. The latter is what happens when an interest group or company hires a contract lobbyist. A contract lobbyist is a professional lobbyist, someone whose

2.3 The Nature of Political Influence

skill in building and maintaining relationships and conveying information and opinions through those relationship channels is at the core of their business. Companies and other interest groups then hire these lobbyists on contract – thus, "contract lobbyist" – to make use of their relationships and skill. The lobbyist then represents these different entities in their political affairs.

In some situations, companies and interest groups prefer instead to grow their own relationships. When this happens, the relationships are often formed by a combination of shared interests and problem-solving. Shared interests can be a good way to form a relationship if the entity is large enough and well known enough to be on the politician's radar already. For instance, a politician may be aware of the largest companies in their district by virtue of their size, and the company and politician may share views on, for instance, taxation.

When that's not the case, however, companies have to figure out how to actively build relationships. One of the best ways to cultivate a lasting and positive relationship with a politician or government agent is to identify what they need or want and help them get it. Political influence-seeking can, accordingly, also be understood as a form of problem-solving. In this way, this understanding subsumes some other explanations of influence-seeking. For instance, a common problem that politicians have – at every level of government – is not fully understanding a political issue or the consequences of taking a position on the issue. This is an information problem: if the politician had more information about the pros and cons of taking a stance, they'd be able to make more informed decisions about whether and how to do that. This sounds a lot like the persuasion model. Another common problem is financing and resources. Elections are expensive, and candidates need money to wage successful campaigns. They also need resources to run their offices and do research. These sound like either the exchange argument or the legislative subsidy explanation. A company can seek influence by helping to solve these funding problems. Although influence-seeking, according to this understanding, is almost infinitely customizable, there are also common problems that politicians and lawmakers face, all of which map onto different common influence-seeking strategies.

2.4 Common Problems and Solutions

The idea that companies engage in problem-solving for politicians and that this problem-solving is the basis for their influence underlies all of the theories of political influence. Information problems are the foundation for the persuasion theory, and, under the assumption that information-gathering requires resources, contribute to the theory of legislative subsidy. Financial problems are the key to the theory of exchange. What these theories don't address, however, is the third problem that politicians have – concerns about perceptions of their job performance. In this section, I discuss each of these problems in turn and explain how they lend themselves to problem-solving and, therefore, serve as a strategy for seeking influence.

2.4.1 Information Problems

Politicians are not experts on much. This isn't meant to insult politicians, it's meant as a statement of fact (Hall and Deardorff 2006). The scope of governmental decision-making – whether at the federal, state, or local level, whether in the executive or legislative branches – is by its nature far greater than the expertise of any individual, let alone every individual lawmaker. As part of their jobs, politicians have to take action and make decisions on issues they know next to nothing about, regardless of their training or professional background. Simply considering how many things governments make decisions about and how many different layers of government there are at an given time, most people making most decisions are not experts at the thing they're considering. These information gaps can, most obviously, be factual, but lawmakers also often lack information about the consequences for them electorally, as well as about the unintended consequences for other issues and for their constituents (Fortunato and Provins 2017).

Factual information is the clearest information gaps that politicians may have on the basis of their lack of knowledge or training in the specialized areas they're asked to take stances on. These gaps can be problematic. Many of the environmental issues that are considered most pressing at all levels of government, for instance, are being legislated by people with little to no training in science, technology, engineering, or math (STEM). Even though there is evidence that

2.4 Common Problems and Solutions

more candidates with STEM backgrounds are running for Congress (Motta 2019) and that this trend may eventually change the composition of Congress, this only addresses the STEM issue areas and may only apply to Congress (and, further, may be at the expense of losing people with expertise in, for instance, law). This means that the actual scientific evidence behind environmental issues – climate change, pollution, and so on – is not exactly in the wheelhouse of most people making those decisions. Without this knowledge, or perhaps without even the background necessary to evaluate the evidence on these issues but with a job requirement to take a stance, it is natural for politicians to fall back on heuristics and ideology. They may also not make the "best" decisions, simply because they don't really know the pros and cons. An example of this is the growing trend of plastic bag bans. On one hand, these bans seem like a good idea because plastic bags contribute to nonbiodegradable plastic waste and they're easily replaced by canvas bags. On the other hand, there is accumulating evidence that those canvas bags may actually be worse for the environment than the much-demonized plastic bag.[18] This additional information might persuade a politician to take a different stance than they might otherwise, but in the absence of information about them – information that would require knowledge of both environmental and economic issues – the information would not be incorporated into their decision-making process.

In addition to gaps in factual knowledge about the issues they have to weigh in on, most politicians, especially at the state and local levels, also don't have complete information about the electoral consequences of their positions. No politician is ever entirely certain about where their constituents stand. This is a problem because taking a position on a policy may matter for whether a politician wins or loses reelection and affect the tenor and difficulty of that battle. If people vote on the basis of whether they agree with what their elected officials are doing, politicians need to know what would gain this support and what would lose it. Since many issues are low salience to most people

---

[18] See Vanek Smith, Stacey and Greg Rosalsky. "The Problem with Banning Plastic Bags." May 8, 2019. The Indicator from Planet Money Podcast. www.npr.org/2019/05/08/721542495/the-problem-with-banning-plastic-bags, and Dillon, Noah. "Are Tote Bags Really Good for the Environment?" September 2, 2016. The Atlantic. www.theatlantic.com/technology/archive/2016/09/to-tote-or-note-to-tote/498557/.

(see, e.g., Guisinger 2009), it is probably not the case that many single issues would, by themselves, have a strong effect, but many issues in aggregate may. Thus, in addition to not having complete factual information about policies, it's important to know that politicians often also lack complete electoral information about those policies.

Further, no political issue exists in a vacuum, so all political stances come with unintended consequences for other issues and for constituents that politicians may not have complete information about. For instance, ordinances banning plastic drinking straws have been put in place by various levels of governments across the United States and the world in response to concerns about plastic waste, especially in oceans. Companies, too, have begun voluntarily announcing phaseouts of plastic straws. Similar to plastic bags, banning plastic straws can seem like an obvious vote for a progressive candidate who supports pro-environmental initiatives and who knows their constituents do as well. The unintended consequences are far less clear. As one lobbyist I spoke to pointed out, local ordinances like these can really wreak havoc on a restaurant's supply chain, and these disruptions can hurt business and be expensive. Additionally, growing criticism of straw bans points out how such bans are ableist, meaning they discriminate in favor of able-bodied people because many people with mobility and strength issues or certain chronic diseases require bendable straws to drink. Banning their use discriminates against these people.[19] A candidate who's unaware of either of these sets of concerns may, accidentally and with good intentions, find themselves in a situation they do not want to be in, either harming the business community, the disabled community, or both.

Lobbying cultivates political influence in part by targeting these information problems. Lobbying solves an information problem by aggregating and delivering the information to the politicians more directly in an easily digestible format (Bertrand, Bombardini, and Trebbi 2014). Although in some jurisdictions lobbying is only recorded if it's carried out by an actual registered professional lobbyist,

---

[19] Danovich, Tove and Maria Godoy. "Why People with Disabilities Want Bans On Plastic Straws To Be More Flexible." July 11, 2018. NPR's "The Salt." www.npr.org/sections/thesalt/2018/07/11/627773979/why-people-with-disabilities-want-bans-on-plastic-straws-to-be-more-flexible.

2.4 Common Problems and Solutions

anyone can lobby a politician or elected official in a less formal capacity. Companies and interest groups may have in-house lobbyists, but their executives, members, or employees (as applicable) can lobby as well if they have a chance to do so. The key is that they provide useful enough information to develop a trusting relationship and provide the information often enough to maintain the relationship.

2.4.2 Financial Problems

Politicians also want to be elected and reelected, which leads to another problem: financing these campaigns. In much of the country, regardless of the level or type of office that politicians are running for, this can be an expensive prospect. Candidates buy ads in print, on television, and, increasingly, on the internet, including social media. Candidates hire campaign staff and must rent and support campaign offices. There are office supplies to buy, transportation costs, and so on. Candidates running in the most expensive Senate race in 2016 (Pennsylvania) spent $47,163,884 collectively. Candidates for the most expensive House race (FL-18) in the same election cycle spent $13,706,697.[20] One of the city council members I interviewed guessed that most of their fellow council members spent over $10,000 on their campaigns and perhaps as much as $30,000, and others I interviewed pointed out that even local elections are becoming more expensive.

It's hard to estimate the degree of the financial problem because it's never quite clear how much it actually costs to run for office. All we observe is how much people spend and the election outcome. Could the person who won still have won if they'd spent less? Maybe. We don't really know. And further, how much it costs is driven by how much people spend because your competitors' spending creates strong incentives for you to spend more in order to match their effort. Spending begets spending, and no one knows what is necessary. Yet suffice it to say that the list of things candidates for office can spend money on in order to win is long and growing.

Because financial problems are pervasive, campaign contributions are a common tool of political influence-seeking in the United States. Companies, their PACs, and their owners can all donate money to

[20] Both figures are from OpenSecrets.org.

candidates for political office, political parties, and issue organizations (Powell and Grimmer 2016). Although it is clear that campaign contributions help politicians raise funds to campaign for office, it is less clear whether and how it translates to political influence. On the politician's end, there is a commitment problem. That is, when a politician accepts a campaign contribution, there is nothing committing the politician to take the company's side. If politicians vote the "wrong" way, the company has no recourse except to not support them in the future. For example, in the months leading up to the congressional vote on the 2010 Affordable Care Act, health insurance companies, which opposed the bill, donated $44,595,421 to congresspeople, about 56 percent to Republicans and 44 percent to Democrats.[21] Even so, the bill ended up passing. The companies that donated the money can't do anything to the politicians who received their money and voted for the bill anyway. The commitment problem makes it unclear if, or why, campaign contributions actually purchase influence.[22]

What campaign contributions can do, however, is establish a relationship and obtain access. Kalla and Broockman (2016), for instance, didn't find donating money to be associated with any particular outcome but instead that a group that identified themselves as having donated had a better shot at being able to meet with the politician. This suggests that donating money can be a way to develop and then maintain a relationship with a politician by becoming known as a group that provides financial backing. When the group wants to talk to the elected official – to give their opinion and lobby – being able to say that they have this ongoing financial relationship can help make that happen.

Campaign contributions are not the only way influence-seekers can attack the financial problem, however. Echoing the argument of Bertrand et al. (2018), a former mayor I spoke to brought up that companies and other interest groups can always donate to nonprofits, such as 501(c)(4)s. The mayor told me a story of another mayor who had started a nonprofit in his own name, which companies then

---

[21] "Insurance: Top Contributors to Federal Candidates, Parties, and Outside Groups: 2010." Open Secrets. www.opensecrets.org/industries/contrib.php?ind=F09&Bkdn=DemRep&cycle=2010.

[22] Or if that is the point at all (Ansolabehere, de Figueiredo, and Snyder 2003).

2.4 Common Problems and Solutions

donated to. That nonprofit then donated to civic groups, funded talent shows, supported community basketball games, and so forth, all with the foundation's name (and therefore also the mayor's) prominently displayed. This, they pointed out, was a completely legal way that a group could gain influence and help a politician win reelection, all without actually donating to anyone's campaign fund. This also allowed those influence-seekers to circumvent spending limits.[23]

A third way that influence-seekers can help politicians with their financial problems without actually donating to a campaign fund is by hosting campaign events, such as campaign kickoffs.[24] These serve two purposes. First, they can serve as fundraisers for the politician in question, allowing the politician to solicit more funds than they otherwise might have and allowing the influence-seeker to claim credit for those funds without needing to file any paperwork and without regard to donation limits. Second, they can save a politician money by paying for something the politician otherwise would have paid for themselves.

Because financial problems are so pervasive, campaign contributions and other forms of financial contributions are a common and accepted form of political influence-seeking. At the same time, they may be falling out of favor, in large part due to their unpopularity with the public. In addition to companies perhaps not wanting to be tainted by association with an unpopular activity, some politicians are beginning to voluntarily put limits on how much money they'll take and, more importantly, from whom. In the 2020 US Presidential election, all twenty-four candidates for the Democratic nomination publicly asserted to Vox that they would not accept money from corporate political action committees.[25] At the local level, one of the city council members I interviewed told me he didn't, as a rule, accept money from developers or any group he knew would have business before the city until a year afterward and sometimes returned contributions because of concerns of undue influence.[26]

---

[23] Anonymous interview #17.
[24] Anonymous interview #13.
[25] Scott, Dylan. "2020 Democrats' Campaign Finance Pledges, Explained." June 25, 2019. Vox. www.vox.com/policy-and-politics/2019/6/24/ 18656919/2020-democratic-presidential-candidates-campaign- donations-finance-pledges.
[26] Anonymous interview #13.

2.4.3 Performance Problems

Of course, politicians also have to do their jobs, and they are held electorally accountable by voters for how well they do that. Legislators at the federal and state levels, for instance, propose and vote on bills and also provide constituent services, and they are judged by voters on how well they do that.[27] Yet, although city and county governments retain some of the same executive and legislative structures as the state and federal levels,[28] they are also held accountable for a broader range of job performance metrics. Therefore, examining local governments can help illuminate the way that job performance problems – problems carrying out the capacities of one's position or public perception of that – can open up opportunities for interest groups to intervene to build relationships and cultivate influence. This section is not intended as a complete list of ways that companies can help with job performance but instead is illustrative of the way it could work at the municipal level and therefore how it might also work at the state or federal level.

Local government politicians at both the county and city level are often held accountable for the quality of life of their citizens in a

---

[27] Not all state legislatures are "full time," meaning that many state legislators hold full-time jobs in addition to their legislative role, and therefore may be held to a different standard or have slightly different job responsibilities and expectations. For more information, see the National Conference of State Legislatures' page on full- and part-time legislators, www.ncsl.org/research/about-state-legislatures/full-and-part-time-legislatures.aspx.

[28] There is even more variation in institutional structure at the municipal level, which means that the discussion here is necessarily general and not applicable to all cities and counties. Some cities have "strong mayors" who have a lot of power and control over policy implementation, whereas cities with council-manager systems usually have a less powerful mayor and a city manager who is a city employee who does much of the implementation. Some city council members are all at-large – meaning each council member represents all the constituents – whereas other city council members represent districts throughout the city. Some city councils have full-time council members with individual staff; other city councils, especially in smaller cities, serve more in a volunteer capacity. For more information and discussion, see DeSantis and Renner (2002). County executives and county commissions are similar, but are the most poorly understood (Benedictis-Kessner and Warshaw n.d.). For more information about the challenges of studying local governments, see Sumner, Farris, and Holman (2019).

2.4 *Common Problems and Solutions* 45

way that state and federal politicians are not.[29] In addition to making policy, two things that local governments are often held accountable for are the local economy[30] and the availability and quality of public services.[31] Politicians in general tend to be rewarded for a strong economy and low unemployment and punished for a weak economy and a lack of jobs. Politicians can also claim credit for trying to attract business investment, even when it doesn't work, because it gives the appearance of trying to grow the economy and create jobs (Jensen and Malesky 2018). Voters also punish local politicians for potholes and bad road quality, indicating that quality of life is a key electoral consideration for local politicians (Berry and Howell 2007; Burnett and Kogan 2016). Although my interviews revealed that municipal elected officials suspect partisanship is becoming a bigger and bigger factor in municipal elections, most of them still believe that people vote on the basis of their overall quality of life within their city. As a municipal city commissioner I spoke to put it, people tend to vote based upon whether they see their needs being met by the government. They ask themselves, Are my taxes reasonable? Am I getting city services? Good parks? Are the schools good?[32] Is the value of my home going up?[33] If so, they support incumbents. If not, they look for change.

Even though local politicians feel as though they are held accountable by their constituents for the quality of public services, many governments fail to provide adequate public services due to forces largely beyond their control. In particular, local governments often do not have sufficient financial resources to actually provide adequate public services (Kim 2017b). In many places, a significant amount of the funding for city and county services comes from the state.

---

[29] Anonymous interviews #16, #19, #20 indicated this most strongly, although it came up in many interviews.

[30] Anonymous interview #19 made this point especially strongly.

[31] Anonymous interview #16.

[32] School quality came up in several of my interviews with municipal politicians, accompanied by some frustration about being held accountable for it because public schools are typically run by an entirely different government "municipality" – the school board – with little to no input or oversight by the city. School boards have their elected officials and their own funding. And yet, despite this, there's a perception by the politicians that their necks were on the line if the schools were bad. For more information on school boards, see Kogan, Lavertu, and Peskowitz (2016, 2018).

[33] Anonymous interview #14, although the sentiment was echoed in slightly different terms by all the municipal elected officials I interviewed.

A county commissioner I interviewed bemoaned the fact that the county had received less funding from the state in 2018 than it had in 2002, despite being entrusted with even more services over that time period – for instance, the standards for foster care had increased – and the cost of living having gone up significantly in that time.[34] Despite often innovative efforts to maintain service provision levels (Kim and Warner 2016), many cities have suffered from reductions or eliminations of public services. Libraries have closed, roads have not been maintained, streetlights have burnt out and not been replaced, parks have been sold to developers, schools have cut staff and instructional days, and trash and recycling pickup have ceased.[35] Local governments can cope with the financial situation by delaying capital improvements and deferring maintenance, including "slowing down the timetable for replacing equipment, reducing the number of potholes filled, and making minor building upgrades" (Nelson 2012, p. 58S). Similarly, many governments implement or increase user fees and taxes to offset the economic effects of recession (Nelson 2012; Kim and Warner 2016). Both options are seen as better choices than cutting essential and necessary services, such as public safety and fire services (Nelson 2012).

Some governments have attempted to increase own-source revenue – money they can raise on their own – or have accepted the necessity of reducing or eliminating services, whereas others have sought out alternative service delivery mechanisms (Nelson 2012; Kim and Warner 2016; Kim 2017b; Bel, Hebdon, and Warner 2018). While these often refer to formal arrangements (Kim 2017b), such as privatization (contracting out public services to a private company) or intra-municipal cooperation (sharing public service provision with other municipalities), informal arrangements are also an option (Gazley 2008), although they may be "thought by some to be too casual and temporary in their nature to be of much value to community agencies or public managers" (Gazley 2008).[36] Yet there is evidence that governments recognize what companies can provide. Before it

---

[34] Anonymous interview #16.

[35] In extreme cases, this kind of underfunding and underprovision can lead to blight and a need for "urban triage." See Cooper-McCann (2016).

[36] Outside the United States, non-state service provision – service provision in tandem with or instead of the state, by actors including NGOs, rebel groups, and corporations – whether formal or informal, is common (Heger, Jung, and Wong 2012; Brass 2014, 2016).

2.4 Common Problems and Solutions

was scrapped, the planned second Amazon headquarters in Long Island City, New York, required Amazon to make infrastructure improvements and build an elementary or middle school as part of its memorandum of understanding with the city.[37]

Just like donating to campaigns to address funding problems or lobbying to solve information problems, companies are well positioned to address issues like service shortages to help politicians with their job performance problems. In some cases, all companies have to do is write a check, similar in both process and amount to how they would if donating to a campaign. Companies providing grants to help with public infrastructure are not uncommon – Domino's Pizza provided several cities with up to $5,000 to repair potholes and do other roadwork in 2018 as part of its "Paving for Pizza" campaign,[38] and KFC funded 350 pothole repairs with a $3,000 check in Louisville, Kentucky in 2009.[39] Although it is difficult to know how prevalent this kind of corporate community development truly is in the absence of systematic data, I estimate that about 19 percent of publicly traded companies have a charitable foundation that allows for this kind of behavior (95 percent confidence interval: 13.3 percent, 24.1 percent), and about 45 percent of publicly traded companies have information on their websites about their community development efforts (38.4 percent, 52.3 percent).[40]

If this kind of service provision does indeed improve quality of life for residents, it should redound to the benefit of politicians, who may also be able to claim credit for the service provision improvements. This can build a relationship if the local officials see the companies as partners and potential sources of future help with public services.

---

[37] New York State Urban Development Corporation et al. "Long Island City Development Project." November 12, 2018. https://d39w7f4ix9f5s9.cloud front.net/4d/db/a54a9d6c4312bb171598d0b2134c/new-york-agreement.pdf.

[38] Zaleski, Andrew. "Why Domino's Pizza is Fixing Potholes Now." June 14, 2018. Citylab. www.citylab.com/transportation/2018/06/dominos-pizza-is-fixing-potholes-now-and-thats-fine/562829/.

[39] Siegel, Robert. "In Fixing Potholes, KFC Thinks Outside the Box." March 26, 2009. Interview transcript from *All Things Considered*. www.npr.org/templates/story/story.php?storyId=102390105.

[40] These estimates come from a random sample of 200 publicly traded companies, which were then hand coded by my hard-working research assistants. The first estimate comes from a completed N of 198 and the second from a completed N of 196.

It is also likely to help companies get on politicians' radar – these kinds of service provision efforts are often carried out by municipalities with funding from the companies or interest groups, implying that the politicians would know about it. This can also build a relationship of necessity as the two become partners, even if temporarily, in carrying out the improvements.

Unlike campaign contributions and lobbying, however, public service provision isn't tainted by its association with corporate political influence. On the contrary, companies engaging in pro-social behavior (or behavior that's perceived as pro-social) can be quite popular. There is evidence, for instance, that being seen as a good corporate citizen can help companies be treated more favorably when they do wrong (O'Connor 2006). There is also substantial social pressure for companies to give back to the communities they operate in.[41] These kinds of activities are also not subject to filing requirements, nor are companies required to disclose things they do in their communities or to help politicians, provided they do not meet the standard of lobbying or campaign contributions. That means companies can selectively highlight the activities that show them in a good light.[42]

Providing public services is just one example of a way that companies (and also other interest groups, potentially) can aim to develop relationships with politicians by helping address their job performance problems. In this case, it specifically operates on the well-documented problems that municipal governments have with providing adequate public services, but it also demonstrates the reasoning behind the broader point: politicians and other policymakers are held accountable by voters for more than just their positions on legislation. Politicians at all levels and in all positions have jobs to do, they have to do those jobs to some standard to continue winning elections, and

---

[41] Larry Fink, the CEO of the influential investment management company BlackRock, illustrated this pressure well in an open letter to companies in early 2018: "Society is demanding that companies, both public and private, serve a social purpose. To prosper over time, every company must not only deliver financial performance, but also show how it makes a positive contribution to society. Companies must benefit all of their stakeholders, including shareholders, employees, customers, and the communities in which they operate." This expectation, he writes, results from "governments failing to prepare for the future, on issues ranging from retirement and infrastructure to automation and worker retraining." See www.blackrock.com/corporate/en-us/investor-relations/larry-fink-ceo-letter.

[42] This also makes it difficult to study this phenomenon, unfortunately.

2.5 Conclusion

there are often resource constraints that stand in the way of their performing to that standard. The legislative subsidy argument makes this point in a slightly more specific way as it pertains to the relationship between lobbyists and legislators: members of Congress would like to give speeches, take stances, draft legislation, and so on, since doing so improves their job performance, and lobbyists can address this by filling some of those roles. More broadly, there are many actions companies and other interest groups may be able to take on their own that help politicians to do their jobs, and addressing these problems can help to build a relationship, which, in turn, can bestow some political influence when it's needed.[43]

2.5 Conclusion

Although popularly viewed as a shadowy quid pro quo, with companies and lobbyists writing large checks and getting votes in exchange, political influence is primarily about relationships. Companies and interest groups that have good and stable relationships with politicians are more likely to have their concerns listened to and taken seriously, and the result is that they may be more likely to get things they want in politics. To use these relationships, companies and interest groups can choose to use someone else's preexisting relationships with politicians – such as a lobbyist, someone who professionally cultivates and maintains relationships and conveys information through those channels – or they can set out to form their own relationships.

A key way that these relationships can be actively formed is by the potential influencer helping the politician they're seeking to influence. This is the logic that underlies the two most commonly accepted forms of political influence, lobbying and campaign contributions, strategies that are so common because they help overcome two common problems: a lack of funding for campaigns and a lack of information (or time and resources to gather that information) about the content of a

---

[43] There is an alternative and much more cynical counter-explanation for how providing public services may work to grant public influence: it's possible that companies can credibly commit to withdrawing the services they provide, effectively blackmailing city and county officials into doing what they want. Yet this claim is a lot bolder than the idea that it solves a problem and builds a relationship and would therefore require substantially more evidence to support.

policy. Yet these are not the only two problems politicians face, and, accordingly, these are not the only two influence strategies. In this chapter, I discuss financial and information problems, along with a third: performance problems. The combination of the three problems opens up a vast universe of possible tools for any entity that wants to develop a relationship with, and therefore try to influence, a politician. Some of these strategies speak to more common problems and are therefore more general, such as campaign contributions and lobbying, whereas others are very specific to the problems of an individual politician or district and are therefore more targeted.

This understanding makes it clear that getting political influence can happen through a variety of channels. Do companies use other people's relationships or cultivate their own? If they choose to cultivate their own, which problems do they target? In the next chapter, I argue that the choices companies make for these questions stem from their concerns about how consumers feel about them. Some of these strategies are more unpopular than others – lobbyists, in particular, are particularly publicly maligned – and companies know it. Companies' fear of boycott, I argue, leads them to either avoid these unpopular strategies in favor of less unpopular strategies, or to avoid being associated with their unpopular strategies.

3 | How Does Public Opinion Shape Corporate Political Advocacy?

3.1 Introduction

"Are you a non-profit? You will be soon!"

This is the message Mary,[1] the Twin Cities entrepreneur from Chapter 1, had for her fellow business owners in Minneapolis. Except she wasn't really joking. The city's regulations, she told me, were excessively costly for businesses, and they tended to eat up profit margins until no profit remained at all. Although the regulations were all intended to solve some social or environmental problem, they had the unintended consequence of increasing her operating costs. The city's minimum wage ordinance, intended to help low-wage workers in a city with a housing shortage and increasing cost of living, increased her labor costs. Ordinances meant to protect the environment from single-use plastics forced her to buy more expensive containers for her restaurant than the ones she preferred. Even a tax on sewage cost her money. Over time these ordinances added up to decrease her profits, she said, until it wouldn't make financial sense to keep the business open at all. She did not intend, after all, to be a nonprofit.

Companies are often affected by political decisions that aren't really about companies at all. Because companies require land, labor, and capital to function, political decisions that impact any of those – measures to help workers, to protect the environment, or to raise funds for public goods through taxation, for instance – typically increase the cost of operating a business. As a result, regardless of the normative good that might be done by these policies, they have negative consequences for companies.

Companies have a lot of options when they find themselves facing a policy that is not in the company's interest. First, they can decide not to engage in politics at all. They can just let it go and accept the

---

[1] Not her real name.

51

52 *How Does Public Opinion Shape Corporate Political Advocacy?*

negative consequences. Some business owners and some businesses[2] choose this route. Sometimes they do this because the policy is not that harmful or because defeating it is not worth the effort. Sometimes the company might decide the consequences are worth the cost of what they perceive as positive social change.

If, instead, the company decides to engage with the political system to address the policy, it has to decide how to do that. Companies have many options for cultivating political influence and advocating for or against policies in an attempt to influence politics and policy. Cultivating political influence is a long game. It's about cultivating and maintaining relationships. Some degree of political influence is necessary for successful advocacy, where advocacy refers to the process of trying to advocate for the company's interests. Although most frequently "advocacy" or "political influence" make people think about campaign contributions and lobbying, there are many options customizable to the company and the situation it finds itself in. Given these options, how do companies decide what to do?

In this chapter and in this book more broadly, I argue that the short answer is: public opinion forces their hand. To that end, in this chapter, I argue that the fear of a public backlash – of mass negative behavior, typically in viral online form, often called a "boycott" or a "firestorm" – looms large in the minds of companies deciding how to advocate for their interests. Although the probability that any given action will result in the kind of public backlash that damages the company is low, it is not zero. That ultimate probability is composed of two separate probabilistic events: the probability that activists notice the company's

---

[2] It can be difficult to talk about a company's decision-making in a way that is generalizable to companies of all sizes and structures because different types of companies have different processes for making decisions. For small businesses that are not publicly traded, for instance, the decisions may be up to one person or a very small group of people, whereas for large companies and even some smaller publicly traded companies, the group of people making the decision and the way they decide can be very different. For that reason, I will mostly speak of "companies" making decisions, rather than specifically about the people or groups making decisions, in order to cast as wide a net as possible without theorizing about the decision-making processes specific to any company. This is the same reason why I switch between using "they" and "it" as the pronoun for the company. "It" refers to the company as an entity, and "they" refers to the company as a group of people making a collective decision.

3.2 How to Use Voice

advocacy and choose to target it for public attention and the probability that the public responds with significant outrage. It is those two probabilities that companies have in mind when they plan their advocacy strategies. In this chapter, I explain all the steps of that process and outline four strategies companies take to advocate for their interests while minimizing those probabilities and, therefore, the overall probability that its advocacy results in damage to reputation.

3.2 How to Use Voice

When faced with a policy that might hurt the company, companies first have to decide whether to advocate for their interests or not. If they choose to advocate, it raises the question of how.[3] As Chapter 2 demonstrated, there is a constellation of options available to companies, all with their own pros and cons. Although political advocacy can have its benefits, if a company is successful in its efforts, it also comes with costs. Notably, any decision a company makes leaves it vulnerable to public opinion, and public opinion can be damaging. The key is for companies to recognize these risks and choose strategies that minimize them. In this section, I explain how that works. Specifically, I explain the steps that lead from advocacy to boycott or "firestorm," an aggressive, negative, and often virtual response to a company's actions. I also explain what makes companies most vulnerable at each stage and, therefore, how companies can act strategically to advocate safely.

When companies choose to advocate for their interests in the political arena, they are faced with making a decision that can lead down a path to public backlash and damage. Specifically, if a company opts to try to influence politics and policy, it may attract the attention of activists, who may successfully enlist the public in vocal opposition

---

[3] In this book, I do not deal with what a company conceives of as its interests. It is worth noting that the size and composition of the group that makes decisions will play a role in how that group conceives of the interests of the corporation. A coop or a company with strong organized labor might conceive of interests more broadly or in different ways than a company with a smaller group of decision-makers drawn primarily from management. Similarly, a small business with one decision-maker may merge their company's interests with their personal politics. This theory speaks primarily to a corporation with a decision-making body that views its company's interests narrowly as their business interests.

54 *How Does Public Opinion Shape Corporate Political Advocacy?*

to the company's actions. This vocal opposition – typically online, sometimes viral, and, for reasons I discuss later, sometimes entirely performative – can then damage the company's reputation and therefore its value.

The key is that each of these steps is probabilistic – companies may or may not attract activist attention, the mass public may or may not get angry enough to make a difference. This means two things. First, because each of these steps is probabilistic, it means that the probability of any given company's actions leading to a public backlash that damages its reputation and therefore the bottom line is fairly small. Yet the probability is not zero – damaging public backlash is unlikely, but it could happen! – meaning that companies that are worried about damage to their reputation have reason to be concerned if they are at all risk-averse. It also means that companies can act intentionally to reduce the probability they're noticed, reduce the probability the public gets angry, and reduce the probability of damage even further. Their fate may ultimately be left up to some element of chance, but there are aspects of the probability they can and do control.

Second, some companies and actions have inherently higher probabilities of being noticed and attracting public anger and therefore higher probabilities that their political advocacy will lead to a damaging public backlash. This means that some companies are more likely to act strategically than others because they see their probability of harm as higher. Taken together, this tells us that companies should engage in intentional strategies to avoid the attention of activists and avoid provoking public anger and that some companies should pursue these strategies more actively than others.

In the next sections, I break down each step in the causal chain illustrated in Figure 3.1. I explain which companies have the highest probability of attracting the scrutiny of activists and which actions have the highest probability of attracting the ire of the public. Then I explain ways companies can act intentionally to reduce these probabilities and therefore aim to advocate for their political interests while minimizing the ultimate probability of reputation-damaging public backlash.

Activists

After a company has decided to advocate, the first step in the causal chain is avoiding the attention of activists. Activists are people who take action to try to bring about change. Some activists try to change

3.2 How to Use Voice

Figure 3.1 The causal chain that links a company's political advocacy efforts with damage to its reputation

the behaviors of powerful people or groups, such as companies. In this context, an activist could be someone who self-identifies as an activist, but they could also be any other person or group who draws attention to a group or company's activities in a critical way with an interest in changing those activities. Often activists target companies for their business practices, but they sometimes also target companies for their political stances or advocacy efforts.

In many cases, the things activists are criticizing companies for are legal, suggesting that activists might instead target their efforts toward changing the laws and constraining companies that way. The problem with trying to change behavior by changing the rules – going through public, political channels to change the laws that bind corporations – is that trying to change laws and ordinances is a difficult, time-consuming process, and companies often find themselves at a disadvantage when squaring off against corporate lobbyists. Instead, many activists prefer to use what Baron (2001) calls "private politics," in which activists target companies themselves and try to coerce companies into changing their behavior on their own by shifting their incentives rather than the laws. Instead of changing pollution standards, for instance, activists might launch a letter-writing campaign against a company that pollutes, drawing negative attention to the company and therefore making polluting less attractive than other options.

When activists engage in private politics, they have a few different options at their disposal. They can protest, engage in civil suits, stage letter-writing campaigns, or call for and coordinate boycotts (Baron and Diermeier 2007; Lenox and Eesley 2009). Each tool targets companies in slightly different ways. Protests, for instance, can interfere with a company's operation – slowing or stopping production, stopping the flow of inputs and outputs, or interfering with customers getting into a retail store. These actions can cast negative light on the company, force the company to divert some resources to attending to the action, and, if the company is publicly traded, can provide additional (negative) information about management and operations to shareholders (King and Soule 2007). The idea is that targeting companies in this way may hurt them enough – through any or all of these various channels – that the company opts to change its behavior independently to avoid that pain, even without the external force of law forbidding their behavior.

Even though a targeted behavior might be common within an industry or even more broadly, activists typically do not target entire industries or all companies that engage in the behavior. Indeed, many companies are never targeted (Lenox and Eesley 2009). There are two reasons for this. First, the activists' actions require time and resources. Any given activist or organization does not have unlimited time or resources and therefore simply cannot target every offending company. Second, if activists target a smaller number of offending companies, they may end up serving as examples – in effect, putting one company's metaphorical head on a pike as a warning to the others. If other companies observe the damage to the targeted companies, they may preemptively opt to change their behaviors in fear that they may be next (Baron and Diermeier 2007). So even if targeting all companies were possible, it might not be necessary or efficient to do so.

Since activists ultimately have to choose targets strategically if they are to serve as good warnings, not all companies are equally susceptible to targeting by activists. Management scholars and sociologists have tried to pin down exactly what it is about companies that make them likely targets. Focusing specifically on coordinated efforts by activists to get a company to change some specific labor or

3.2 How to Use Voice

manufacturing process – such as the use of sweatshops or polluting – several studies have found that larger, more prominent companies with stronger brands tend to be targeted at higher rates than smaller, less prominent companies (Baron and Diermeier 2007; Lenox and Eesley 2009; Bartley and Child 2014). These companies are easier to monitor, serve as better examples, and are more well known, which might aid in getting the public to support the activists' efforts and also make them better warnings to their peers.

Size Expectation: Large companies have a higher probability of being a target of activist campaigns.

Brand Expectation: Companies with strong and recognizable brands have a higher probability of being a target of activist campaigns.

Other companies may be under increased scrutiny for other reasons and therefore more likely to attract the attention of activists. For one, companies that have previously been the target of activists' efforts may remain under scrutiny – either because they're known or because they're considered likely to reoffend. Although some research finds that protests of previously targeted companies are less likely to hurt share prices because the protests provide no new information about the company or its management (King and Soule 2007), it is still likely that frequent offenders are subject to additional monitoring and scrutiny. This means that companies that have previously offended may be under increased scrutiny and, therefore, more likely to be targeted.

Previous Target Expectation: Companies with a history of being targeted by activists have a higher probability of being a target of further activist campaigns.

Companies led by women are also subject to additional scrutiny and therefore potentially disproportionate targeting. There are several reasons why women-led companies may be scrutinized more than others. First, women are disproportionately appointed to leadership positions when companies are in a bad situation. Ryan and Haslam (2005) call this situation "the glass cliff," indicating that women first must burst through the "glass ceiling" to even ascend to leadership positions, at which point they are placed in particularly vulnerable or perilous situations (the "cliff"). This means that women might ascend to leadership positions within companies because bad things are happening or about to happen, and therefore those bad things might increase scrutiny of the company, separate from attributes of the leadership (Ryan and Haslam 2007). Even though this suggests that women-led companies might be subject to additional scrutiny for reasons unrelated to their leadership, it still implies that companies led by women are likely to face additional scrutiny and therefore might be disproportionately targeted.

Second, women in leadership positions may be subject to greater monitoring and scrutiny due to a combination of misogyny and gender stereotypes, which might bring greater scrutiny of them as leaders and the companies they lead. Research shows that women CEOs may face increased scrutiny of their job performance (Ryan and Haslam 2007) but also of more mundane characteristics, such as their appearance. Gender stereotypes also sometimes peg women as being less corrupt (Esarey and Chirillo 2013; Barnes and Beaulieu 2014), which, when paired with misogyny (or even just schadenfreude), can lead to women being monitored more to watch for them to slip up. In sum, because women as women face higher scrutiny, so too may their companies.

Third, women in leadership positions may themselves be more visible, and thus lead to higher visibility of their companies. This visibility can come, in part, from their relative rarity. Of the 2020 Fortune 500 list, 38 of the 500 companies (7.6 percent) were led by women.[4] This renders the women who are in charge of these companies relatively high profile on their own, in large part because of the exceptional careers and attributes they had to possess to get where they are and in smaller part because they become human interest stories. Further, because of their rarity, the appointment of a new woman CEO can generate significant news, as does the year-over-year change as women CEOs become more common yet still unusual. For instance, in 2019, *Fortune Magazine* noted that "The Fortune 500 Has More Female CEOs Than Ever Before," celebrating a 37.5 percent year-over-year increase from 24 in 2018 to 33 in 2019. Finally, women CEOs may be more visible because they may come to their positions alongside discussions of diversity and equity, where their selection itself may

---

[4] Benveniste, Alexis. "The Fortune 500 Now Has a Record Number of Female CEOs: A Whopping 38." August 4, 2020. CNN Business. www.cnn.com/2020/08/04/business/fortune-500-women-ceos/index.html.

3.2 How to Use Voice

be subject to additional attention. Insofar as these women are highly visible, their companies may share that spotlight, and therefore be more likely to be scrutinized, similar to how large companies and companies with strong brands are likely to face scrutiny.[5]

Gender Expectation: Companies with women CEOs have a higher probability of being a target of activist campaigns.

In sum, some companies are more likely to be monitored and subject to scrutiny than others, even if they all engage in the same behavior. This is why, although trying to influence politics and policy is a common feature of corporate life, only a fraction of companies that engage in it end up being targeted. Every company has some underlying probability of being targeted by activists, but, as I have explained in this section, some companies have higher probabilities of being targeted, in large part because they are subject to more monitoring and scrutiny. These companies are likely to be larger, have recognizable brands, may have been the subject of activist action in the past, and/or be headed by women or non-white men. This increased probability means that, if their company engages in political advocacy, they are more likely to be observed and targeted. Other companies – smaller, with less identifiable brands, not previously targeted by activists, and/or headed by white men – have lower probabilities of being targeted and are thus more likely to have their actions go unnoticed, unscrutinized, and untargeted. Every company gets a coin toss every time it tries to influence politics, but they are not all tossing the same coin. Some companies with high probabilities might get lucky sometimes, and some companies with low probabilities might find themselves at the center of an activists' campaign, but it remains true that some companies are more likely to be targeted than others.

---

[5] The same expectation can be stated of CEOs with other marginalized identities – especially Black and Latine CEOs or LGBTQIA+ CEOs. They are also relatively rare, and thus they also may face damaging stereotypes. For instance, there is evidence they face the same "glass cliff," where they are appointed to lead poorly performing companies (Cook and Glass 2014) as well as losing teams (Cook and Glass 2013). Yet I do not state this as a formal expectation because of the difficulty of testing it. Whereas data on CEO gender is widely available, information on other attributes typically is not. With that in mind, I have opted to not test this expectation rather than test with especially problematic data. I leave this expectation, therefore, to future research.

60   *How Does Public Opinion Shape Corporate Political Advocacy?*

All the companies can really control is their own actions. The rest is left up to the activists to notice and publicize and the mass public to care.

The Mass Public

The second step in the progression from corporate activism to damaging public backlash is the mass public. Activists can call attention to a company's perceived misbehavior, but the success of any organized action depends upon the call resonating with the public and attracting enough participants. It's the organized action itself – the boycott, the protest, the letter-writing campaign – that threatens a company, not necessarily the effort to organize the action. In general, the more participants, the more effective the action is at changing corporate behavior.[6] So, if activists notice a company's actions and criticize them, will the mass public respond?

There are two key elements that determine whether the mass public will sign on and participate. First, what the company did to be targeted and whether it is sufficiently motivating. And second, the character of the organized action and what the people are being asked to do.

As discussed in the previous section, many activists target corporations because of their labor or environmental activities. This makes sense because corporate labor and environmental practices can have devastating effects on individuals, populations, and the world more broadly. The consequences are severe, and the necessity of stopping those practices is paramount. Yet this may lead to a somewhat circumscribed group of potential participants, which becomes smaller as the activity in question becomes divorced from the overall societal problem (e.g., a specific environmental practice vs. "climate change"). There are plenty of people who care a lot about those issues and want to be involved, but there are also plenty of people who do not.

---

[6] This is not universally true. Some forms of political activism are especially targeted and perform best with small, dedicated groups. This is especially true for direct actions that require secrecy, as larger groups make keeping the secret harder.

3.2 How to Use Voice

Efforts to call companies out for their efforts to influence politics, however, cast a wider net. Not everyone knows or cares much about sweatshops or pollution, and even less so as the practice becomes more specific, but the topic of political influence and corporate political advocacy inspires strong views. The subset of the population who may not care too much about environmental or labor problems may still care about politics, hold political views, and care about the political system. Efforts by a company to influence politics is, therefore, something that can reliably rile up a sizable chunk of the mass public.

Some people find corporate political advocacy upsetting because they feel companies have greater access and influence than individual constituents. This violates a core value they hold about democracy, that democracy is a system of "one person, one vote," where elected officials represent and answer to their individual constituents. When companies seek to influence policy, it represents a deviation from this ideal. It also represents a level of access that most people don't (and can't) have. This is frustrating because it can feel like people are not truly represented in politics and have no say over policy, whereas companies and others with extraordinary access are perceived as largely writing their own rules and designing the systems that are supposed to constrain them. Coupled with rising income inequality, this lack of access, control, and influence leads to a spectrum of negative emotions, from rage to resignation. This suggests that the act of seeking political influence – regardless of why it's being sought – may be an egregious enough violation of a deeply held value to provoke the person to boycott.

This view, that corporate influence over politics and normative conceptualizations of democracy are at odds, is illustrated by a 2018 *Atlantic* article by political theorist Yascha Mounk (2018). Entitled "America Is Not a Democracy," it begins with a story about a company exerting influence over politics in a New England town. Mounk concludes about the town and the process by which the company retained its contract to supply water, "a nasty suspicion had taken hold: that the levers of power are not controlled by the people." There is also some existing survey evidence that supports the idea that people find corporate influence and normative concepts of democracy to be incompatible. A 2015 *New York Times* poll found that 84 percent of respondents thought money had too much influence in American political campaigns today, and a 2016 Gallup report found that about 60 percent of those polled reported that they were dissatisfied with the size and influence of major corporations (Riffkin 2016). It follows that a majority of people would also oppose the role of corporate money in politics because large and influential corporations have significantly more money to invest in political influence and advocacy than the normal person.

For many more people, however, it isn't the act of seeking influence itself that people find egregious but rather the political positions implied by it. Many of the common forms of political advocacy, such as campaign contributions and lobbying, are publicly inseparable from partisan stances. In other words, when the agriculture cooperative Land O'Lakes donated money to Iowa Representative Steve King, a Republican known widely for his racism, their money was seen by many as an endorsement of his politics and racism, even if, most likely, the company's aim was to maintain a relationship with a member of Congress in a district where many of their farmers operate.[7] At minimum, Land O'Lakes was seen as not viewing his stances as a deal breaker, which itself is seen as a political stance. In this case, the source of anger that precipitated the boycott was not that the company tried to influence politics at all – indeed, Land O'Lakes, like many companies, has donated to many elected officials without significant backlash – but specifically that they gave money to a politician whose views are reprehensible to many. Their attempt at corporate advocacy was read as an endorsement of a particular brand of far-right Republicanism.

Why do people care about companies' implied partisanship? There are two reasons. First, in many contexts, people have choices about how they spend their money, and they think it is important to support companies that share their views. If a company takes stances that the person disagrees with, they may feel that it is necessary to have their money follow their values and only spend money at companies that align with those values. For instance, many progressives refuse to eat at Chick-fil-A because of its historical stances on LGBTQIA+ issues. Because the company's stances have historically been in opposition to their values, these people avoid Chick-fil-A and instead purchase their food elsewhere. This is an element of political consumerism

---

[7] Land O'Lakes did not respond to my request for an interview.

3.2 *How to Use Voice*

(Stolle and Micheletti 2013). Yet a second and equally important reason is that opposing a company's political stance or identity – especially publicly – is an expression of an individual's political identity. For many people, political expression and partisanship are fundamental to their self-image and personal identity (Federico and Ekstrom 2018), and many people find their partisanship centered more on opposing one party than supporting another. Evidence for this phenomenon, which is termed "negative partisanship" – the idea that our political identities and expression are rooted in opposition to the opposing party – has been found beginning in early childhood (Holman et al. 2019). Combining the importance of political expression with negative partisanship and increasing political and social polarization (Mason 2018) means that taking a stance against a company that supports your opposing party can be an important statement of political expression. In these statements of opposition, we can find not only our own personal identities but also companionship and a sense of camaraderie and companionship with our co-partisans. Opposing a company that donates to Republicans can reinforce identity and create community among Democrats and vice versa. Our choice to support a boycott reinforces to ourselves our values and what we stand for, and our choice to discuss it helps situate us within a group.

Johnston, Lavine, and Federico (2017) explain the polarization of economic policy choices this way: "The rise of cultural division between Democratic and Republican elites has created a context in which economic opinion is increasingly a means by which engaged citizens signal their allegiance to a cultural in-group" (p. 45). In other words, taking a stance on economic issues allows people to define themselves publicly, something that is especially valued in a politically and culturally polarized environment. This logic extends to which companies or brands a person will buy from, proclaim they would never buy from, or, in some cases, lie about buying from. In her essay "Girl 6," Tressie McMillan Cottom illustrates the expressive political stance implied by her purchases:

> A few months ago I could not get the City of Richmond to give me a trash can. They call them "supercans," which sounds like it has a lot of cool powers but just means it can hold three Amazon Prime boxes. This is good because I am really working on being a socialist black feminist. It would help if my comrades did not see my Amazon Prime

boxes in my trash can. As it is, I am careful never to link to my book page on Amazon or take a selfie where you can see the traitorous blue tag in the background. I made that book link mistake once on social media and I am still apologizing for not linking to the unionized Powell's bookstore. (Cottom 2019, p. 203)

The implication is clear: good progressives, especially socialist Black feminists, don't buy from Amazon. Buying from Amazon, and especially being seen doing so, conveys cultural and political values in opposition to how she wants to be seen. This is not strictly for class or political reasons but rather because many progressives disagree with Amazon's labor and businesses practices. This accords with Johnston, Lavine, and Federico (2017), who go on to explain that political engagement is about expressing "core aspects of the self" through political statements. Most people don't refuse to buy from Amazon, encourage others to not buy from Amazon, or hide Amazon boxes because they believe their consumer choices will somehow punish Amazon for its political, environmental, and labor missteps; instead, they hide their Amazon boxes because it signals to others and reinforces to themselves the kind of person they are. They are not someone who would buy from Amazon because good progressives don't do that, but instead they are the kind of person who buys from "the unionized Powell's bookstore." As Cottom acknowledges, the use of consumerism as a method of political positioning is important both psychologically, for helping an individual define their sense of self, but also for social positioning.

When a company is called out publicly for taking a political stance or trying to influence politics, it provides an opportunity for people to engage in political signaling and tell those around them who they are and what they stand for. In other words, a call to "boycott" a company is an invitation for an individual to participate as a way to declare their partisanship and where they stand in the political–cultural milieu, largely by declaring what kinds of corporate behaviors and stances they oppose.[8] In other words, Democrats and progressives don't signal their partisanship and views to others by praising a

---

[8] This is similar to arguments made by Johnen, Jungblut, and Ziegele (2018), drawing on the moral panic framework of Goode and Ben-Yehuda (1994), about participation in online firestorms driven by a moral compass and desire for social recognition.

3.2 How to Use Voice

company for donating to Democrats, but instead by deriding a company for donating to Republicans. It's this ability to publicly take a stance in opposition to political values that allows the action to alert those around them – especially if they're like-minded – that the signaler is of a particular type. If someone posts to social media that they will not buy products from Goya because their CEO endorsed Donald Trump, for instance, they are telling the people around them that they are liberal.

Yet getting people to participate in organized actions – even if it's a chance to signal which team they're on – is difficult. Most forms of political organization require commitment and effort from individuals. And this commitment and effort can be antithetical to mass recruitment. Research shows that individuals are more likely to join an organized action when the benefits outweigh the costs (Klein, Smith, and John 2004). The benefits are mostly psychological – including a belief that the company's actions are sufficiently egregious to warrant the action, that taking an action might lead to change, and/or a personal sense of fulfillment. The costs, however, can be more concrete. Participation in protest requires time, effort, money, and social energy. Some people may be willing to withstand these costs for the potential psychological benefit, but many more may not.

On the other hand, the rise of the internet and social media have enabled forms of protest that are essentially costless. Although low-cost, low-commitment shows of support are neither new nor limited to the internet (Christensen 2011), the internet has created many new venues for what Kristofferson, White, and Peloza (2014) term "token" support and others call "slacktivism" (Morozov 2009). This kind of activism is criticized as "feel-good online activism that has zero political or social impact" (Morozov 2009), in part, perhaps, because it is mostly intended to signal a person's preferences to people in their networks, not to make meaningful social change (Christensen 2011). However, even if it doesn't signal a deep commitment to the issue or translate into other forms of activism (Christensen 2011; Kristofferson, White, and Peloza 2014), it is so easy that it puts up few of the hurdles of more traditional activism, meaning it's easier to attract large crowds of people to an action.

The ability to attract large crowds of people to participate means that what this online activism may lack in depth of commitment it can make up for in breadth and virality. In other words, the internet – and, in particular, social media – has enabled a great many people to costlessly assert their stance on an issue. Instead of traveling to a protest or writing a letter to a company, people can share, copy-and-paste, or write short statements to share on social media, which is considerably easier and less resource-intensive. Since so many more people can do it, the result can be a giant (virtual) crowd and a substantial ruckus.

Often, this online activism in opposition to a company's political advocacy takes the form of a call to boycott a company. Boycotts are a common way that individuals respond to perceived bad behavior on the part of companies. According to Dietlind Stolle and Michele Micheletti's (2013) *Political Consumerism*, boycott is a form of political consumerism that people engage in as a response to a perceived "vacuum" of government leadership. Stolle and Micheletti define political consumerism as "consumers' use of the market as an arena for politics in order to change institutional or market practices found to be ethically, environmentally, or politically objectionable" (p. 39). Boycotting and other forms of political consumerism are intended to force companies to change their behavior in response to market factors, such as loss of sales, in the absence of government action to force the companies to change their behaviors. In three surveys conducted in 2016–2017, Endres and Panagopoulos (2017) found that between 32 and 36 percent of respondents reported boycotting in the previous year, a range that increased to 39–50 percent when the sample was limited to registered voters.

Yet it is not at all clear that online calls to boycott result in meaningful changes to consumer behavior. Indeed, professed boycotters often face criticism that they never would have purchased from the company in question in the first place, therefore, invalidating their claims of boycott. "It's a gay bar, Pamela," a meme that swept the Twin Cities in 2019, illustrates this. This was one Facebook commenter's response to an older white woman from rural Minnesota who posted that a Minneapolis bar and nightclub that had lampooned President Trump[9] had "lost her business." The internet delighted in this, recognizing this woman had likely never been to the bar (The Saloon) in the first place, let alone was a frequent enough visitor to

---

[9] Specifically, they put a "Trump Baby" balloon on their roof in preparation for a speech Trump was scheduled to give in downtown Minneapolis.

3.2 How to Use Voice

have business it could lose, given both what they inferred about her identity based on her Facebook profile as well as her distance from Minneapolis. The response – "It's a gay bar, Pamela" – marked the perceived absurdity of her statement. It went viral and even ended up on t-shirts.[10]

This criticism – even when it is in jest – misunderstands the point of an online boycott. Calls to boycott, especially online, are in large part performative. This is not to say that people are not earnest and do not change their behavior, but the intent in calling for or talking about boycott (separate from one's consumer choices) is to express anger at the company and demonstrate solidarity with others who are similarly opposed. They are efforts focused on trying to convince others – including governments and other companies – not to buy from the company in question. Above all else, they are public statements that allow someone to declare where they stand politically. Pamela, of course, was not actually intending to inform anyone about her drinking and partying habits; instead, she was making a public statement in support of Donald Trump by opposing a company that had lampooned him. Someone making statements about boycotting Land O' Lakes for donating to Steve King or boycotting Goya for its CEO's endorsement of Trump, similarly, is not necessarily providing reliable information about what kind of butter or chickpeas they buy but rather telling everyone that they are not a Republican or a white supremacist.

This definition of boycott is consistent with the history of the term, which originally was not moored to the idea of purchasing behavior or consumerism at all. The word "boycott" comes from the English land agent Captain Charles Boycott, who attracted the ire of his Irish tenants for his policies. To punish him, his tenants contributed to his economic and social ostracism, in large part by refusing to work his land (Hyde and Wehle 1933). Just as the Irish tenants in the late nineteenth century did, an online boycott effort aims to economically and socially ostracize a company – to mark it as tainted, to clarify that people in a certain social and political group (or looking to sell to them) should not associate with it, to brand it as associated with

---

[10] Jones, Hannah. "How 'It's a Gay Bar, Pamela' Became the Twin Cities' Favorite Meme." October 22, 2019. City Pages. www.citypages.com/news/how-its-a-gay-bar-pamela-became-the-twin-cities-favorite-meme/563571331.

an out-group. In other words, in an online boycott, an individual's consumer decisions matter less than the negative public attention to a company from many people stating they would boycott, if only hypothetically.

Not all attempts to rile up the public over a company's political advocacy will gain the same momentum, however. Understood as a chance to signal political type and positioning, we should expect that efforts to support especially partisan-linked policies should attract the most attention, as will contributions to prominent and especially partisan politicians. Either of these actions positions the company most clearly to be used for political positioning since little explanation of the egregiousness of the offense is necessary. Policies without a clear partisan identity or politicians who are less well known or less clearly partisan-linked (i.e., not standard-bearers), on the other hand, have a lower probability of a mass backlash since opposition to things associated with them are not as useful for easy political positioning.

Expectation: The mass public has a higher probability of reacting when the event provides a clear signal of their political type.

> **Sub-Expectation:** The mass public has a higher probability of reacting when the company supports a policy that is clearly partisan-linked.
> **Sub-Expectation:** The mass public has a higher probability of reacting when the company is clearly associated with a well-known and prominently partisan politician.

Although the company may be able to engage in marketing efforts to prevent or tame an online boycott campaign, whether the campaign gains steam and people talking about boycotting a company is largely outside of the company's control. As discussed previously, all the company can do is choose its own actions carefully, with attention to potential downstream consequences. Yet, if boycotts aren't about lost sales, why do they care anyway?

Reputation Damage

The third step is not a strategic choice – there is no forking decision in Figure 3.1 but rather a scope condition related to both the company

3.2 How to Use Voice

and the nature of the public backlash. Will the uproar damage the company? In other words, does the company care?

Boycotts, as they are conventionally understood, as consumers ceasing to consume for some principled reason, target companies in an obvious way. If people who were buying from a company suddenly *stop* buying from that company, the company's revenues will drop. Companies' revenues are mostly based on selling things, so that drop in revenue could theoretically be severe, and companies might opt to change their behavior to win back those customers (and then some, perhaps) in order to recover. This is, of course, in theory – it's very hard to tell if the people who say they're going to boycott actually will, or if, indeed, they would ever even be in a position to buy from the company in the first place. But as a theory, it is sensible. If people say they won't buy, and they don't buy, this hurts sales and revenue, and drops in revenue are bad.

Yet it would be a mistake to believe that a company's value is strictly the sum of its revenues. Many companies also own intangible assets that contribute to the firm's value. Intangible assets are things of value to a company (and that increase its value) but do not have a physical form. These can include a company's intellectual property, trade secrets, and brands. All of these things can rise and fall in value and can contribute to the company's value rising or falling. For instance, the Coca-Cola company has famously guarded its "secret" recipe for over a century, including showing off a vault purportedly containing the recipe in its museum in Atlanta.[11] This kind of very public secrecy is not uncommon – KFC, Mrs. Field's, WD-40, and many others all also have very public trade secrets – as the trade secret is valuable both as a method of maintaining competitive advantage and as a way to shape public perception of the company (Hannah et al. 2014; Crittenden, Crittenden, and Pierpont 2015).

Companies are so particular about how they are perceived because a company's brand is among the most valuable assets many companies have (Budac and Baltador 2013; Fournier and Srinivasan 2018). "Brand" can refer to the names of product lines that a company owns, such as how Johnson & Johnson owns Neutrogena, Tylenol,

---

[11] See "Vault of the Secret Formula." 2020. World of Coca-Cola. www .worldofcoca-cola.com/explore/explore-inside/explore-vault-secret-formula/.

and Listerine, but a company's "brand," more broadly, refers to a combination of aspects of how people think about the company. This is multifaceted and includes their knowledge, their belief in its quality, and the associations they have with the company, as well as their perceptions of its "personality" (the group of human traits they would ascribe to the brand), its reputation, its image, and many other aspects (Keller 1993; Aaker 1997; Keller and Lehmann 2006; Ettenson and Knowles 2008). Brands can be painstaking to develop and expensive and difficult to maintain, and companies often devote significant resources to the task of brand management because brands can help companies compete in a crowded marketplace and build loyalty (Romaniuk and Nenycz-Thiel 2013). This suggests that companies with especially valuable and well-known brands should be the most concerned about reputation damage because these have the most to lose.

Brands (and reputations) can also be fragile. This is because they are intangible and exist primarily in the public imagination, meaning that all it really takes to damage a company's brand and reputation is enough people thinking about the company in a different and negative way. In some cases, associations with a brand or company can shift without the company doing anything at all (Pandya and Venkatesan 2016). Yet, if companies do engage in activities that people disagree with, the intangibility of brands and reputations means they can be hurt by "firestorms," large groups of people expressing dissatisfaction with a company on social media (Pfeffer, Zorbach, and Carley 2014), that often manifest in calls for boycott or rejections of the company or brand (Delgado-Ballester, López-López, and Bernal-Palazón 2019). Even divorced from any consumer activity, Hansen, Kupfer, and Hennig-Thurau (2018) found that large firestorms can have not only short-term negative effects for the company's brand but also effects that are detected two years later. Although the intent of these firestorms is not necessarily to damage the company's reputation but rather to express unhappiness and vent, damage is done nonetheless (Delgado-Ballester, López-López, and Bernal-Palazón 2019).

The overarching problem is that these kinds of firestorms can lead to a company losing control over its reputation, as the public, rather than the company, determines what the company's reputation is and stands for in the public imagination. Of course, in some circumstances

3.2 How to Use Voice

in which companies purposely make political statements, the firestorm may be intentional or at least not necessarily damaging and may be part of a deliberate branding effort. In the example of the Minneapolis bar and nightclub with the Trump balloon, for instance, it is likely the action was intended at least in part to generate publicity, whether positive and negative. Angering a swath of conservatives was not an unintended consequence of the action; it might well have been the point.

Yet, in other cases, when companies are not intentionally taking political stances but are instead trying to advocate for a particular policy, this loss of control over the message and brand can be especially damaging. This represents a lack of control over an important asset, which can be a serious threat to a company's value for several reasons. For one, reputations are valuable in and of themselves, and so a decline in the public perception of the company (and its brands) can decrease its value and therefore hurt the overall value of the company. In addition, shareholders may respond negatively to the information provided by the firestorm (King and Soule 2007), and a hit to the brand identity or reputation might hurt a company's ability to recruit and retain talent (Keller and Richey 2006; Franca and Pahor 2012).

Brand Expectation: Companies with valuable and well-known brands should be most concerned about reputation damage.

A related issue specific to politically motivated firestorms is that they can lead to a company being permanently associated with a particular party or group of people, such that it becomes persona non grata to many. This circles back to Cottom's point about how socialist Black feminists don't buy from Amazon. Similarly, many white liberals do not buy from Walmart, and many conservatives do not buy from Nike. It is nothing to do with an ongoing boycott and everything to do with a company's image and associations. These images and associations can shift as the result of firestorms, such that people, in the aftermath, may not even know *why* they do not or will not buy from a particular company, just that they (and people like them) don't. Even if the "boycott" doesn't result in people changing their consumer behavior, subsequent public rebranding might change consumer patterns in the long term.

Firestorm Strength Expectation: Boycotts are most likely to damage a company's reputation when the backlash is "strong," meaning a high volume of tweets or other content, especially over a sustained period of time.

Partisan Rebranding Expectation: Boycotts are most likely to damage a company's reputation when the boycott creates an association between a company and a political party.

Although companies can intervene to try to stop these firestorms, sometimes intervention can make the entire situation worse, and best practices about how companies should engage with firestorms is still a topic of active debate (see, e.g., Rauschnabel, Kammerlander, and Ivens 2016; Scholz and Smith 2019). A further complication is that companies may also be asked directly to comment if the media pick up the story, only causing the energy and attention to build (Pfeffer, Zorbach, and Carley 2014). As a result, it is in the best interest of most companies to avoid firestorms rather than attempt to respond in the moment or afterward.

To summarize, if companies choose to engage in politics, they face the prospect of unleashing an unpleasant chain of events. If they advocate for their political interests by trying to influence politicians, there's a chance that activists will notice and publicize it. If activists notice and publicize it, there's a chance that the mass public will pick up on it and use it as an opportunity to signal their political "team." And if the mass public picks up on it, there's some probability it'll result in long-term reputation damage. The probability that each of those events happens may not be especially high – and it varies at each stage in the process – but it is not zero. That means that any time a company takes a political stance, it stares down the possibility of reputation damage. In the next section, I explain what that means for how companies engage with the political system.

Choosing Tactics

All of this puts companies in a difficult position. On one hand, companies have very good reasons to want to avoid a firestorm. If they do not engage in politics or policy, their actions won't be noticed or publicized by activists, the mass public won't pick up on it, and there will be no resulting reputation damage.[12] Yet at the same time, companies

---

[12] This is all assuming that any backlash is based on actual events and not fiction or speculation. In an era where misinformation thrives, this is a strong

3.2 How to Use Voice

still have political issues that concern them and good reasons to advocate for their interests. Fear of downstream consequences does not actually do anything to change that. It makes advocacy more perilous but not less necessary.

So what do companies do when faced with the potential for serious consequences of an action they perceive as, nonetheless, necessary? Some companies might "look down the game tree" at how their choices might play out, think about what that might mean for their company, and opt to not take the chance at all, avoiding political advocacy entirely and just accepting the policies they are given. This is likely if the consequences of the policy are minor, for instance. The potential costs of advocacy exceed the costs of policy compliance. Yet other companies consider the same potential chain of events and still do not see non-intervention as a viable strategy. These companies have to decide how to use their voice while trying to avoid a chain of events that ends in social media outrage. This creates incentives for companies to act strategically to reduce their probability of triggering a firestorm.

Recall the schematic outlining the chain of events in Figure 3.1. Each of these steps is probabilistic, meaning that companies might attract the attention and criticism of activists or they might not. The mass public might respond with a firestorm or it might not. At every stage, each individual company and each type of action has its own specific probability of advancing on the path toward reputation damage. Certain types of companies (larger, branded, previously targeted, headed by women) have a higher probability of being targeted by activists. Certain types of activities (clearly partisan-linked, associated with an especially prominent or divisive politician) have a higher probability of resulting in substantial public backlash. Companies want to minimize the probability of a large public backlash – get it as close to zero as possible – which means they want to minimize the probability of being targeted, the probability of a resulting public backlash, or both while simultaneously maximizing the probability of successfully obtaining their preferred outcome. Yet companies cannot control what activists

assumption. Yet relaxing this assumption, and assuming companies may be targeted based only on partial truths or fiction, reinforces the idea that companies may need to be even more careful to avoid the ire of activists and the public.

or the mass public do. All they can control is their own actions, with an eye toward reducing the probability of an eventual public backlash.

For companies that decide to advocate rather than accept politics and policy as they are, this puts them in the realm of managing how their advocacy is perceived. In other words, once the decision is made to advocate, the question becomes how to advocate in a way that minimizes risk. In the absence of concerns about public backlash and with sufficient resources, companies would generally prefer to engage in direct lobbying and campaign contributions because this is efficient and direct, it follows a known and understandable playbook, and it requires none of the compromise or delegation inherent in working with or through third parties. Yet the fear of public backlash creates an incentive for companies to act strategically and deviate from this play-book and to manage the appearances and perceptions of their actions. I argue that there are two primary ways companies do this. First, they can aim to evade activists by making it look like they did not engage in political advocacy. Second, they can aim to defuse the public by mak-ing it look like they did *something* but make it unclear whether that thing is actually worth getting worked up about. In the next sections, I discuss each of these in turn.

3.2.1 Evading Activist Attention

The first thing that companies can do to minimize risk when they engage in political advocacy is to aim to avoid the attention of activists. They can do this by making it appear as if they did not actu-ally engage in any political advocacy. Activists – a group that includes anyone who monitors companies' activities and may publicly criticize them in an attempt to change their actions – can be especially thor-ough in their monitoring, but they aren't omnipresent or omniscient. Whether they notice and publicize a company's advocacy efforts is probabilistic. Some companies have a higher probability of evading detection because they are monitored less thoroughly. Even some com-panies that are under more scrutiny may still sometimes fly beneath the radar just by chance. Yet, while companies cannot control what the activists notice or what they do, they can control their side of it. That is, they can take steps to avoid detection by appearing to engage in no political advocacy activity at all. This is political advocacy in stealth mode, and there are two ways of doing it: first, by hiding advocacy entirely, and second, by creating distance between the company and its advocacy efforts.

3.2 How to Use Voice

3.2.1.1 Hidden Advocacy

The first way companies can advocate without appearing to advocate is to hide their activity, such that it appears that no advocacy occurred. There are many perfectly legal ways that companies (or any interest group) can get involved in political advocacy without leaving a paper trail, allowing them to advocate without being seen to advocate. Although many conventional forms of advocacy have associated disclosure laws, anyone knowledgeable enough about those laws can craft activity that skirts the disclosure requirements.

For instance, if companies donate money to a political candidate, most jurisdictions require the company to file paperwork that says they did that. Yet some of those same laws specify minimum thresholds that must be met for disclosure to be necessary. For instance, the Federal Election Commission's (FEC) guidance for candidates specifies that small contributions collected at a fundraiser do not need to be linked to the individual or group donating but rather can be reported as an aggregate for the event.[13] If a company donates less than that amount of money, it would not necessarily generate a record. In some places, companies could donate multiple times below the minimum threshold and appear to never have donated at all.

Similarly, if companies employ a lobbyist or directly lobby someone in a political or governmental office, they may be required to file paperwork. If they retain a lobbyist, many states require that companies file paperwork to that end, even if the lobbyist doesn't take action for the company. Yet sometimes there is a specific definition of "lobbyist" and "lobbying," and lobbying can happen unofficially without being reported if it's not carried out by registered lobbyists. In other places, lobbying does not need to be reported unless each individual lobbyist meets a time threshold: if they don't spend a certain amount of time lobbying, they don't need to report it. In other words, if someone who isn't actually a lobbyist lobbies, in some places this doesn't count as lobbying and therefore doesn't have to be reported. In other places, if not enough money or time is spent on the lobbying, it doesn't need to be reported. In other places, establishing a nonprofit to educate lawmakers – where education is a loose synonym for

---

[13] Federal Election Commission. "Recording Receipts." Accessed August 28, 2020. www.fec.gov/help-candidates-and-committees/keeping-records/recording-receipts/.

76 How Does Public Opinion Shape Corporate Political Advocacy?

lobbying – is not legally considered lobbying and therefore doesn't have to be reported as such.

Of course, some jurisdictions have even more minimalist laws, and some have robust laws or statutes that make it difficult for the public to find any information that was disclosed. Activity that is legally disclosed but is only accessible to the people to whom it is disclosed and not the public is still, effectively, invisible. Advocacy in the absence of laws, in the presence of laws without public data, or within the loopholes of laws can all allow companies to financially support candidates or politicians, or otherwise advocate for policy without their being a clear, public record saying their company did any of those things. Without that clear, public record, it is much harder for activists to know the activity is happening. If they don't know it's happening, they aren't scrutinizing it and they can't publicize it.

That said, this is not without its own particular danger. If companies and other organized interests could easily and painlessly advocate without anyone knowing, it isn't clear why anyone would ever do otherwise. One problem is that working within loopholes is inefficient and difficult to do. It requires clear knowledge of the laws and enough interest in working within them to take steps like donating underneath minimums.[14] Engaging in political advocacy only within places without disclosure laws or only in places where the disclosures are hard to find does not help companies who want to advocate for policy in other places. And, finally, hiding activity carries with it the potential of even greater backlash if the company is found to be strategically evading reporting requirements. In the short term it solves the problem, letting companies engage in conventional advocacy strategies while reducing the probability of eventual public backlash and reputation damage. Yet, especially for companies that are under particular scrutiny already, getting caught trying to hide activity could result in a huge public relations problem and firestorm of its own.

Hiding Expectation #1: Companies that are concerned about political boycotts should be more likely to try to evade reporting requirements.

[14] Full disclosure: many of my interviews mentioned these minimums and definitions, but I struggled to find clear guidance for many jurisdictions on the internet independently.

3.2 How to Use Voice

3.2.1.2 Distanced Advocacy

The second way companies can advocate without appearing to advocate is to structure their activity such that it appears that advocacy did occur but that it was carried out by someone other than the company. If the first strategy can be summarized as "we didn't *do* anything," this strategy shifts the emphasis – instead saying "*we* didn't do anything." By using third parties with preexisting relationships with politicians, companies can seek out political influence indirectly. Having someone else actually do the work de-links the activity and the company's name, obscuring the origins of the influence-seeking, creating distance between the advocacy and the company, and protecting the company from backlash. Although activists and the public will be able to tell that advocacy work happened, they will be unable to easily tell which companies were involved. Grumbach and Pierson (2019) found, for instance, that the ability to donate through these kinds of intermediaries allows companies to appear more moderate than their interests actually are.

There are several different types of third parties that companies can work through. One is an industry group. Industry groups are groups of companies in the same industry or with certain key characteristics in common that result in their having similar political interests. The American Beverage Association, for instance, is an industry group that represents the interests of companies such as Coca-Cola and its subsidiaries that make and sell non-alcoholic drinks. The National Restaurant Association, along with its state-level branches, represents the political interests of restaurants and some other companies in the hospitality industry. Chambers of Commerce often represent the interests of businesses across industries that have a geographic or political jurisdiction in common rather than industrial characteristics. These groups advocate on behalf of their members along their shared political concerns. Companies that channel their political advocacy through industry groups benefit from the group's lobbying efforts but don't have their name directly linked to them. If a restaurant association lobbies on behalf of its members, for instance, any associated records of the lobbying indicate that the group has lobbied but does not list its members. Although some industry groups have public directories of their members – the American Beverage Association, for instance, does – others, like the

National Restaurant Association, do not, meaning that connecting individual companies with advocacy on their behalf can be difficult or impossible.

Yet companies do not have to rely on interest groups as their third-party intermediary of choice (and, indeed, some companies may not have the choice at all[15]). Any third party who is not a professional lobbyist and has a preexisting relationship with the politician in question can be useful for advocacy without records. The key, again, is that companies use those preexisting relationships instead of forming their own, and therefore only engage with the politicians indirectly and informally. A politician's personal connections (friends, family, etc.) or anyone else that has the politician's ear can be a good resource for this since a politician's friend or member of their child's school's parent-teacher association does not need to file disclosure paperwork.

The public can also act as a third party when enlisted by companies to advocate on their behalf. By mobilizing the public, companies aim to enlist the public to advocate on their behalf as this too serves the company's interest in advocacy but creates no record linking the advocacy to the company. One way companies can do this is by purchasing advertising to convince the public to take a stance on an issue and contact their representatives about it. This uses the weaker preexisting ties that constituents have with their elected leaders, but it can make up for the weakness of the tie with the quantity of phone calls, emails, or social media messages about that issue. Another way companies can appear to mobilize the public is through a process called "astroturfing," in which "participants pretend to be ordinary citizens acting independently" (Keller et al. 2020). Astroturfing is especially popular on online platforms and can mobilize public support by creating the appearance that public support already exists, as, potentially, an alternative to buying ads. Just like with using industry groups or people who know the politician personally, enlisting the public can help companies spur advocacy on their issues while obscuring the fact that the company is behind the advocacy.

---

[15] As work on trade by Baccini, Pinto, and Weymouth (2017), Osgood et al. (2017), and Kim and Osgood (2019) all illustrate, industries may not always share preferences on salient political issues, and so industry groups may only be an option in situations where a consensus does exist.

3.2 How to Use Voice

Again, this strategy has the benefit of avoiding backlash, but it carries with it all the risks inherent in delegation and, in the case of industry groups, collective-action problems as well. In other words, working indirectly through a third party has the benefit of distancing a company from its advocacy efforts, but the drawback is just that: it distances a company from its advocacy efforts. It entails the company giving up control over its message and timing. The delegate may not get the message right. They may not take action at all. Working through third parties, therefore, reduces the risk of boycott at the cost of increased uncertainty.

Hiding Expectation #2: Companies that are concerned about political boycotts should be more likely to engage in political influence-seeking through third parties.

3.2.2 Defusing the Public Response

In addition to (or instead of) evading activists, companies can try to defuse the public response. Unlike evading activists, defusing the public response does not require companies to hide their activities but instead aims to make it unclear whether their actions warrant criticism and backlash. In the previous section I explained that the evasion strategies can be summarized as "we didn't do anything" (regardless of emphasis). This strategy can be summarized as "we did something, but it wasn't (that) bad." This relies on the idea that people respond publicly to corporate advocacy because it provides an opportunity for them to signal their political type. If a company can remove that element – advocate while not giving people an opportunity to use it to position themselves within the current political–social milieu – they may be able to avoid a firestorm. In this section, I explain two ways that advocacy can happen while minimizing the risk of firestorm. The first is taking actions that may not be perceived as advocacy at all and the second is engaging in visible advocacy while avoiding especially partisan figures.

3.2.2.1 Creative Advocacy

The first way to engage in advocacy while defusing the public response is to engage in advocacy that may not present itself as advocacy. In other words, companies can use unconventional advocacy

80　*How Does Public Opinion Shape Corporate Political Advocacy?*

and influence-seeking strategies that allow them to build and access relationships with politicians but that do not take the form of conventional advocacy (i.e., lobbying, campaign contributions). Since people get publicly upset and boycott because a company takes a stance in its advocacy that is partisan and therefore allows the individual to use that to define themselves politically, advocacy strategies that don't *look like* advocacy should defuse the reaction by not providing that opportunity.

Philanthropy and community service, for instance, are good strategies for masking political influence. These can help to build relationships with politicians, but they come with plausible deniability. Most people are unlikely to recognize donating to a philanthropic cause or filling potholes, cleaning a park, or tutoring students as forms of political influence. They don't look at all like a company taking a political stance. Criticizing companies for their philanthropic or community service activities is not straightforward, further, because those who would criticize them for their political actions may not want to be seen as dissuading philanthropy or community service more generally.

The drawbacks of these strategies are that they require more creativity, may require more effort, and may not be as broadly useful as either campaign contributions or lobbying. Money and information help all politicians, which make those two strategies good go-tos. The kinds of community engagement efforts that might help any given policymaker can vary across jurisdictions. Cleaning a park might help build relationships with some politicians, while others might need help with community safety, road maintenance, or schools. Knowing what will help requires deeper knowledge and, most likely, people with different skill sets.[16]

In sum, any activity that cultivates a relationship with a political official but avoids the appearance of influence-seeking and stance-taking can help companies manage the competing necessities of influencing politics and avoiding criticism, although potentially at the cost of logistical difficulty and increased uncertainty about effectiveness.

---

[16] There are, however, organizations that exist to facilitate corporate volunteerism, which can help with this. The Corporate Volunteerism Council – Twin Cities is one such organization.

3.2 How to Use Voice

Defusion Expectation #1: Companies that are concerned about political boycotts should be less likely to pursue campaign contributions and lobbying and more likely to pursue strategies such as community development and philanthropy.

3.2.2.2 Careful Advocacy

Finally, companies can engage in visible, conventional advocacy but try to defuse the response by being careful of what associations their advocacy implies. The aim here is to make it less likely people will see the company's advocacy – if it is brought to their attention by activists – as an invitation to declare their political type. Since people have their attention pulled in multiple different directions at any given time, not every call to action by activists will successfully attract a crowd. Therefore, companies may be able to reduce the probability, intensity, and duration of public outrage, which, in turn, reduces the company's risk of reputation damage. As Hansen, Kupfer, and Hennig-Thurau (2018) found, not all firestorms are equally damaging: only those that really gain steam, garner a lot of tweets and retweets, and last for a decent amount of time actually have significant consequences. So, if companies can reduce the probability the mass public responds at all or reduce the level of offense such that it attracts a smaller crowd, they may be able to avoid the worst of the damages.

The key to this strategy is to engage in conventional political advocacy while avoiding associating with political standard-bearers. Because people become publicly angry about corporate advocacy in order to define their own partisanship and ideology, companies want to avoid interacting with anyone or anything that allows people to latch on to that person or thing as a stand-in for a broader ideology.[17] In other words, if a company needs to engage in political advocacy by donating to or lobbying Democrats, they should avoid being linked to politicians or policies that carry within them a clear association with Democratic or progressive-leaning politics. The same is true of Republicans.

The reason for this is that, even if companies cannot or do not try to avoid detection, there is always a chance that the firestorm will not

---

[17] In literature, this is called a synecdoche.

start at all or that it will not attract sufficient attention to be damaging. It's probabilistic, but it's not random. That is, companies may not be able to predict exactly which activities will attract attention and public response, and they cannot control what people do, but they do know that creating associations in the public imagination between their company and any particular ideology can potentially be damaging. If they donate money to prominent Democrats or progressives, they may risk outrage by conservatives who use their public anger about the donation as a way to signal to their peers where they stand. If the company lobbies prominent Republicans or conservatives, the company risks progressives viewing it as an invitation to tell people about their politics. If companies can avoid associations with people or ideas with clear partisan associations, however, it reduces the probability of a firestorm by making it less inviting and less seemingly egregious. People are less likely to use a company's political donation to declare their ideology to their social networks if it is to a politician no one has heard of. If too many characters are required to explain who a politician is, it might not make a good tweet.

Defusion Expectation #2: Companies that are concerned about political boycott should be less likely to associate themselves with partisan-linked political issues, even if those issues concern the company.

Defusion Expectation #3: Companies that are concerned about political boycott should be less likely to associate themselves with very partisan and/or divisive politicians.

These strategies also work together. For instance, if a company has an interest in opposing a policy that's especially partisan-linked and is likely to generate a significant backlash or if it has a need to influence a politician who is a prominent partisan, the company can aim to advocate creatively, at a distance, or hide their advocacy activity.

3.3 Conclusion

Companies frequently face government policies that affect them and spur them to advocate for their interests. In this chapter, I address the question of how they reason about their choices about how to advocate. The cost of doing politics, I argue, is the potential for public backlash, often called a "boycott" colloquially or a "firestorm"

3.3 Conclusion

academically. In this chapter, I explore how companies' political advocacy activities can lead them down a probabilistic chain of events that leads to that public backlash. If a company gets involved in politics, it faces the probability that activists may notice and publicly criticize their actions. If activists do criticize their actions, the company then faces the probability that the mass public will be outraged enough to perpetuate a major online call to boycott or other type of firestorm. Each company and each activity has its own probability of being noticed and then experiencing public backlash – some companies and some activities face higher probabilities than others – and what actually happens when companies engage in politics is often beyond the companies' control. What the companies can control is how they engage with politics.

With that in mind, I outline four strategies companies use to reduce the probability of continuing down the potentially damaging path. I call them hidden advocacy, distanced advocacy, creative advocacy, and careful advocacy. The first two, hidden advocacy and distanced advocacy, are aimed at avoiding the attention of activists, whereas the latter two are aimed at reducing the probability and size of a potential public backlash should the activities come to light. Each of these is a strategy companies can take to reduce the overall probability that their decision to advocate politically results in a public backlash that damages their reputation, which is a valuable and intangible asset.

In the next three chapters, I test each of these components separately. Chapter 4 further interrogates the idea of politically induced public backlash, demonstrating that public backlash does tend to be driven by partisan concerns rather than concerns about fairness or influence on its own. I also use social media data to investigate what information people actually provide when they talk about boycott and how these map onto ideas of signaling political type. Chapter 5 digs deeper into whether and why companies care about politically induced boycotts and online firestorms, looking both at the types of companies that are most likely to be targeted for these efforts as well as those most likely to suffer from reputation damage. Chapter 6 then puts these together and seeks to weigh the evidence for whether companies' influence-seeking strategies are actually consistent with the proposition that they are trying to avoid public boycott.

4 Why Does the Public Care About Corporate Political Influence?

4.1 Introduction

"Oh look, it's the sound of me Googling 'how to make your own Adobo'", tweeted US Rep. Alexandria Ocasio-Cortez.

Adobo sauce, a common condiment, is actually fairly easy to make yourself – you mix and heat some hot peppers, herbs, and spices with broth and vinegar, then blend[1] – but Rep. Ocasio-Cortez did not tweet that on July 9, 2020, with the intent of tracking down the best ratio of ancho chiles to garlic or an authoritative source on whether she should include cinnamon. Instead, Ocasio-Cortez was trying to demonstrate that people *could* make their own, and they should make their own instead of buying premade Adobo sauce from Goya Foods. This was a tweet supporting a boycott.

She was one of the first high-profile people to respond to remarks from the CEO of Goya Foods praising President Donald Trump, helping to launch a boycott of the food company, maker of chickpeas and other food staples, including Adobo sauce. When Robert Unanue, the CEO, appeared at the White House Rose Garden, he praised Trump, saying, "We are all truly blessed ... to have a leader like President Trump who is a builder ... We have an incredible builder, and we pray. We pray for our leadership, our president".[2] Google searches for the word "Goya" spiked shortly thereafter.[3] #BoycottGoya and #Goyaway began trending on Twitter. Unanue called the boycott a suppression of his free speech and refused to apologize. Trump and his daughter, Ivanka, both publicly supported Goya. Within a few weeks, the popular and media interest had mostly fizzled out.

---

[1] Bayless, Rick. "Red Chile Adobo Sauce." www.rickbayless.com/recipe/red-chile-adobo-sauce/.

[2] Goldman, David. "Goya Foods Boycott Takes Off after Its CEO Praises Trump." July 10, 2020. CNN Business. www.cnn.com/2020/07/10/business/goya-foods-boycott-trump/index.html.

[3] Google Trends.

84

4.1 Introduction

This pattern is common: a company is perceived as taking a political stance, activists publicly criticize the company for its actions, and the mass public responds with calls for boycott. Sometimes the company's stock takes a hit if it's publicly traded, sometimes it doesn't, and often there is an argument about whether it did or not. In most cases, the criticism and effort are not sustained long term. Consumer behavior may not shift at all, or, if it does, it may not shift meaningfully or permanently.

The Goya boycott is especially telling, though, because some of the participants clearly recognized that the point of the boycott, at least for them, was not to punish Goya at all. As an NBC News article articulated, "The 'Boycott Goya' movement, some Latinos say, is more about taking a stand against the president's bigotry than about punishing a once-beloved brand."[4] Boycotting Goya, or stating support for the boycott, was not so much about causing any short- or long-term damage to the company but more about voicing one's political views.

Many consumers recognize that their purchases are a reflection of their political and social values (Stolle and Micheletti 2013). Political consumerism – the idea that people use their consumer behavior as a form of political participation intended to change corporate or government behavior – is a growing phenomenon. The most common way people engage in political consumerism is by aligning their purchases with their values. For instance, people may choose to consciously purchase from local or Black-owned businesses (following the "buy local" and "buy Black" movements), they may become vegetarians, or they may prioritize buying fair-trade products.

Yet, in addition to actual consumer behavior changes, people can use statements about these choices – about boycotting, about supporting boycotts, about the choice to not buy from certain companies – as a way to position themselves socially and politically. Sometimes these statements align with consumer behavior, but sometimes they do not. For instance, some people who supported the Goya boycott may not have been regular buyers of Goya products to begin with. That means that their choice to not buy from Goya, and statements

---

[4] Reyes, Raul A. "Latinos Boycotting Goya Say It's Not about Politics. It's about Standing against Trump's Hate." July 18, 2020. NBC News www.nbcnews.com/news/latino/latinos-boycotting-goya-say-it-s-not-about-politics-it-n1234052?cid=sm_npd_nn_tw_ma.

to that effect, were largely symbolic: a way of stating intentions and contributing to a conversation. These statements tell people more about the boycotter's politics and where they envision themselves in the social–political atmosphere than they do about their consumer choices.

In this chapter, I bring evidence to bear on that point – that online boycotts are primarily a source of information about an individual's politics and a method of informing others in their networks about their politics and values. I also test two specific expectations from Chapter 3: that the mass public has a higher probability of reacting when the company's advocacy efforts convey (a) support for a policy that is clearly partisan-linked and/or (b) a close association with a politician who is well known and associated with a party.

In the rest of this chapter, I provide more information about the central claim of this chapter, outline a few key counterarguments, give an overview of my two sources of data, and then explore what we can learn both from experimental tests and observational social media behavior.

4.2 The Claim

People profess to boycott in response to perceived partisanship from companies, and these boycotts are primarily a form of partisan and ideological signaling, not an expression of actual consumer behavior.

The central claim of this book – and perhaps the most counterintuitive one – is that boycotts in response to corporate advocacy and influence-seeking are neither really about influence-seeking nor really about boycotting.

What do I mean by that?

First, it is not the act of advocating or seeking influence over politics that actually angers people enough to compel them to boycott. To be sure, many people do find corporate influence and the act of companies advocating for or against policy to be upsetting. Especially in an age of growing economic inequality, there is a lot of anger about the power that companies and wealthy individuals appear to have over politics and policy, while normal people appear to have limited influence. Yet that, I argue, is not at the core of calls to boycott a company because of its political advocacy.

4.2 The Claim 87

Instead, when companies assert themselves in the political arena, the thing that tends to trigger a boycott is the perceived partisanship of the action. Most forms of corporate advocacy are observationally inseparable from an endorsement of a party or ideology. Campaign contributions, for instance, create a link between a company and a politician that is easily interpreted as an endorsement of that politician's agenda and ideology. The connection between lobbying for a policy and endorsement of that policy (or lobbying against and public disapproval) is similarly obvious. Even if the intent of the campaign contribution is not to endorse a candidate's entire ethos – even if it is only to seek favor for a particular purpose – the appearance is still of an endorsement. The link between the company and the politician or the issue is the only thing people see, not the intent or background. It is this perceived partisanship that pushes people to boycott.

Second, boycotts are not always really boycotts. That is, boycotts are conventionally understood as being a statement about cessation of consumer behavior. If you buy from a company and then you decide to boycott the company, that means you stop buying products from that company. Yet this is a very narrow understanding of boycott and one that does not square with the social functioning of a call to boycott or a profession of intent to boycott. Understood that way, a boycott is more a statement of values than it is a statement of consumer behavior. It is a way for people to express disapproval of a company and even encourage others to avoid doing business with the company. A boycott is not about consumer activity, or not entirely about consumer activity, so much as it is about signaling someone's values and ideology. In this way, someone can boycott a company they have never purchased from, or indeed ever would purchase from, because saying that you're boycotting is, in large part, using the language of consumerism to declare opposition to a corporate action.

Why do people feel the need to publicly signal their disapproval of a company's partisanship?

The first reason is that, when people have a choice of where to spend their money, many people will prefer to spend their money in ways that align with their own values. The opposite is also true: when given a choice, many people will choose not to give their money to companies they perceive as having views that run counter to theirs. It can often be easier to identify the second type than the first. When a company donates or lobbies and it becomes public knowledge, that provides people with information about the company that they can act on. In the absence of that information (or a concerted marketing effort), identifying companies that align with your values can be hard. Identifying and avoiding companies that do not is easier, and some people choose to do this for that reason.

The second reason is that supporting a boycott of a company is a form of political speech and a way that people can define themselves politically. People are especially polarized, both socially and politically (Mason 2018), such that most things that someone likes and does – or dislikes and refuses to do – ends up being part of a particular political identity. This applies especially well to shopping and consumer behavior. The companies we buy from or don't buy from are a statement of our political and social identity. When a company's activities become known, expressing support for a boycott (or opposition to it) can do two related things. First, it can help reinforce our political identities to ourselves, and second, it can allow us to signal our political allegiances to others.

The first is important because, for some people, political expression is fundamental to their self-image and personal identity (Federico and Ekstrom 2018). Choices of which companies to buy from, especially when information about their perceived partisanship becomes available, is a form of political expression and identity. Choosing to support a boycott, whether or not one actually changes their behavior (or, in fact, has the ability to do so), reinforces political identities and therefore serves an important psychological function.

The second is about signaling in-group loyalty and creating a sense of community and camaraderie among like-minded people. In other words, in addition to being a form of political expression that reinforces who we are to ourselves, it also signals our political type and where we stand on political issues to other people. Denouncing a company and proclaiming an intention to boycott tells other people the kind of person we are, and when the action prompting the proclamations is a political association, it serves as a signal of the direction and strength of someone's partisan identity. Thus, not only does supporting a boycott in response to political advocacy help reinforce individual identity, but it also forges and reinforces an individual's position within a group.

Accordingly, not all attempts at corporate advocacy will spur a boycott because not all forms of corporate advocacy provide the same fertile opportunity to define oneself. For one, not all corporate

4.2 The Claim

advocacy becomes publicly known, and only advocacy that permeates the public consciousness can serve as a signaling opportunity. Second, not all corporate advocacy is equally valuable as a signal. That is, corporate advocacy that creates a link between the company and a well-known politician with a clear partisan stance (a "standard-bearer") is a better boycott opportunity than a link between that same company and a lower-profile or less partisan politician. Similarly, lobbying or other advocacy that associates the company with an especially partisan-linked policy is more likely to generate a boycott than one that has murkier partisan associations. In both cases, this is because the need to explain the reason for boycott makes it a less obvious signal of one's ideology.

All this suggests that people should dislike companies more if the company engages in political advocacy that links them with politicians or policies that are counter to someone's own partisanship and that they should be most likely to support boycotting companies that take advocacy actions that counter their own partisanship.

Expectation 1: People are more disapproving of companies that engage in political advocacy that counters their own partisanship.

Expectation 1A: People dislike companies that engage in political advocacy that links the company with politicians or policies that counter their own partisanship.

Expectation 1B: People should support boycotting companies that engage in political advocacy that links the company with politicians or policies that counter their own partisanship.

Yet the decisions of any individual are not of particular concern to companies. It is, instead, the actions of the mass public – a large group of individuals – that shape corporate decisions. That means that any corporate action that has the highest probability of creating negative associations and support for boycott among individuals should result in the highest probability of mass public reaction.

Expectation 2: The mass public has a higher probability of reacting when the incident provides a clear signal of their political type.

Expectation 2A: The mass public has a higher probability of reacting when the company supports a policy that is clearly partisan-linked.

90   *Why Does The Public Care?*

Expectation 2B: The mass public has a higher probability of reacting when the company is clearly associated with a well-known and prominently partisan politician.

What follows from all of this is two tactics companies can use to engage in political advocacy while short-circuiting the public response. I call these "Creative Advocacy" and "Careful Advocacy." I explained them in greater detail in Chapter 3, but the basic idea is that these are ways to acknowledge the factors that lead to a negative public response – the need for political expression and the ease of political expression when expressing anger toward partisan figures or policies – and work with them. "Creative Advocacy" suggests that companies can engage in political advocacy without regard to who they are advocating or what they are advocating for if they cloak their advocacy in uncertainty about its motives. In other words, companies can use some of the other strategies detailed in Chapter 2 – things that help politicians solve their problems – but that are not commonly understood as political advocacy tactics, and in doing so, they can fly beneath the radar. "Careful Advocacy," on the other hand, allows companies to engage in conventional advocacy strategies (campaign contributions and lobbying), but it relies on a careful choice of who to advocate and what to advocate for, carefully avoiding anyone who might make an advocacy effort an easy target for political expression.

4.3 Why and How It Might Be Wrong

There are also good reasons to believe this claim is wrong – that people don't dislike or boycott based on a company's political influence-seeking, or, if they do, that it is unrelated to political expression and signaling but instead driven by something else, such as a dislike of political advocacy and corporate political influence in general. In this section, I outline a few reasons why these expectations may be incorrect and how that might show up in the data.

1 **People Don't Care Enough:** The first counterclaim is that corporate advocacy and a company's implied partisan stances simply do not matter enough to any individual person to provoke them to boycott. The claim in this chapter is that not only do people care, but they actively dislike corporate political advocacy, and they dislike it enough to boycott a company.

4.3 Why and How It Might Be Wrong

There are good reasons to think this is true. Most of the high-profile boycotts have historically focused not on politics exactly but on events that are, quite literally, matters of life and death. For instance, after the 2013 garment factory fire at Rana Plaza in Dhaka, Bangladesh, which killed at least 1,100 people and injured perhaps twice as many more,[5] there were coordinated efforts to boycott the fast-fashion companies that contracted with that factory and factories like it.[6] Other boycotts of major multinationals have similarly been prompted by corporate actions that seemed likely to cause injury to people, animals, or the environment.

Trying to exert political influence and advocate for policy, whether it's by donating to a candidate, lobbying, or something else, seems qualitatively distinct from these other rationales. Given that even those boycotts were not universally adopted, it raises the completely reasonable concern that something more trivial, like campaign contributions, might not be nearly consequential enough to shape an individual's choice to support a boycott. If most individuals won't boycott on the basis of a person's death or environmental devastation, it seems reasonable they might not be willing to boycott on the basis of lobbying.

If it is true that people don't care enough about political influence-seeking to boycott, that can show up in different ways in the data. For one, we shouldn't see boycotts emerging around political advocacy. We should also see that, if asked, people don't express an opinion about political advocacy in general or about particular instances of it.

2 People are Too Committed to the Products They Buy to Boycott: The second counterclaim is that, regardless of how people feel about political influence-seeking, they aren't willing to (or can't) give up the products they buy. Brand loyalty may lead people to make excuses for companies they like, even if they don't like the company's behavior. That means that, even if people know, care, and don't like political influence-seeking and even if they consider the political advocacy

---

[5] www.ilo.org/global/topics/geip/WCMS_614394/lang–en/index.htm.

[6] Pasick Quartz, Adam. "What to Improve Working Conditions in Bangladesh? Boycott the Gap." May 2, 2013. https://qz.com/80621/want-to-improve-working-conditions-in-bangladesh-boycott-the-gap/.

sufficiently egregious to prompt them to boycott in principle, they may not consider boycotting. In this situation, the decision to boycott is mostly disconnected from the emotion about the corporate activity. Boycott, here, is strictly a material consideration.

Yet the argument in this chapter is not really about consumer behavior, it's about political expression. Strictly speaking, there is no reason a person can't "boycott" a company they buy products from, using my definition of boycott as a statement of principled opposition. Someone can support a boycott and publicly denounce Amazon, as Cottom did in the previous chapter, but still have the telltale boxes in their house. According to my theory, these are not necessarily at odds.

That said, it may still be the case that loyalty to a product, brand, or company (or a lack of choice) might lead someone to not even state an opposition, particularly if they are concerned about seeming hypocritical. It is also certainly the case that some products, companies, and brands are easier for consumers to boycott than others. For instance, no matter what political actions a pharmaceutical company takes, a sick person who buys medicine from that company is unlikely to boycott. People who really like and appreciate a particular store and its products may be more likely to excuse its behavior. If this is true, survey data should suggest that, even if people dislike corporate advocacy, they should be unlikely to boycott.

3 People Dislike Corporate Advocacy, But It Isn't About Political Expression: The third counterclaim is that people do, in fact, dislike corporate advocacy, and may be willing to boycott on that basis but their dislike and motivation to boycott is divorced from political or partisan concerns. Certainly, the idea of political advocacy in itself is upsetting to many because income inequality is rising and political power often appears to be clustered among the "haves," leaving the "have-nots" adhering to laws and policies they feel were crafted without their interests in mind.

It is also the case that people may be upset by and boycott on the basis of a dislike of political power and yet still be driven by political concerns. This would only invalidate the theory if, on aggregate, people cared not at all about the implied partisanship of the advocacy and only about the fact of the advocacy itself. If the two exist alongside one another, that is simply a second (possibly complementary) causal mechanism rather than a reason the theory is wrong. Yet, if the data

4.4 Sources of Evidence 93

demonstrated that people care strictly about the fact of political advocacy and power and not at all, or significantly less, about the implied partisanship, then that would suggest the dominant mechanism in the theory is probably incorrect.

4.4 Sources of Evidence

In this chapter, I consider two sources of evidence. The first is evidence from a survey, which tested the individual-level mechanism and predictions. The second is social media data, which tested the group- and boycott-level dynamics.

4.4.1 Evidence from Survey

Although the underlying theory in this book is about group dynamics, the foundation is based on individual decision-making. After all, you can't have large groups of people supporting a boycott without individuals deciding to express support. Thus, survey data allowed me to test the individual-level predictions, Expectations 1A and 1B: that it's partisanship, in particular, that leads to dislike of companies engaging in advocacy and to support for boycotting those companies. It also allowed me to test the assumptions underlying the Creative Advocacy and Careful Advocacy strategies. While Careful Advocacy logically follows from Expectations 1A and 1B – if people express stronger dislike and a greater willingness to boycott when the action is clearly partisan-linked, it follows that they should express less distaste and be less likely to boycott when it's not – Creative Advocacy does not. Moreover, Creative Advocacy relies heavily on the (testable) assumption that people psychologically designate some corporate actions as intended to influence politics and that they do not like those activities. The survey data allowed me to test this assumption directly.

To test the individual expectations and the assumption about activities intended to influence politics, I fielded a survey of 1,000 US residents over the age of 18 in June 2019 using the Lucid platform. Lucid allowed me to create a convenience sample of people whose demographics matched the demographics of the US population as a whole. This wasn't a random sample – meaning that every person in the United States did not have an equal probability of being selected into the survey. It was instead a convenience sample that was considered both large enough and demographically representative enough to draw inferences from.

I ended up with 1,004 respondents. Like the United States as a whole, just over half of the sample identified as women (51.4 percent) and just under half of the sample identified as men (48.2 percent). A small percentage of the population (0.43 percent) identified as non-binary. The average age of one of my respondents was 44; the youngest was 19 and the oldest was 97. The sample was fairly evenly distributed across the political spectrum, with just under half the sample identifying as either strongly or leaning Democratic (48.8 percent), 35.4 percent identifying as strongly or leaning Republican, and the remaining 15.8 percent of the sample identifying as neither. The sample was also roughly evenly distributed across income categories. 12.8 percent of respondents reported household incomes of over \$100,000 per year and 9.8 percent of respondents said they had a household income between \$75,000 and \$99,999. Between 17 and 22 percent of respondents reported being in the four categories with incomes lower than that.

4.4.2 Evidence from Social Media

Although data about individuals helps to test expectations about individual motivations, it misses crowd dynamics. Since the overarching theory is really about the mass public – it's the reaction of the crowd that companies worry about, not that of individuals – I also turn to social media data. Social media data is useful because it is where boycotts originate and flourish in modern times. It is through statements on social media that people can support a boycott in order to signal their partisanship and become a part of a community. Therefore, data from social media allowed me to test the components of Expectation 2 – that mass boycotts are most likely to occur when they allow people to signal their political type and are therefore most likely to circle around prominent, partisan politicians and strongly partisan-linked policies. These data also allowed me to assess the content of posts, to assess what kinds of information people provide when they talk about boycott, and how they frame it, to provide some evidence for whether people do seem to understand these posts as political signaling rather than a statement of consumer behavior.

4.4 Sources of Evidence 95

Although there are many social media platforms, I specifically looked to the social network platform Twitter for a few reasons. First, as Barberá (2015) explains, "Twitter has become one of the most important communication arenas in daily politics" (p. 76). He goes on to point out that Twitter is unique in that it includes not only ordinary citizens but also political actors. It also includes companies, brands, celebrities, and other elites. This puts these groups of people (and entities) in conversation with one another, either directly or indirectly, in a way that breeds and perpetuates political conversations. Accordingly, Twitter has been the origin and primary hub for the most high-profile discussions of boycotts in recent years. The ease and costlessness of writing a tweet, or retweeting another tweet, makes participation simple, and the social nature of the platform enables boycott support as a form of social and political signaling. It allows people to call companies out directly, and it allows politicians, celebrities, and other elites to participate. As a result, Twitter, more than other social platforms, has become where activists go to publicize the things they have learned and where those boycotts catch fire.

Other reasons to study Twitter are practical in nature. Unlike Facebook, for instance, public tweets are a public forum for discussion that is easily observable. It enables discussions of anything, including boycotts, to happen in full view, where anyone can join in. This also means that tweets, unlike Facebook posts, are easy to view, download, and analyze. Second, Twitter allows people to demarcate keywords using "hashtags" that allow their tweets to contribute to a broader conversation. These hashtags create communities of people discussing similar topics, which can create and perpetuate conversations and movements. Hashtags themselves can go viral, and the virality of hashtags is sometimes used as a measure for the social importance of an idea or movement.

To collect the data, I scraped Twitter for tweets that included the word "boycott" every day for one month in the summer of 2019. This allowed me to identify the universe of boycotts that occurred in this time frame. In total, I collected 188,689 public tweets that included the word "boycott." All these tweets had US-based IP addresses, indicating that they most likely originated within the United States, and they were collected from June 10 through July 9, 2019. Because of caps on how many tweets can be collected in a given period of time, it's possible this wasn't the entire sample of boycott tweets, but it is a thorough, representative, and nearly complete sample. This sample excluded tweets that were themselves retweets or reposted, unmodified copies of existing tweets.

4.5 Why Do People Respond Negatively to Corporate Advocacy?

The first causal hurdle is the individual's reaction to a company's behavior or their perception of its behavior. A key mechanism in my theory is that people, if they have the opportunity to respond to knowledge of a company's corporate advocacy, are angered by it specifically because of its political flavor. People don't like corporate political advocacy not because it is advocacy or because it implies out-sized power but rather because it is perceived as a company endorsing a candidate, party, or position. People then seize on these examples of corporations seemingly endorsing a political stance as an opportunity to define themselves politically, both internally as well as externally. They support and join boycotts in large part as a form of political expression.

Although the theory itself hinges on the group dynamics of this – if one person gets upset and supports a boycott, it does not matter much, but if a large group does, it matters a lot – the group can't exist without the individual. That means it's imperative to nail down the individual mechanisms here. First, that people don't like corporate political advocacy specifically because of its partisan flavor. Second, that boycotts are a form of political expression more than a statement of consumer behavior. And a third thing to establish with the survey data is that companies can advocate without angering the public if they use unconventional advocacy strategies.

First, to test the partisan angle, I exposed people to real-life information about corporate campaign contributions to determine how they respond to information about corporate advocacy, both when it does and does not align with their own partisanship. Specifically, I inform people (accurately) about campaign contributions Walmart's PAC made during the 2018 election cycle. People were either told that Walmart donated \$45,000 to the Democratic National Campaign Committee or to the National Republican Congressional Committee. Both of these statements are true, but people were informed of only one. The first hurdle is to establish that people actually disapprove of

4.5 Why Do People Respond Negatively

this, suggesting that everything that follows that disapproval is plausible. If people by and large do not disapprove of it, it does not even make sense to ask why they disapprove, and there is no reason to believe they would then support a boycott. If that is established, the expectation is that people should disapprove of the contribution when it's to the party they do not align with but not disapprove when it's to their own party. This suggests that it's not the campaign contribution itself that is angering people but instead its partisanship. To assess whether this is truly about consumer behavior, I also looked at whether people report that this would make them more or less likely to shop at Walmart and analyzed that as a function of whether they were frequent shoppers to begin with. If people who never or rarely shop at Walmart report they would be less likely to shop at Walmart as a result of this information, I interpreted that as a boycott that is more about political expression rather than consumer behavior.

Second, to test whether companies can avoid public anger by pursuing unconventional strategies, I asked people to respond to brief, fictional stories about cities proposing real-life policies and companies responding to those policies. Each story was structured the same way, where the reader was told what the company does, informed about the policy the city was planning to enact, and then told about how that policy might negatively affect the company. Each story concluded with a sentence about something the company did in response.

In some cases, the company responded in a way that is accepted as conventional political advocacy, by donating money to a candidate or lobbying. In other cases, the company responded by taking a targeted approach that was less likely to be perceived as political advocacy. In a fifth case, the company "responded" in a way that wasn't linked to political influence at all but was included as a control and read somewhat like a non-sequitur. The last sentence – the corporate response – was assigned randomly, and survey-takers were asked to rate their approval of the policy, the city, and the company. This allowed me to test two contentions. First, because I chose the city policies to clearly align with partisan priorities (minimum wage increases, which are associated with progressive politics, and crackdowns on undocumented immigrants, which are associated with conservative politics), I expected to find further evidence of partisan sorting in disapproval. That is, I expected people to disapprove of the company more when it opposed a policy backed by the survey-taker's party.

Second, I expected this disapproval to diminish or perhaps even go away entirely if the company's response was the nonconventional advocacy angles as compared with the conventional advocacy angles.

4.5.1 Test A: Reaction to Real-Life Information

First, I exposed people to real-life information about corporate campaign contributions to assess overall disapproval about corporate political advocacy and to test whether that disapproval was specific to counter-partisan support. Specifically, I informed people about campaign contributions Walmart's PAC made during the 2018 election cycle. People were either told that Walmart's PAC donated $45,000 to the Democratic National Campaign Committee or to the National Republican Congressional Committee. Both of these statements are true. Expectation 1A states that people will disapprove of the campaign contribution more when the $45,000 was donated to the party they don't associate themselves with. Further, I expected that this information, when it countered their own preferences, would change their professed consumer behavior (Expectation 1B). In other words, I expected that Democrats who are told that Walmart donated to Republicans and Republicans who are told Walmart donated to Democrats would be more likely to say it makes them less likely to shop at Walmart.

I chose Walmart for three reasons. First, Walmart is a large company that many people frequent, regardless of where they live. Because they sell everything, everyone in my survey is likely to have heard of Walmart and to be a potential customer of Walmart's. Second, Walmart's PAC's political donations tend to be fairly bipartisan, meaning they donate to both Democrats and Republicans. This means I could honestly present survey-takers with a situation in which the company donated the same large sum of money to both parties. Third, because the PAC donated the same amount of money to both political groups, I could use the partisan group – which contains the party in the name – rather than assuming people know the partisanship of specific politicians. This also allowed me to sidestep concerns that would present themselves if the donations had been to politicians, including attributes or reputations of politicians that would have made drawing causal claims about partisanship more complicated.

Overall, there was no real evidence that people systematically approved or disapproved of the PAC contribution. Figure 4.1 shows

4.5 Why Do People Respond Negatively

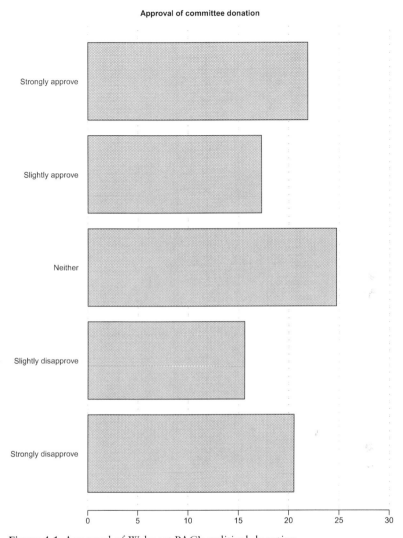

Figure 4.1 Approval of Walmart PAC's political donation

the percentage of survey-takers who strong approved, slightly approved, neither approved nor disapproved, slightly disapproved, or strongly disapproved of the contribution. Although the modal category is "neither," it only slightly beat out the two most extreme categories, with the more moderate approval and disapproval categories not far behind. In other words, approval was spread pretty

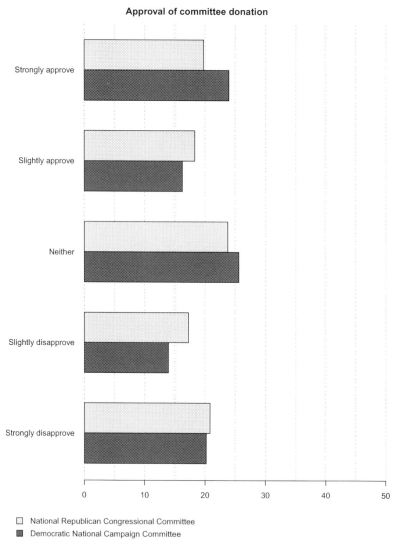

Figure 4.2 Approval of Walmart PAC's political donation by recipient

evenly across all categories. The same was true when approval was broken down by recipient – whether it was the Democratic or Republican committee who was given the money – as illustrated in Figure 4.2. Between 15 and 25 percent of people fell into almost every category, with no category or recipient dominating. People, again, were fairly evenly spread.

4.5 Why Do People Respond Negatively

Table 4.1 *Results of ordered logistic regressions predicting a survey-taker's approval of Walmart on a five-point scale, ranging from strong disapproval (1) to strong approval (5). The omitted category for partisanship is "Neither Democrat nor Republican." All models control for age, gender, education, household income, race, whether the survey-taker is a frequent Walmart shopper, and whether the survey-taker reported disapproving of campaign contributions. DNCC, Democratic National Campaign Committee; NRCC, National Republican Congressional Committee*

	Dependent variable:			
	Approval of PAC donation			
	(1)	(2)	(3)	(4)
Treatment: NRCC	−0.043	0.117	−1.405***	
	(0.121)	(0.301)	(0.188)	
Treatment: DNCC				−1.706***
				(0.224)
Republican	0.507***	−0.410		
	(0.185)	(0.268)		
Democrat	0.289*	1.036***		
	(0.173)	(0.245)		
NRCC × Republican		1.624***		
		(0.370)		
NRCC × Democrat		−1.493***		
		(0.350)		
Observations	901	901	439	324

Note: $^*p < 0.1$; $^{**}p < 0.05$; $^{***}p < 0.01$

This is not a relic of the simplicity of the bar plot either. The first column in Table 4.1 shows the results of an ordered logistic regression predicting an individual survey-taker's approval level as a function of a variety of demographic variables, including party and the party of the campaign recipient. There is no evidence of a treatment effect – people who were told that the money went to the National Republican Congressional Committee were not, on average, more or less inclined to approve of the contribution than those told it went to the DNCC. Yet there is some evidence of a partisan effect: both Republicans and Democrats were more likely to approve of the contribution when compared with people who identified as neither.

The reason for this, of course, is that the treatment effect itself is partisan and the treatment effect is aggregating two sharply contrasting subgroup effects. That is, there is no overall treatment effect because the treatment affects Democrats and Republicans differently. Democrats disapprove when told that the PAC donated to Republicans and Republicans disapprove when told that the PAC contributed to Democrats. Since the treatment was assigned randomly, Democrats and Republicans were equally likely to receive either treatment, and therefore the responses were split roughly evenly between the two groups, canceling each other out.

When the effect of the treatment was parsed out by party, the partisan treatment effects were overwhelmingly clear. Democrats strongly approved of a contribution to Democrats and strongly disapproved of a contribution to Republicans. Republicans strongly approved of a contribution to Republicans and strongly disapproved of a contribution to Democrats. In each case, strong approval of the co-partisan contribution was the modal category by a wide margin and strong disapproval of the counter-partisan contribution by a similarly wide margin. The percentages were similar too, around 30–35 percent in each case. The plots in Figure 4.3 look like mirror images of one another.

This finding also stood up to statistical analysis, which eliminated potential confounding. Although the effects were about the same in both groups, it helped to rule out findings that were driven by differences between the groups in other ways. The results were not, for instance, attributable to Republicans in the sample being older on average than Democrats (although they are, slightly) or Democrats in the sample being less disapproving of campaign contributions as an idea (although they are, slightly). I modeled this two different ways. First, I used the same ordered logistic regression to predict approval of Walmart, with the same variables, but I also interacted the treatment with the survey-taker's party, allowing the effect of the treatment to vary by party (Column 2 in Table 4.1). Second, because interaction effects can be complicated to interpret, I ran the same model as before but on samples of Republicans and Democrats separately (Columns 3 and 4 in Table 4.1, respectively). For the split-sample models, I also switched the treatment and control, so that for Democrats the treatment was donating to Republicans and the control was donating to

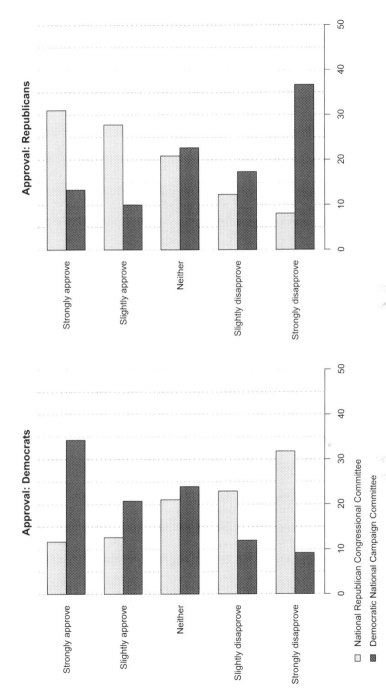

Figure 4.3 Approval of Walmart PAC's political donation by recipient and partisanship of survey-taker

104   *Why Does The Public Care?*

Democrats and for the Republicans the treatment was donating to Democrats and the control was donating to Republicans.

Although the statistical interpretation was slightly different, the substantive findings were the same. The interaction model found that the treatment (donating to the Republican committee) had no independent effect, but it increased approval among Republicans and decreased approval among Democrats, both of which were statistically significant. In the model with only Democrats in the sample, the effect of the Republican treatment was a large decrease in approval of Walmart. In the sample with only Republicans, the effect of the Democrat treatment was a large decrease in approval of Walmart. All these effects were highly statistically significant.

Yet disapproval and professed consumer behavior are not the same thing. They are, of course, related. Very few people (3.8 percent) who expressed disapproval of the PAC donation said it would make them *more* likely to shop at Walmart, and almost no one (literally three people, or 0.081 percent) who approved said it would make them less likely. Among those who disapproved, however, the plurality of people (49.3 percent) said it would make no difference in their shopping patterns. Although people who strongly approved were far and away most likely to say the donation would make them much more likely to shop at Walmart (122 people – 58.7 percent, and more than twice as many people who said it wouldn't make a difference), among people who slightly approved of the donation, the majority (59.1 percent) again said it would make no difference in their patterns. So, disapproval implies a greater probability of professing boycott, but it is far from a foregone conclusion that someone who disagrees will profess to change their behavior.

This, again, masks partisan behavior. As Figure 4.4 illustrates, in both parties, regardless of treatment, most people say this will not change their shopping behavior. Yet again, the same patterns emerged as when looking at disapproval, although the effects were somewhat weaker. People who were told that the donation was to their party reported being more likely to shop there, or much more likely, regardless of party. What is more interesting, though, is the differences among people who reported being less likely or much less likely to shop at Walmart as a result of the information, and this really drives home that this is an issue of distaste with partisanship, not a distaste with campaign contributions themselves. Among Democrats,

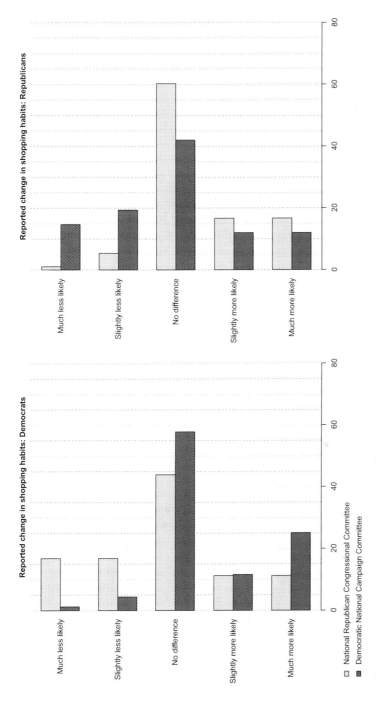

Figure 4.4 Reported change in Walmart shopping frequency as a result of knowing about political donation, broken down by treatment

only 1.2 percent, upon learning of the PAC contribution, said they were much less likely to shop at Walmart when the donation was to Democrats and only 4.4 percent said they were slightly less likely in that circumstance. Yet, when told that the donation was to Republicans, 16.8 percent reported being much less likely to shop there and 16.8 percent reported being slightly less likely. This is a huge increase. The numbers were almost exactly the same for Republicans, among whom 1.1 percent were much less likely to shop at Walmart and 5.4 percent were slightly less likely after having learned of a donation to Republicans, but upon learning the donation was to Democrats, the numbers jumped to 14.6 percent for much less likely and 19 percent for slightly less likely. This is clearly not a story of disliking political contributions but of disliking political contributions to the opposing party.

The same findings came out of the ordered logistic regression results shown in Table 4.2. As before, these results consisted of one model in which party and treatment were interacted (Model 1 in Table 4.2) and then a set of split-sample models isolating the treatment effect among Democrats (Model 2 in Table 4.2) and among Republicans (Model 3 in Table 4.2) separately. In the interaction model, the treatment itself had a negative coefficient, but it was not statistically significant, indicating that, among those who identified as neither Democrat nor Republican, knowing that the PAC donated to Republicans might make them slightly less likely to "boycott" (or reduce their shopping frequency), but the effect was not statistically distinguishable from zero. The coefficient on Democrats, in this model, shows that Democrats in the control group – told that the PAC donated to Democrats – were less likely to boycott, as expected. The interaction terms tell the same story. Republicans who were told that the PAC donated to Republicans were less likely to boycott, whereas Democrats who were told that the PAC donated to Republicans were more likely to boycott, and all of those effects were statistically significant. In the split-sample models, the finding was the same: Democrats who were told that the PAC donated to Republicans were more likely to boycott (Model 2) and Republicans who were told that the PAC donated to Democrats were more likely to boycott, and both effects were highly statistically significant.

In addition to partisan behavior, these findings also mix together two groups of people for whom the question of whether to shop at Walmart is different: people who shop at Walmart often and people

4.5 Why Do People Respond Negatively 107

Table 4.2 *Results of an ordered logistic model predicting a survey-taker's professed likelihood of shopping at Walmart in the future. Dependent variable is a five-category response to the question "Does this information make you more likely, less likely, or equally likely to shop at Walmart?" but it has been ordered so that higher categories reflect being less likely to shop at Walmart. The omitted category for partisanship is "Neither Democrat nor Republican." All models control for age, gender, education, household income, race, whether the survey-taker is a frequent Walmart shopper, and whether the survey-taker reported disapproval of campaign contributions*

	Dependent variable:		
	Less likely to shop at Walmart (five categories, increasing in likelihood of "boycott")		
	(1)	(2)	(3)
Treatment: NRCC	−0.159	1.147***	
	(0.330)	(0.200)	
Treatment: DNCC			1.102***
			(0.229)
Republican	−0.031		
	(0.293)		
Democrat	−1.226***		
	(0.268)		
NRCC × Republican	−1.032***		
	(0.400)		
NRCC × Democrat	1.333***		
	(0.382)		
Observations	900	439	323
Sample	Full	Democrats	Republicans

Note: *p<0.1; **p<0.05; ***p<0.01

who rarely shop at Walmart. For the first group, the decision of whether to tell an internet survey-taker how their Walmart shopping behavior might change as a result of information is more concrete. The answer itself is probably a mixture of actual intention and signaling, but the question itself is not abstract or hypothetical. If you shop at Walmart frequently and someone asks you if that is likely to change, you can reflect upon your shopping behavior and think about how likely it is to change, regardless of how well your response maps onto that intention.

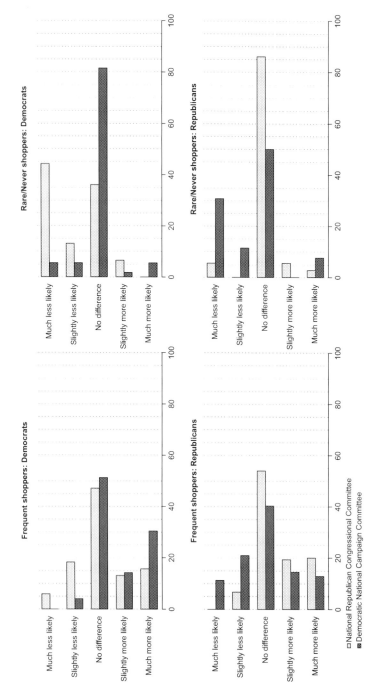

Figure 4.5 Reported changes in Walmart shopping behavior in response to the PAC information, broken down by treatment, party, and survey-taker's Walmart shopping frequency

4.5 *Why Do People Respond Negatively* 109

On the other hand, people who rarely or never shop at Walmart are, in effect, answering a slightly different question. If you don't shop at Walmart, the decision of whether to shop at Walmart less than you do is more abstract. You are much less likely to be thinking about the baby formula or eggs or shampoo you need to buy. Instead, the question is more of a hypothetical: If you were faced with a decision to shop at Walmart, what would you do? This, I argue, is where we're likely to see more evidence of reported change in shopping habits as a form of partisan signaling.

The differences between these groups – and how we might interpret their responses – are illustrated in Figure 4.5. The top row is Democrats, the bottom row is Republicans, the left column is people who frequently shop at Walmart (at least once a month), and the right column is people who shop at Walmart rarely or never (3–4 times per year or less). The differences between people who frequently and rarely shop at Walmart is striking, reflecting that frequent shoppers are being asked to make a practical choice and statement about their consumer choices, whereas those who never shop at Walmart are being asked an abstract question about principles. Accordingly, regardless of party, those who rarely or never shop at Walmart are far more likely to report that this information makes them much less likely to shop at Walmart as compared with those who shop more frequently. Almost half of Democrat never-shoppers who were told that the PAC had donated to Republicans said the information made them much less likely to shop at Walmart. For Republicans in the corresponding counter-partisan scenario, 30.8 percent reported they were now much less likely to shop at Walmart and 11.5 percent said they were slightly less likely.

This is even clearer when looking at the statistical model. For this model, I subset the data into Democrats and Republicans, like before, and focused on the interaction between the treatment and whether someone was a frequent Walmart shopper. As before, I ran an ordered logistic model predicting the five-ordered categories of reported changes in shopping behavior with the same control variables but interacting infrequent Walmart shopper with the treatment.

In Table 4.3, Model 1 is Democrats and Model 2 is Republicans. In the Democrats model, those who were told that the PAC donated to Republicans were more likely to say they would reduce their shopping frequency compared to those who were told that the PAC donated

110

Why Does The Public Care?

Table 4.3 *Results of an ordered logistic model predicting a survey-taker's professed likelihood of shopping at Walmart in the future. Dependent variable is a five-category response to the question "Does this information make you more likely, less likely, or equally likely to shop at Walmart?" but it has been ordered so that higher categories reflect being less likely to shop at Walmart. All models control for age, gender, education, household income, race, whether the survey-taker is a frequent Walmart shopper, and whether the survey-taker reported disapproval of campaign contributions. DNCC, Democratic National Campaign Committee; NRCC, National Republican Congressional Committee*

	Dependent variable:	
	Less likely to shop at Walmart (five categories, increasing in likelihood of "boycott")	
	(1)	(2)
Treatment: NRCC	0.861***	
	(0.225)	
Treatment: DNCC		1.082***
		(0.253)
Infrequent Walmart Shopper	1.175***	0.993***
	(0.324)	(0.350)
NRCC × Infrequent Shopper	1.185***	
	(0.448)	
DNCC × Infrequent Shopper		0.101
		(0.557)
Observations	439	323
Sample	Democrats	Republicans

Note: $^{*}p < 0.1$; $^{**}p < 0.05$; $^{***}p < 0.01$

to Democrats. The same was true, in reverse, for Republicans, with Republicans who were told that the PAC donated to Democrats more likely to report that they would boycott. In both samples, infrequent Walmart shoppers in the control (co-partisan) group reported that they were less likely to shop at Walmart in the future, perhaps suggesting that people who do not shop at Walmart are more sensitive to any political contributions, regardless of partisanship. Only among the Democrats, however, was the interaction between the treatment and

4.5 Why Do People Respond Negatively   111

infrequent shopper significant, indicating that Democrats who were infrequent Walmart shoppers were even more likely to report they would shop at Walmart less after being told that the PAC donated to Republicans. The same was not true of Republicans, who were equally likely to report boycotting regardless of how often they shop at Walmart.

4.5.2 Test B: Reaction to Fictional Situations

For the second test, I asked people to respond to brief stories about fictional cities proposing real-life policies and companies responding to those policies. The fictional situations added context to the abstract concepts in Test A. Each situation described a certain type of company, a policy that negatively affected that company, and how the company was affected. (For more information and full scripts, see Appendix A.) The first scenario, for instance, reads as follows:

> Company A is a retail food chain. It has a retail operation in Oak City. Oak City has recently announced a proposal to institute a tax on sugary drinks, which will slightly increase the cost of buying sweetened beverages. This tax may reduce sales for Company A, as people may buy fewer sugary drinks.

The paragraph then concluded with one of the following five sentences, assigned to respondents at random:

- Company A donated money to city council members who oppose the tax.
- Company A lobbied city council members in opposition to the tax.
- Company A recently sponsored a youth soccer team in Oak City.
- Company A is considering relocating its store to nearby Birch City.
- Company A released a quarterly profit report last month.

In this and the other two situations, the options represent particular types of responses that companies can take. The first two – donating money to city council members who oppose the tax and lobbying city council members in opposition to the tax – represent traditional influence-seeking strategies. The third is an example of the kind of targeted strategy a company might take: providing a service for the community that might help a local politician. (In all the tables, I refer to this as the "pro-social" approach since all three involve some form of positive community engagement.) The fourth is the conventional idea that companies can leave when they don't like a policy. The fifth, crucially, is a nonresponse. This is parallel to the other four sentences in that it concludes the paragraph, but it features the company taking some action that is not a direct response to the policy proposal or is, at minimum, not a method of political influence-seeking.[7]

Respondents were asked a series of questions after reading the situation – chief among them being to rate their approval of the company and to rate their approval of the policy. Because the "responses" were randomly assigned, differences in how people viewed the company should be solely attributable to their perceptions of the company's response.

These data can answer two questions. First, as the Creative Advocacy suggestion assumes, do people disapprove more of companies that they perceive as engaging in political influence-seeking? If they do, people who are told that the company donated money to candidates that oppose the policy or lobbied against the policy should rate the company more unfavorably than people who are told that the company did other things, and, in particular, more unfavorably than when the company takes a nonaction. This is why the "nonresponse" response is so important, because it serves as a comparison. People who perceive the company as engaging in political influence should disapprove of the company more than if the company did nothing. Testing this assumption is important because it underlies the logic of companies being able to advocate while avoiding public backlash by merely appearing to not be advocating or trying to cultivate political influence.

Second, is this dislike conditional upon partisanship, policy approval, or neither? Expectation 1A says that disapproval should be conditional upon partisanship: people dislike companies that do things that they perceive as stances in opposition to their own individual partisanship. For the three scenarios, I intentionally chose two policies that tend to be associated with political parties and ideologies – a $15

---

[7] The exception to this is Situation 2, in which the company opts to increase its own minimum wage, which may be viewed as a response and an effort to preempt the policy shift. See Malhotra, Monin, and Tomz (2019). This was chosen because it is a common response and therefore makes the scenario seem more realistic.

4.5 *Why Do People Respond Negatively* 113

minimum wage, associated with progressive Democrats, and a policy that cracks down on undocumented immigration, associated with conservative Republicans – and one that is more ambiguously partisan in nature (a sugary drinks tax, which draws opposition from progressives for being regressive and from conservatives for being government intervention). Yet in no situation do I explicitly mention partisanship or parties. In other words, no one can use party approval as a heuristic for whether they should approve or not. If people disapprove of companies taking stances that counter their personal partisanship, self-reported Democrats should be more critical of the company when it opposes the Democrat-associated policy (minimum wage) but more accepting when it opposes the Democrat-opposed policy (restricting undocumented immigration), and Republicans should be the opposite. An alternative explanation is that people are personally invested in a policy – not partisanship – and dislike companies that oppose policies they support. This is a different logic, and one that does not support the idea that opposition to companies is a partisan issue. If it isn't partisanship but actual policy approval, then people who approve of a policy should be critical of a company trying to influence politics against a policy they agree with and vice versa. If it's neither, disapproval of political influence should be independent of party affiliation or policy approval.

In Table 4.4, each column represents one of the three situations – a retail food company opposing a sugary drinks tax, a retail company opposing a minimum wage increase, and a manufacturing company opposing a measure to crack down on undocumented immigration. The coefficients indicate how much more (or less) favorable people feel about the company based on what they were told it did in response compared with people who were told that the company took an action that was not a response (releasing a quarterly profit report, voluntarily raising wages, releasing a new product).[8] These models, as well as all the others, controlled for a variety of demographic variables – although the results were not especially sensitive to their inclusion or exclusion –

---

[8] Voluntarily raising wages is more of a response than the other nonresponses since it indicates the company is responding to a proposed mandated increase by taking the action without the mandate. This may also increase favorability of the company in a way that the other nonresponses do not, which helps explain the larger coefficient sizes in the models for Company B.

114   *Why Does The Public Care?*

Table 4.4 *The effect of a company's actions on respondent approval.*
Each coefficient is compared with the group of people presented with a
"nonresponse" action. Models are ordered logistic regressions with five
categories and control for gender (woman vs. non-woman), education,
household income, and race (white, including bi-/multiracial vs.
non-white). Full results with controls are given in Appendix B

	Dependent variable:		
	Approval of:		
	Company A (Sugary drinks tax) (1)	Company B (Minimum wage) (2)	Company C (Undocumented immigration) (3)
Donated money	-0.730^{***}	-1.267^{***}	0.085
	(0.194)	(0.199)	(0.187)
Lobbied	0.058	-1.110^{***}	-0.006
	(0.184)	(0.191)	(0.185)
Pro-social	0.759^{***}	0.151	0.257
	(0.193)	(0.187)	(0.181)
Considering relocation	0.0003	-1.342^{***}	-0.022
	(0.186)	(0.193)	(0.191)
Observations	896	900	900

Note: $^{*}p < 0.1$; $^{**}p < 0.05$; $^{***}p < 0.01$

and pooled people with different party identifications and different
levels of approval of the underlying policy. Negative coefficients indicate that people who were told that the company took a certain action
felt less favorably toward the company on average than people who
saw the nonresponse.

The most consistent finding in these models was that donating
money to candidates that oppose the policy seemed to make the company less popular. This was true in the first two scenarios, as indicated
by the negative and statistically significant coefficients. Yet the small,
positive, and statistically insignificant coefficient for Company C indicates that donating money probably didn't change perceptions of the
company over its taking no action (releasing a new product) in the
third situation. Taking the pro-social or targeted influence-seeking
approach seemed to make the company more popular in all three

4.5 Why Do People Respond Negatively 115

situations, but the positive coefficient was only significant at conventional levels for Company A, in which the company fought the sugary drinks tax. In the other two situations, the coefficient was positive but not necessarily statistically distinguishable from zero. Lobbying did not consistently depress popularity as compared with the nonresponse group and neither did considering relocation, except, in both cases, for Company B, which had especially large coefficient estimates due to the popularity of its nonresponse option (voluntarily raising minimum wages). Yet, overall, in the full sample, the pattern of results – even just looking at the signs on the coefficients and ignoring statistical significance – did not support the contention that conventional advocacy strategies make a company less popular.

Do these effects change when we focus instead strictly on groups of people who support the policy? Table 4.5 considers this by limiting the data set to only people who approve of the policy in question – the policy that the company opposes and is taking action to fight.[9] If opposition to influence-seeking and advocacy is driven by being on the opposite side as the company when it agitates against a policy, that implies that people who support the policy in question should oppose the company's influence-seeking. Yet the results in Table 4.5 – limited strictly to the group of people who, for each policy, said it was "sort of" or "very" good – are also not clear, strong evidence. Unlike in the full sample, the coefficient on the two conventional influence-seeking actions, donating money and lobbying, were more consistently negative in this sample. Donating money and lobbying both caused the company to be viewed more negatively than the nonresponse action in every case, although the effects were only statistically significant in the case of Company B and the minimum wage. (This is not necessarily surprising since the other samples were smaller, as were the effect sizes. Determining that effects are distinguishable from zero is more difficult unless the effect is especially large.) The results for considering relocation in response to a policy were the same – relative to a nonresponse, respondents viewed the companies less favorably in each case, although, again, the effect was only statistically significant in the second model. By contrast, the pro-social action had a positive coefficient in every model, indicating that the company who did positive

---

[9] Interpretation of results is identical with an interactive model.

Table 4.5 *The effect of a company's actions on respondent approval among respondents who support the policy the company opposes. Each coefficient is compared with the group of people presented with a "nonresponse" action. Models are ordered logit with five categories and control for gender, education, household income, and race. Full results with controls are given in Appendix B*

	Dependent variable:		
		Approval of:	
	Company A (Sugary drinks tax)	Company B (Minimum wage)	Company C (Undocumented immigration)
	(1)	(2)	(3)
Donated money	−0.385	−1.552***	−0.123
	(0.295)	(0.242)	(0.262)
Lobbied	−0.101	−1.538***	−0.282
	(0.269)	(0.239)	(0.254)
Pro-social	0.958***	0.135	0.047
	(0.268)	(0.227)	(0.249)
Considering relocation	−0.106	−1.785***	−0.323
	(0.299)	(0.243)	(0.261)
Observations	422	630	500

Note: $^*p < 0.1$; $^{**}p < 0.05$; $^{***}p < 0.01$

things within the community was viewed more positively than if it did nothing, but these results were only statistically significantly for Company B. Overall, the evidence suggests that people who disagree with the company on policy are likely to disapprove of influence-seeking, as the theory suggests, although, again, the evidence is not overwhelmingly strong.

Yet the theory, as written, does not speak directly to policy support but instead to partisanship: Democrats should disapprove when companies try to influence politics in ways that suggest support of Republicans, and Republicans should disapprove when companies try to influence politics in ways that suggest support of Democrats. In the situations presented earlier, there is no explicit mention of party, but there is one policy that is linked with Democrats (minimum wage increase) and one that is linked with Republicans (cracking down on undocumented immigration). A third – a sugary drinks tax, which

4.5 Why Do People Respond Negatively 117

Table 4.6 *The effect of a company's actions on respondent approval among respondents who belong to the party associated with support for the policy the company opposes. Each coefficient is compared with the group of people presented with a "nonresponse" action and models control for policy approval. Models are ordered logit with five categories and control for gender (women vs. non-women), education (omitted category: no college), household income (omitted category: less than $20,000), and race (white, including multiracial white vs. non-white)*

	Dependent variable:	
	Approval of Company B (Minimum wage)	Approval of Company C (Undocumented immigration)
Donated money	−1.464***	−0.216
	(0.294)	(0.335)
Lobbied	−1.812***	−0.595*
	(0.295)	(0.321)
Pro-social	0.042	−0.189
	(0.267)	(0.306)
Considering relocation	−1.523***	−0.391
	(0.280)	(0.323)
Observations	439	324
Sample	Democrats	Republicans

Note: $^*p < 0.1$; $^{**}p < 0.05$; $^{***}p < 0.01$

adds a "sin tax" on top of the normal cost of buying drinks like soda or juice – is less strongly linked to a particular party because it includes things both loved and hated by each party.[10] Accordingly, Table 4.6 looks at how Democrats respond to Company B's opposition to the minimum wage increase and how Republicans respond to Company C's opposition to the immigration measure.[11] In both cases, I controlled for policy approval in an attempt to more clearly estimate the effect of each treatment in partisan groups as partisanship, separate from policy approval.

[10] Some Democrats dislike the policy because it is regressive, meaning that it ends up primarily targeting people who make less money. Republicans, on the other hand, dislike the policy because it represents government intervention into the market and personal freedoms.

[11] Interpretation of results is identical with an interactive model.

The evidence for Expectation 1A was similar to the evidence in the policy-approval test and stronger than the test in the full sample. As in the policy-approval model, the signs for donating money, lobbying, and considering relocation were all negative, indicating that, when the company does those things, it is viewed more negatively than when it does nothing. All three of these were statistically significant for Company B, and lobbying was statistically significant for Company C, even though it was the smallest sample size in this section. This indicates that Democrats and Republicans have the same response, reacting negatively to a company doing something to counter a policy associated with their party.

Taken together, the experimental tests with the situations data suggest that there is evidence of varying strength supporting both of the relevant expectations. The evidence on whether people generally dislike companies that engage in political influence is mixed. The test on the complete sample shows that people do, in general, dislike companies that donate money to candidates. The evidence that people in general dislike lobbying is less clear. They do seem to dislike it when it's compared with the company taking a popular action, and it doesn't seem to make the company any less popular than when it takes no action at all. The evidence is stronger that revulsion to political influence is driven by partisanship and specifically that it's partisanship and not policy approval. People who approve of a policy demonstrate the same patterns of approval and disapproval as the general population – disliking donating money (in general) and with mixed findings on lobbying. Yet, for the two situations in which the policy can be used as a heuristic for partisanship, the patterns of opposition are clearer.[12]

4.6 Are Boycott Tweets Political Signaling?

In the experiments, I provided people with information about a company's behavior, whether real or fictional, and then asked them to respond. Experiments are excellent at establishing causal relationships and therefore testing the underlying theoretical mechanism. These experiments, like most experiments, were by their nature unrealistic.

---

[12] The results also held when controlling for policy approval, suggesting it really is partisanship doing the work.

4.6 Are Boycott Tweets Political Signaling?

In this case, there are two reasons why the experiments alone were insufficient and thus needed to be paired with observational data. First, in the real world, people do not receive information about corporate political activities from a seemingly disinterested, non-partisan researcher, let alone in a randomized and controlled format. The ways people come across this information vary, if they come across it at all, and the presentation is unlikely to be entirely depoliticized. Although that may mean the reactions people had in the experiments may actually be more muted than they would be if the information were presented in a politicized format and intended to spur a reaction – suggesting that a more realistic experiment may have provided even clearer results – it still points to the necessity of looking at partisan reactions in the real world.

Second, in the real world, people do not express their thoughts and feelings via a Likert scale on a survey platform. Instead, they talk to their friends, they change their behavior, and they take to social media. Thus, although the experimental data allowed me to test the link between political information and opinions, it did not allow me to observe whether those opinions would translate into social media posts or whether the social media posts functioned as a partisan signal. Those are two components of the theory that are, however, important to test because companies do not particularly care if people quietly disapprove. They care only if people act on that disapproval and particularly if they act in a public way that damages the brand.

Twitter data fills that void. While using social media data didn't allow me to manipulate – or even know – what kinds of corporate political information people are exposed to, it did let me analyze how people respond to it. In other words, I couldn't see whether people tweet in response to corporate political information because I didn't (and couldn't) know what the universe of possible corporate political information they *could* respond to was or how they were exposed to it. Yet I could answer two related questions. First, are tweets about boycott that mention partisanship – and therefore provide straightforward partisan signals when retweeted – shared more frequently than other boycott tweets? And second, does the language used in political boycott tweets suggest people are trying to declare where they stand politically or not, and how does this compare with the language in nonpolitical boycotts?

4.6.1 Do People Share Political Boycott Tweets More Frequently?

The first question these data can answer is whether politically oriented boycott tweets are more likely to be retweeted than other boycott tweets. Although people frequently say that retweets are not endorsements, retweets are a quick and easy way for someone to repeat another person's message to their own feed with their own name attached to it. If not an endorsement, it at least signals to someone's Twitter followers that the message they are retweeting is one they wish others to look at. It also requires only one click and no composition of an additional message. If someone wants to signal something to their followers or broadcast a message, retweets are the easiest way to do that.

If people are using boycotts as a way to signal a political stance to themselves and the people around them rather than simply changing their consumer behavior accordingly, then we should observe boycotts that explicitly reference partisanship to receive more retweets than other boycotts. If, instead, people support boycotts as a way to convince others to change their behavior or for any other function, then all kinds of boycott tweets should be roughly equally likely to be retweeted, other relevant factors held constant.

To test this, I defined a very minimalist list of partisan words: Trump, liberal(s), libs, conservative(s), maga,[13] democrat(s) dems, and republican(s). This list is clearly not an all-encompassing dictionary of political or policy terms, and that's intentional.[14] The list contained nothing about policy, race, racism, the police, or other topics that were tied up in many boycotts during this time period and that were also, often, heavily politicized. These strict coding rules were an attempt to isolate a group of tweets that were obviously partisan in nature rather than those that might require reading between the lines. Yet even with that minimalist list of words, 20 percent of tweets were "political," meaning they contained at least one of those words.[15]

---

[13] MAGA, which stands for Make America Great Again, is an acronym used often on and off Twitter by supporters of Donald Trump.

[14] The list was derived by randomly sampling selections of tweets to identify the prevalence of political words.

[15] Of those, most (90 percent) contained only one.

4.6 Are Boycott Tweets Political Signaling?   121

Retweets themselves are relatively uncommon – only 18.6 percent of the boycott tweets in the sample were retweeted even once – and yet all the statistical models illustrate that partisan tweets are retweeted significantly more than other tweets. Regardless of how I modeled it,[16] as Table 4.7 shows, partisan tweets were retweeted more than tweets that did not use that language. Since the models all accounted for the characteristics of the person tweeting, as well as the content of the tweets themselves, in that I controlled for whether a tweet mentioned the four most popular corporate boycotts during this time (Nike,[17] Home Depot,[18] Wayfair,[19] and Starbucks[20]), this means, in effect, that partisan language increased the number of retweets, even among similar tweeters talking about the same thing. In the first model, which contained all boycott tweets by any user, the model predicted that a tweet that used partisan words would be retweeted three times more than one that did not. In the second model, which was restricted to verified users, a partisan tweet was predicted to receive 108 more retweets than one that did not. And the third model, which contained only verified users with tweets that have been retweeted at all, the model predicted receiving about 134 more tweets using partisan language than no partisan language. The logged model and the negative binomial model, although less straightforward to interpret, also had positive and highly statistically significant coefficients, indicating that partisan tweets were associated with an increase in retweets.

---

[16] The dependent variable is a count with lots of zeros but a huge range of values, so I employed several different model specifications to deal with those features. I used both ordinary least squares (Models 1–4) and negative binomial (Models 5–6). Models 2, 3, 4, and 6 limited the sample to only verified users, which were more likely to be retweeted at all. Models 3 and 4 omitted all tweets that received no retweets in order to look at the effects *conditional upon being retweeted*, and in Model 4, I logged the number of retweets to further rein in outliers. Each model controlled for the quantile of followers relative to others in the model sample as a way to deal with followers, and the models that were not limited to verified users controlled for verified status. Each model also controlled for whether the tweet mentioned Home Depot or Nike, since both were highly partisan, very popular boycotts during this period and therefore are likely to both generate more retweets and contain partisan language. The results were substantively identical in each model.

[17] 14.5 percent of tweets mention Nike.

[18] 5.3 percent of tweets mention Home Depot.

[19] 2.4 percent of tweets mention Wayfair.

[20] 4 percent of tweets mention Starbucks.

Table 4.7 Six models, each with the count of retweets as the dependent variable. Models 1–4 are ordinary least squares linear models, Models 5–6 are negative binomial models. Follower quantile estimates are omitted for space. Omitted category for followers is the lowest decile for the particular sample, meaning people who are in the lowest 10 percent of follower counts.

	Dependent variable:					
	# of Retweets OLS		# of Retweets (logged) OLS		# of Retweets negative binomial	
	(1)	(2)	(3)	(4)	(5)	(6)
Partisan	3.110***	110.416***	139.538***	0.660***	0.319***	1.150***
	(0.510)	(23.115)	(32.351)	(0.086)	(0.021)	(0.101)
Home Depot	4.453***	145.498***	199.974***	0.024	0.062*	1.140***
	(0.909)	(41.222)	(58.815)	(0.157)	(0.037)	(0.179)
Nike	−0.802	−34.439*	−48.397	−0.422***	0.214***	−0.640***
	(0.576)	(18.767)	(29.447)	(0.079)	(0.024)	(0.083)
Wayfair	3.443***	193.878***	273.907***	0.598***	−0.229***	0.517**
	(1.330)	(50.281)	(74.087)	(0.198)	(0.056)	(0.221)
Starbucks	4.722***	296.245***	392.532***	0.698***	−0.026	1.801***
	(1.034)	(43.530)	(60.888)	(0.163)	(0.043)	(0.189)
Constant	−0.769	−33.786	−57.330	0.821***	−1.423***	0.055
	(0.650)	(23.830)	(35.168)	(0.094)	(0.029)	(0.113)
Observations	188,689	4,369	2,921	2,921	188,689	4,369
Sample	All	Verified	Verified w/ RTs	Verified w/ RTs	All	Verified
R^2	0.013	0.050	0.062	0.160		
Adjusted R^2	0.013	0.047	0.057	0.156		
θ					0.088***	0.230***
					(0.001)	(0.005)
F Statistic	166.259***	16.477***	13.663***	39.646***		

Note: *$p < 0.1$; **$p < 0.05$; ***$p < 0.01$

4.6 Are Boycott Tweets Political Signaling? 123

What this tells us is that tweets with partisan language received more retweets than tweets that lacked partisan language, even when controlling for both the message – what the tweets were about – and characteristics of the messenger. This suggests that partisanship, and the act of explicitly invoking partisanship, made a tweet more likely to be shared. In other words, it wasn't the type of boycott, the act that the company engaged in, or even the person who was calling attention to the behavior but, instead, the explicit use of partisan language that made a tweet more retweetable. This suggests that part of the social function of a retweet in the context of boycott is to broadcast some partisan message to followers. In other words, the evidence from Twitter is consistent with the idea that people support boycotts in part to position themselves in partisan space.

4.6.2 Does the Language of Boycott Tweets Suggest Partisan Signaling?

The Twitter data also provides a good opportunity to understand the social and psychological function of boycott in this setting. Do people tweet about boycott as a way of signaling their political type to others? If people really are using calls for boycott as a way to position themselves politically and signal to others what their politics are, that should show up in the way people write tweets when they are composing original tweets. Although the tweets tended to sometimes be light on the specifics of why someone was boycotting – as in, the exact event or piece of information that caused them to link a company with a party – they were heavy with political content. The key finding from the boycott tweets I analyzed was that politically oriented boycotts are characterized by the use of insults: disparaging the other side as a way of solidifying someone's belonging to an in-group. This is consistent with the theory that people demonstrate who they are to those around them in large part by disparaging the "other side."

Tweets about Nike and Home Depot, the two largest boycotts in the data, were useful for understanding how it is that people tweet about boycotts. In both cases, the initial cause of the boycott was a newspaper article about a political action associated with the company – a campaign contribution made by the co-founder of Home Depot Bernie Marcus and a decision by Nike to pull a line of patriotic shoes – that spurred a boycott by people on one side of the ideological spectrum (liberals angry at Home Depot, conservatives angry at Nike), which then was met by a corresponding counter-boycott, in which people on the other side of the ideological spectrum weighed in. The news coverage then pivoted to covering the boycotts themselves, which gave publicity to the boycotts, apparently allowing them to grow and become more partisan. As a result, there were many tweets to study, and both liberals and conservatives got pulled into the conversation. This provided plenty of text to read and analyze.

It is worth noting, first, that both Home Depot and Nike are among the companies most vulnerable to boycott according to the theory. Nike and Home Depot are both very large companies with very recognizable and valuable brands. According to data distributed by Brand Finance,[21] Home Depot was the tenth most valuable brand in 2020 and Nike was 16th. Further, neither Nike nor Home Depot is a stranger to boycott. As the theory explains, companies that have previously been the target of boycotts tend to remain on the radar of activists, facing greater scrutiny and typically experiencing additional boycotts. If each had women CEOs, they would be the perfect storm of predictors of future boycotts. So, it should be of no surprise to anyone that these boycotts occurred.

The most noticeable thing in both cases was the insults. Discussions within both boycotts were dominated by people insulting those in the opposing camp. In the Home Depot case, those insults were primarily directed at the boycotters by conservatives. In the Nike example, the insults were initially hurled at Nike, Colin Kaepernick, and progressives more generally by conservatives and then at the boycotters by liberals. This phenomenon was most noticeable, in both cases, in the counter-boycott. Unlike a *buycott* – in which people intentionally buy products from a company in order to support its stances – neither counter-boycott was centered on discussions of purchasing or even about supporting the company and its actions. Instead, the counter-boycotts were almost exclusively comprised of insults – conservatives mocking liberals for boycotting Home Depot and liberals mocking conservatives for boycotting Nike. In both cases, the language of the tweets made it clear that most of the tweets were from people within a particular group talking to other people within their

---

[21] Accessed via Statista, September 29, 2020.

4.6 Are Boycott Tweets Political Signaling?

group, disparaging members of the other group as a form of bonding and signaling.

The initial boycotters, progressives who disagreed with Marcus' contribution, were especially portrayed in caricature by the anti-boycotters. A recurring theme in the anti-boycott tweets was the common misunderstanding of boycott: that progressives don't shop at Home Depot anyway. The fifth most retweeted tweet conveyed this sentiment: "I love how liberals are trying to boycott a store we all know they never go to. The only liberals who shop at hardware stores are members of Antifa. #BoycottHomeDepot."[22] Another likened a liberal boycott of Home Depot to "a vegan boycott of Longhorn Steakhouse." The opponents of the Nike boycott made similar points about the ineffectiveness of the boycott. Referencing the calls to burn Nike apparel and the frequent conservative boycotts of Nike, one user summarized the sentiment well: "the 17 people who actually had Nikes during the first boycott already burned theirs, so they'll probably need to buy a new pair to burn this time."

In both cases, people relied on stereotypes of the other party, as well as code words, insults, and nicknames that are unique within their community. Conservatives portrayed liberals as effete, disconnected from reality, and either poor or reliant on government aid, and used terms such as "soyboy." For instance, one Twitter user noted that in all their time shopping at Home Depot they "have yet to see a man-bun on any of the customers." Others were sure that Home Depot didn't sell "items to fix up their Section 8 living abodes," "items to improve your cardboard box homes," "soy lattes," or the necessary supplies to "modify their safe spaces or change the air in their bubbles." Even if they did sell those things, the people who reported they were boycotting Home Depot "are the same people who have no idea what a hammer and nail is used for," "have no idea which end of the hammer to hold let alone which end of the nail to hit," "have never even hammered a nail into a wall," and don't know a hammer from "a skill saw" or "a screwdriver." Liberals, on the other hand, portrayed conservatives as poor "rednecks" who were opposed to exercise. As one user put it, "It's not a boycott if you can't afford it." Both sides portrayed their opponents as dumb and gullible. Clearly, these tweets

---

[22] "Antifa" is a political protest movement that opposes fascism and right-wing ideology.

were about cementing an individual's in-group status within the group by disparaging the other side.

Yet the thing that made Home Depot and Nike so fruitful for analysis – that they are both large and especially partisan boycotts – might also make them unique. Smaller boycotts, for instance, are unlikely to have counter-boycotts, which is where most of the insults arose in both cases. Analyzing tweets from unique boycotts is useful for making observations, but it is difficult to make claims about the generalizability. Which of these findings is about the social function of tweeting about boycott and what is specific to the two cases at hand?

This is the reason I returned to the entire set of tweets that contained the word boycott, pooling people talking about large, established boycotts, as well as smaller boycotts. The broader data set can validate the finding from the cases – that insults are especially likely in partisan boycotts because of their ability to signal someone's partisanship to their peers. It turned out that the insults being used to express distaste for the other party and solidify in-ground solidarity with the individual's party was a pattern that held in the data more broadly. When compared with boycott tweets that did not contain partisan language, boycotts tweeted with partisan language, as defined in the previous section, were not only more likely to be retweeted but were also more likely to contain insults. Table 4.8 shows the results of a logistic regression predicting the presence of common insult words: idiot, stupid, dumb, and imbecile.[23] The results showed that partisan tweets increased the probability of including insults when compared to tweets without partisan content. It also reaffirmed that the Home Depot and Nike tweets were especially insult-laden and that verified users were less likely to use insults. To assure this result was not strictly

---

[23] I developed this list by reading through random samples of tweets and recording common insults. The words tended to focus on intelligence. I do not have an especially good explanation for this, except that part of the in-group/out-group signaling here has to do with shoring up the in-group's value by dragging down the out-group, and, in this particular situation, making them out to be unintelligent is logical given that these are criticisms of intentional actions. Partisan-linked insult words were also relatively common – libtard, magat, and snowflake, in particular – but I chose to omit them because their correlation with partisanship was already evident in their construction.

4.6 Are Boycott Tweets Political Signaling? 127

Table 4.8 *The results of a logistic regression predicting the presence of common insult words (idiot, stupid, dumb, and imbecile) as a function of partisanship. Follower quantile estimates are omitted for space. Omitted category for followers is the lowest decile for the particular sample, meaning people who are in the lowest 10 percent of follower counts*

	Dependent variable:	
	Insults opponent's intelligence	
	(1)	(2)
Partisan	0.340***	0.395***
	(0.034)	(0.039)
Verified	−0.412***	−0.476***
	(0.135)	(0.166)
Home Depot	0.352***	
	(0.056)	
Nike	0.486***	
	(0.036)	
Wayfair	0.629***	0.617***
	(0.077)	(0.078)
Starbucks	0.775***	0.814***
	(0.055)	(0.061)
Constant	−3.782***	−3.850***
	(0.046)	(0.054)
Observations	188,689	151,524
Sample	All	Omits Home Depot and Nike
Log Likelihood	−22,859.820	−17,092.260
Akaike Inf. Crit.	45,751.640	34,212.530

Note: $^*p < 0.1$; $^{**}p < 0.05$; $^{***}p < 0.01$

driven by people in the Home Depot and Nike samples being especially mean to each other, the second model in Table 4.8 includes a sample

4.7 Conclusion

Overall, the evidence in this chapter strongly supports the theory. First, the experimental evidence demonstrates clearly that people disapprove of a company's political advocacy or other activities primarily for partisan reasons. That is, people do not oppose corporate campaign contributions or lobbying primarily because they take exception to the idea of corporate power in politics; instead, they oppose it when it opposes their own individual partisanship. In other words, people do not especially dislike Walmart's PAC making a political contribution, but Democrats dislike Walmart's PAC donating to Republicans and Republicans dislike Walmart's PAC donating to Democrats. This holds even when looking at local politics, in fictional cases, and without partisanship stated.

Second, the experimental data supports the assumption that people are not opposed to companies engaging in activities that may be advocacy or influence-seeking but are not explicitly so. A wide range of activities can be used to influence politicians based on their particular needs, and one of the strategies I argue that companies use to avoid backlash is to pursue advocacy strategies that are less common and less reviled. The experimental evidence, particularly in the fictional vignettes, supports the idea that engaging in unconventional advocacy may allow companies to influence politicians while sidestepping negative public opinion.

Third, the social media data supports the contention that the psychological and social function of talking about a boycott online is political signaling. In other words, people talk about boycotts to reaffirm to themselves and to demonstrate to others where they stand in

---

[24] In unreported robustness checks, I investigated whether partisan tweets were simply more negative or more vulgar than other tweets but not necessarily more insulting. Using Quanteda for sentiment analysis (Benoit et al. 2018), I found that partisan tweets were higher on disgust and anger but not higher on negativity. Using Carlin's (1972) 7 Words as a dictionary, I found that partisan tweets were actually significantly less profane than other tweets, whereas another sample of slightly less vulgar profanity terms indicated no statistically significant difference between the partisan and non-partisan tweets.

4.7 Conclusion

the political space. I show that more explicitly partisan tweets about boycott – even when tweeted by similar users and about similar, or even the same, topic – tend to garner significantly more retweets than posts that do not use partisan language. This demonstrates that it is not necessarily the company's actions that matter for large, popular boycotts on social media but rather the ease of opportunity to take a political stance.

Finally, the social media analysis illuminates one way that people use those partisan tweets to signal: by insulting the "other side," people make it clear which side they are on. I used the two largest boycotts during this time period, those against Nike and Home Depot, to illustrate this phenomenon, and then I tested it on the data more broadly. I found that boycott tweets with partisan language were more likely than other boycott tweets to contain insults, specifically insults that targeted the other group's intelligence. It is by insulting the other group, and particularly by calling them idiots, that people demonstrate to themselves and to those around them that not only do they belong to their group but also that their group is superior to the other group.

Yet all this raises the reasonable question of whether any of it matters. Do companies care if people disapprove of their stances? Does it matter at all if large and contentious, insult-laden discussions of a company grow on Twitter? In the next chapter, I tackle the question of why companies would care about what people think and whether what people say on Twitter even matters.

5 | Why Do Companies Care About Public Opinion?

5.1 Introduction

A company that doesn't pay attention to its consumers is a company that won't be around long term. All companies, for instance, eventually evolve with the times or go out of business, ensuring that they still sell things people want to buy. Telecommunications companies that once dealt primarily in supplying homeowners with landline phones have had to change with the times, recognizing that landlines are going the way of the dinosaur and instead focusing their energy on more popular applications of similar technology, including the internet, television, and cell phone service. AT&T, the giant telecom company, originally stood for American Telephone & Telegraph, but they don't make much of their money from telegraph service anymore.[1] Had they dug in their metaphorical corporate heels and doubled down on telegraphs even as consumer interest declined, it's unlikely they'd be the telecommunications giant they are today.[2]

Yet consumers don't just care about products. As illustrated in the previous chapter, consumers also care about how a company operates in the political sphere. Many people don't like it when companies get involved in politics, or, at least, as I demonstrated in the previous chapter, many people don't like when companies get involved in politics that differ from theirs. In the survey I conducted, 52.9 percent of people – just over half of those surveyed – disapproved of companies engaging in the political process when their interests are at stake. Consumers dislike corporate political influence even more when

---

[1] Actually, they make none of their money from telegraph service.

[2] Eastman Kodak is often cited as a counterexample of a company that refused to evolve and declined precipitously as a result. See, for example, Brancaccio, David. Dec 20, 2011. "Decline of Kodak Offers Lessons for U.S. Business." Marketplace. www.marketplace.org/2011/12/20/decline-kodak-offers-lessons-us-business/.

5.1 Introduction 131

they disagree with the company's stance. People also frequently take to social media to express their disapproval of companies doing things that they interpret as political stances and can use these posts as a way to establish their position within political space.

But do companies care?

If it were just an issue of people not liking a company's political activities, it might not matter too much to companies. Companies sell things, and they care about whether people want to buy them, but there's no particularly good reason to expect them to care if their consumers agree with their political stances. Yet companies do care about revenue and reputation (Diermeier 2011), and many people do translate their dislike of corporate political influence into a willingness to boycott. An interest in boycott spurs a discussion about the boycott, which brings unwanted negative attention to the company. Even if the boycott itself does not directly affect sales – that is, even if people who say they are going to boycott do not actually change their consumer behavior immediately or at all – the damage to a company's brand and reputation that can arise from such a boycott can be damaging in itself and might also indirectly – down the line – affect sales or shareholder views. It follows that it's in a company's best interest, then, to avoid doing things it thinks might provoke a boycott.

In this chapter, I address the question of whether companies actually care – or even know – that people might boycott on the basis of their political actions. First, I explain in more detail which companies should, theoretically, be the most and least concerned about the risk of boycott. In short, concern about boycott comes at companies from two different directions: some companies are more likely than others to be targeted by activists and therefore more likely to have their activities publicized and criticized, and some companies are more likely than others to be damaged by any ensuing boycott. Many of the variables that predict these two different angles of vulnerability are the same: bigger companies and companies with especially valuable brands are both more likely to be targeted and more likely to be damaged. Yet some companies are more likely to be targeted but not necessarily more likely to be damaged (companies led by women, for instance) and some companies are more likely to be targeted but might actually be less likely to be damaged. Companies that have been targets of activists before are more likely to be on the activists' radar and thus more likely to experience a boycott, but the previous boycott

132   *Why Do Companies Care About Public Opinion?*

might actually make them relatively immune to future boycotts if the boycott provides no new information to shareholders or does not actually make the mass public update their image of the brand.

I also explore the evidence for these claims and illustrate that companies do, in fact, care. First, I use corporate documents – specifically documents filed with the Securities and Exchange Commission (SEC) – to demonstrate that companies with certain attributes are more likely to be concerned about the threat of public backlash, whereas others are not. Further, I find that these companies are more likely to link concerns about social media with concerns about brand damage and reputation, which supports the idea that concerns about backlash are driven by concerns about brand, not necessarily revenue. Although this doesn't demonstrate that companies are concerned specifically about the response to their politics or political activities, it does provide strong evidence that they are concerned about themes related to public backlash.

Second, I use evidence from interviews with corporate government affairs professionals and others with first-hand experience of companies seeking political influence. The key finding from the interviews is that concern about boycott is not in any way limited to companies in the retail sector or other companies that sell directly to the public, reinforcing the claim that the mechanism about boycott is not directly about sales but rather about reputation, brand, and the indirect damage to profits that they may confer. Further, I find that companies are not only worried about boycott broadly but are also well aware that their political activities might get them into hot water with consumers.

In the next section, I explain the central claim behind this chapter, followed by an explanation of the different ways in which it might be wrong. I then discuss the sources of evidence I use to assess the support for the claim and my findings.

5.2 The Claim

> Boycotts are concerning to companies primarily because of brand damage.

In the previous chapter, I demonstrated that people disapprove of companies taking actions that counter their personal partisanship and

5.2 *The Claim* 133

that a primary function of supporting a boycott is to signal individual partisanship. The key question that follows from this is – So what? Do companies even care that people might boycott or, even less, just talk about boycotting? The central claim of this chapter is that companies do care about boycott, and, moreover, it may not even matter if people actually change their purchasing habits or just talk about it. Boycotts matter even if the purported boycotters don't change their consumer behavior because discussion of boycott can threaten a company's brand and reputation.

Boycotts are conventionally understood to be about individual purchasing decisions. If someone decides they do not agree with something a company is doing, they can decide to shift their purchasing behavior and no longer do business with the company. When people refuse to do business with the company, it deprives the company of that revenue, and, therefore, the idea is that the reduced revenue due to the boycott causes the company sufficient pain to cause it to shift its behavior. Under that understanding of boycotts, people can only really boycott companies whose products and services they at least semi-regularly purchase and consume. For a boycott to actually harm a company through that direct revenue mechanism, the people who decide to boycott should be people who, under other circumstances, would have done business with the company. Given that so many companies in the economy are primarily in the business of selling to other companies or the government and that the average consumer is only likely to buy products sold by a fraction of the remaining companies, most companies should have no real reason to fear a boycott.

Yet there are no limits on which companies people can *talk about* boycotting. As demonstrated in the previous chapter, anyone can propose or support a boycott of any company, regardless of what the company does or whether the person ever would, or could, do business with it. And this, too, can damage companies but not by directly affecting sales and revenue, like a traditional boycott. By contrast, an internet boycott – one that is mostly talk – damages companies by harming their brand and reputation. For many companies, their brand is among the most valuable assets they have (Budac and Baltador 2013; Fournier and Srinivasan 2018) – it is a combination of all the ways people think about a company and all the things they associate with a company, and it's a key way that companies differentiate themselves in a crowded marketplace (Keller 1993; Aaker 1997; Keller and Lehmann 2006; Ettenson and Knowles 2008).

But because brands are intangible and rely on the positive feelings and associations of customers, they are also fragile. It does not necessarily take much for those associations and feelings to change. A reassociation of the company with values that its consumers do not hold or a group people do not like – for instance, a political party – can do significant damage to the brand, both short and long term, through different mechanisms, separate from the consumer behavior of purported boycotters. First, because the brand in itself is a valuable asset, anything that hurts the brand value also hurts the company's finances. Second, if the damage and reassociations of the brand are lasting, it might harm consumer behavior and sales in the longer run, even among people who did not actively boycott or may not even have necessarily been aware of the boycott. Third, if the company is publicly traded and if the boycott provides new information to shareholders that make it doubt the company and its management, it may hurt the company's stock price.

Online boycotts – people speaking negatively about the company, separate from any consumer choices – have the potential to hurt the company's brand in that way by drawing negative attention to the company and its actions. Because of that, it doesn't necessarily matter if any of the people supporting a boycott of a company change, or could change, their consumer behavior, provided enough of them are talking enough. Boycotts that become especially large may even attract media attention, leading to further scrutiny and press coverage of the company and its perceived misdeeds, leaving open the potential for further disagreements and bad press on the basis of what is revealed in the articles. The potential for this, I argue, is enough to change a company's behavior in an attempt to avoid online boycotts, because even the *prospect* of losing control over such a valuable asset and letting the crowd define what the company is and what it stands for is frightening for all the potential damage it could do.

Expectation 1: Concerns about boycott, especially on the internet, come from fears of brand and reputation damage.

That is all to say that many more companies should theoretically fear boycotts than a model of boycott as consumer behavior would suggest, simply because an individual's purchases are not the only

5.3 Why and How It Might Be Wrong

mechanism that hurts the company. That said, not all companies are equally likely to be targeted by activists for their behaviors – meaning not all companies are equally likely to be called out and criticized for their corporate advocacy (or anything else) – and not all companies suffer equally if their brand is damaged. Large companies and companies with valuable, recognizable brands get hit from both directions on this – they are more likely to be targeted and they tend to face greater damage because they have more invested in their brands and therefore more to lose. That means that those companies, all else equal, should experience the greatest concern about boycott. Companies led by women are more likely to be targeted by activists, but they are not theoretically more likely to suffer brand damage, and therefore companies led by women should be more likely to fear boycott than companies led by men, controlling for other relevant variables.

Expectation 2: Companies with valuable, recognizable brands and large companies should express the greatest concern about boycott.

Expectation 3: Companies led by women should express greater concern about boycott than companies led by men, all else equal.

5.3 Why and How It Might Be Wrong

On the other hand, there are also reasons to believe none of this is true. Maybe companies don't know, or don't care, about boycott, for instance. If that's the case, even if consumers might boycott in response to political action, there's no reason to believe it would actually affect corporate decision-making. In this section, I provide an overview of a few reasons why the claim might be wrong.

1 Companies Don't Realize the Threat: One reason why companies might not fear boycott in response to their political activities is that they don't realize it's a threat. Companies can't fear a bogeyman they don't know about, after all. Even if there is a relationship between a company's efforts to intervene in politics and consumer behavior, as demonstrated in Chapter 4, it might well be the case that companies themselves don't make that connection.

How might companies not know? It could be that they don't often intervene in politics and therefore they have never experienced boycott themselves, or that they do aim to influence politics but have never experienced negative consequences from doing so. If the boycott affects other companies that try to do politics, those boycotts and the consequences may not be visible to other companies, or other companies are not paying attention. In sum, there are a variety of reasons why companies just might not realize this is a threat, and if they don't realize it's a threat, it makes sense that they wouldn't be concerned about it and we wouldn't expect it to influence their behavior.

2 **Companies Don't Care:** A second reason why companies might not fear boycott, even if they know that influencing politics might in principle provoke people to boycott, is that they don't actually think the boycott is a serious threat. They might doubt that it'll materialize or doubt that it'll become large enough to actually matter. Companies might expect that they are sufficiently skilled (or sufficiently lucky) that a boycott threat wouldn't affect them. They might think that by virtue of characteristics of their company – what they sell, who they sell it to, or the nature of their revenue streams – that a boycott is unlikely or wouldn't actually be harmful if it did happen. If this is the case, we'd expect companies to acknowledge that a boycott might happen but not express actual concern about it.

3 **Companies Can Easily Recover:** A third possibility is that companies realize and care, but they have systems in place that would allow them to easily counter the boycott and recover, such that the boycott itself would not meaningfully threaten either the company's revenue or its reputation. If this is the case, a boycott might hurt a company in the short term but not the medium or long term, and the company can recover without significant effort. In other words: boycotts might happen and they might be damaging, but the damage does not really matter. Any damage from the boycott wouldn't matter much, and certainly not enough to really concern anyone at the company. If this is the case, companies should demonstrate awareness of the connection between politics and boycott but experience only minor, fleeting concern

4 **Companies Benefit from Boycotts:** It is also possible that boycotts aren't negative at all. Boycotts might actually *help* companies. There is some evidence, for instance, that "brand polarization" – a brand having "lovers" and "haters" – which can easily occur as a result of a politically motivated boycott, as the counter-boycotts in Chapter 4 illustrate, might actually provide some benefits to companies

(Osuna Ramírez, Veloutsou, and Morgan-Thomas 2019). As they note, "polarizing brands are noticeable and are able to generate vigorous emotional and behavioral reactions from the side of the consumers, as strong brands are expected to do." Companies may be able to use a boycott to, for instance, strengthen their marketing toward the group of people who oppose the boycotters. It could also be the case that companies use their political influence-seeking as a signal of their type to consumers and therefore the boycott by people who oppose their position may, in a sense, be either deliberate or just anticipated collateral damage. In other words, a company may want to signal that it is a progressive company and use lobbying for pro-labor or pro-environmental efforts or prominently donating to progressive figures as a way to shore up their progressive credentials and therefore appeal to a progressive market. In this case, they may experience consumer backlash from conservative consumers but that backlash may not matter to the company and may pale in comparison to the benefit of further advertising to progressives. If this is the case, companies should demonstrate awareness of the connection, but rather than concern, may actually demonstrate interest.

5.4 Sources of Evidence

To evaluate these claims, I used two different sources of evidence, both of which offer insights into corporate decision-making and how companies "feel" about boycott but in slightly different ways. First, I analyzed corporate reports. Specifically, I used 10-Ks, which are reports publicly traded companies have to file with the Securities and Exchange Commission (SEC). 10-Ks allowed me to evaluate a large number of companies to assess their stated concern about boycott. Second, I turned to interviews with representatives from corporations, which allowed for a more in-depth view of a smaller number of companies to get at the internal decision-making and cognizance of the link between advocacy and boycott.

5.4.1 Evidence from 10-Ks

The first source of evidence I used was aimed at statistically evaluating the expectations about the kinds of companies that are most likely to express concerns about boycotts. 10-Ks are reports that publicly traded companies are required to file with the Securities and Exchange Commission (SEC).[3] The aim of 10-Ks is to ensure that shareholders are informed when they make their investment decisions. The information within them, accordingly, tends to focus on things shareholders would need to know before they choose to invest in a company. Among other things, this includes financial information, information about the company's business operations and activities, and a list of its board members and management. Companies are required to list any active litigation they are involved in and often detail mergers and proposed new business activity in the coming year. These are also where, for instance, the Dodd-Frank efforts to stop trade in conflict minerals turns up as a mandatory section in the 10-Ks.[4]

One section, Item 1A, focuses on risks the company foresees that might negatively influence its profitability in the coming year. The idea is that shareholders should know what might hurt profits since that might hurt share prices, and that might influence whether (and how much) they want to invest in a particular company. Companies are required by law to list all the potential risks to their profitability that they foresee as potentially being issues in the coming year. Unlike evidence from corporate surveys, which often have a low response rate, 10-Ks are not optional. 10-Ks also include incentives for both honesty and comprehensiveness: dishonesty or knowingly failing to disclose a risk opens a company up to potential investor fraud lawsuits. ExxonMobil, for instance, has been accused of shareholder fraud for not disclosing the risks of climate change in its SEC reports.[5] 10-Ks are written by lawyers in technical, legal terminology with a focus on corporate liability: in other words, they are documents intended to protect the company from lawsuits but simultaneously to not deter investment, and therefore, I argue, they provide a good incentive to be honest but not overstate the problem. They are, therefore, the most

---

[3] Publicly traded companies are companies that are listed and traded on the New York Stock Exchange (NYSE), the National Association of Securities Dealers Automated Quotation System (NASDAQ), or the American Stock Exchange.

[4] For more information on the conflict minerals requirements, see Bloem (2019).

[5] Wamsley, Laurel. "Exxon Is On Trial, Accused of Misleading Investors About Risks of Climate Change." October 22, 2019. NPR. www.npr.org/2019/10/22/772241282/exxon-is-on-trial-accused-of-misleading-investors-about-risks-of-climate-change.

5.4 Sources of Evidence

complete, thorough, and honest accountings of companies' perceived threats and liabilities, political or otherwise.

5.4.2 Evidence from Interviews

Although the 10-Ks allow for an assessment of which companies cite concerns about boycott, they offer limited insight into why. They also provide the hardest test since companies should be expected to only list boycott as a risk when they believe it's their responsibility to inform shareholders of that risk but not under other circumstances since overstating risks to profitability might deter investment. Interviews provide a different look into corporate dynamics and decision-making and allow for deeper insights into the concerns of a smaller number of companies. Specifically, I conducted in-depth interviews with corporate representatives about their company's political concerns and efforts to advocate for their interests in the political system.

One difficulty with conducting interviews is that the theory itself suggests that companies that are most concerned about the public response to their political statements should be least likely to speak to me. As one person I interviewed put it when they initially declined to be interviewed, "We don't usually talk about politics in relation to our company as it is generally bad for business." By contrast, the theory predicts that the companies that should be least concerned about the consequences of their advocacy should be the most willing to consent to an interview. They should also be the least likely to discuss concern about boycott. This means that this is a particularly hard test of the theory because the theory itself predicts that I should find no evidence that any company cares about boycott (even if what I collect is consistent with the theory), and the people I would expect *would* express concern about boycott should be entirely missing from my sample. It turns out that it is difficult to learn about something that many people have an interest in not speaking to you about, but the fact that people don't want to talk about it is, in itself, informative.

I conducted two waves of interviews for this book – one in the summer of 2019 and the second in the summer of 2020. In the first round, I sampled companies by industry and recruited the largest companies in each industry. Even after intentionally oversampling companies with strong brands (and especially those in the retail and food service industries), I was unable to recruit a single representative of a large, branded, consumer-facing company. By contrast, as expected, people in industries that the theory predicts should be less concerned about consumer backlash and therefore less sensitive about political influence were more likely to agree to talk to me, although recruiting government affairs professionals to interview had a low yield rate overall. Out of about forty requests,[6] I ended up with four interviews with in-house government affairs people, current and former – about a 10 percent yield. Most of my requests were ignored, although it merits a brief note that, of the six companies that explicitly declined my requests, all but one were companies the theory predicts would make people unwilling to talk – a national food chain, a company that makes and sells many popular food brands, a regional grocery chain, a hotel chain, and an education company.[7] Although this isn't to say that they declined for this reason – one company in particular told me that their government affairs team is small and was currently entirely focused on a pressing policy issue – it is consistent with the theory.

In the second round of interview requests, I randomly sampled 400 publicly traded companies and sent requests to each of them. Instead of explicitly focusing on the types of companies the theory suggests should respond to the threat of public backlash, choosing companies at random made it easier to understand patterns in response and non response. Of the 370 companies that had publicly available and functioning email addresses, only 31 responded (8.4 percent). Of those 31, 18 declined (58.0 percent) to speak with me. The companies that agreed to be interviewed were, with exactly one exception, companies with brands unlikely to be known outside of their industry and companies that did not sell directly to consumers but instead did their business primarily or exclusively with other companies or governments. Although this allows me to discuss the threat of boycott within that subset of industries, it does not allow me to understand the threat of boycott in other industries that, theoretically, ought to be the most

---

[6] It's difficult to know exactly how many requests were sent, since I only have records of my own requests, but I also enlisted others who sent requests to their personal contacts on my behalf, and I don't know how many of those there were, or to whom.

[7] The sixth had recently left her position and was uncomfortable discussing her former employer.

5.5 Which Companies Fear Public Backlash? 141

threatened. Yet this in itself, again, is instructive: companies that are concerned about public backlash to their political activities likely will be hesitant to discuss those activities. The one representative from a company that was consumer-facing and had a valuable, recognizable brand was the exception that proved the rule. That representative was clear with me that their company did not engage in political activity as a rule, a claim that was backed up by the data. This, therefore, does not fit the trend of companies in that space being concerned about the interpretation of their political activity by the public since they don't engage in any. In the absence of a more even distribution of interviews across industries, I supplemented the government affairs interviews with secondary interview evidence from lobbyists and journalists. Although they could not speak directly to how particular companies strategize, their answers reflected their perceptions of what the decision-making for these companies looks like. Since many of the lobbyists I spoke to also viewed their role as encompassing public affairs consulting, many of them had fairly in-depth knowledge of what companies are thinking about. Together, the interviews told a clear story about how companies perceive the consequences of their political actions.

5.5 Which Companies Fear Public Backlash?

The risk factors section of the 10-Ks is especially well suited to figuring out what a company perceives to be its threats. In these documents, companies outline in detail all the possible threats to their company in the coming year. The audience is shareholders or potential shareholders, and, in drafting these documents, the lawyers balance an interest in being forthcoming in order to avoid lawsuits from shareholders who believe they've been misled about a known risk with an interest in not scaring away shareholders. From these documents, we can learn, for instance, that Dunkin' Donuts (more formally Dunkin' Brands Group, Inc.) is concerned about local styrofoam bans ("[banning] the use of certain packaging materials (including polystyrene used in the iconic Dunkin' Donuts cup) ... would be costly to comply with ...") and the Rocky Mountain Chocolate Factory worries about increases in the minimum wage ("Because a significant number of our employees are paid at rates related to the federal minimum wage, increases in the minimum wage would increase our labor costs.").

Domino's, the pizza chain, is very concerned about the price of cheese, which, combined with labor, makes up 60 percent of the costs of most of their restaurants. Abercrombie & Fitch, the clothing company, is implicitly concerned about climate change. It lists natural disasters, pandemic disease, and unseasonable weather among their risks since the former two could both disrupt their supply chain and drive down consumer traffic, whereas the latter might reduce demand for seasonal clothing. The Ford Motor Company notes concern about cyber incidents "caused by malicious third parties using sophisticated, targeted methods to circumvent firewalls, encryption, and other security defenses, including hacking, fraud, trickery, or other forms of deception." Alphabet, the holding company that owns Google (and still has the stock symbol GOOG), cites the popularity of ad-blocking software as a significant risk since most of its revenues are derived from ad sales.

With companies citing everything from local minimum wage laws to terrorism, 10-Ks are thus a prime opportunity to figure out which companies are concerned about boycotts and how and why they see those boycotts harming their business. Coupled with data on the size, management, and industry of the companies (obtained from the database Orbis), we can also figure out how these concerns covary with characteristics of interest. Are larger companies more concerned about boycott? Are companies led by women more concerned about boycott? And why? Is the concern driven by worries about sales, or reputation?

I assembled the risk factors section from all available 10-Ks for every company that was traded on the three major stock exchanges in the United States as of summer 2018.[8] The documents do not change much from year to year, and coverage is spotty prior to 2010, and so, along with an interest in combing the documents with data on corporate characteristics, I used data only from calendar years 2018 and 2019. The plurality of companies in the data were major banks,

---

[8] Although some aspects of the formatting are standardized, such as section heading names, other aspects, like font, word processing software, and other aspects of how the report is actually rendered, are not. In a mass data scrape like this one, this means I had to write broad rules to capture the correct section, and sometimes this results in errors. In my data, this mostly means the scraper would sometimes extract part of the Table of Contents instead of the actual section. In rare cases, it extracted Item 7 instead of Item 1A.

5.5 Which Companies Fear Public Backlash? 143

Table 5.1 *Top five industries in the data and representative companies from that industry*

Industry	Number (percent)	Representative companies
Major banks	2,039 (7.5 percent)	Bank of America, US Bank, Wells Fargo
Real estate investment trusts	1,599 (5.9 percent)	Lamar Advertising Company, Public Storage, Simon Property Group
Major pharmaceuticals	1,449 (5.3 percent)	Johnson & Johnson, Allergan, Eli Lilly
Industrial machinery/components	1,062 (3.9 percent)	Northrop Grumman, Raytheon, Eaton
Oil and gas production	936 (3.4 percent)	Zion Oil percent Gas, Occidental Petroleum Chesapeake Utilities Corporation

real estate investment trusts (a broad category that included companies that own and operate malls, storage facilities, and billboards), and major pharmaceutical companies (Table 5.1). Although this sample of companies is representative of publicly traded companies, it may not generalize perfectly to the broader population of companies since companies that opt to be publicly traded may be different from companies that don't (Pagano, Panetta, and Zingales 1998).

The text of those 10-Ks provides insight into what the company perceives as risks to its profitability, and including the threat of boycott within that text therefore indicates that the companies consider boycott to be a potential threat to its business and shareholders. The main claim of this chapter is that boycotts, understood as social media statements, are primarily a threat to companies through their threat to reputation and brand and less through direct sales and revenue. Each expectation within the theory argues that certain characteristics of companies – size, brand value, and having women leadership – should, therefore, increase the company's risk.

To understand how companies perceive the threat of boycotts on social media, I took each sentence of each document as its own unit and I coded two quantities. The first linked social media boycotts with brand damage. I coded for whether, within an individual sentence, the terms "social media," "boycott,"[9] or "protest" were used in tandem with "brand damage" or "reputation."[10] The second linked social media and boycotts with revenue and sales by looking for those terms used in tandem with each other. Many 10-Ks use each of these terms at some point within the 10-Ks; the point of looking at their co-occurrence within the same sentence is to indicate that they are, somehow, linked.[11]

Of the 18,653 10-Ks from 2018, 22 percent mentioned the term "boycott," "protest," or "social media" at least once. Only 3.1 percent mentioned boycott (after filtering out anti-boycott provisions and the BDS movement), but 14.6 percent mentioned social media and 5.5 percent mentioned boycott. By contrast, companies were exceptionally concerned about both reputation and brand damage, as well as revenue and sales. Almost all of them (89.7 percent) expressed concerns about their reputation or damage to their brand, illustrating what a paramount concern these things truly are to companies, and even more mentioned revenue and/or sales (96.0 percent).

The question, then, is how these ideas are linked. When companies discuss social media, boycott, and/or protest, are they concerned about brand damage and reputation, or revenue and sales? Or both? Or neither?

The answer is: both! Some companies linked social media and boycott with brand damage and reputation, some linked them with revenue and sales, and twenty companies (1.08 percent of the sample) did both. Yet the social media terms were paired with brand and reputation damage considerably more often than with revenue and sales. Of companies that cited a concern about social media, protest, and/or boycott, 27 percent mentioned brand damage or reputation in

---

[9] I screened out references to the Boycott, Divestment, and Sanctions (BDS) movement and references to anti-boycott clauses.

[10] I also coded for the use of the term "firestorm," but none used that term.

[11] This is an overly strict test in the sense that two ideas can be linked in the text without occurring in the same sentence but instead may be linked by occurring within the same paragraph. I opted to look within sentences and err on the side of being overly strict because the nature of the 10-Ks lends itself to many fairly long paragraphs that are not necessarily cohesive for our purposes (although I do not doubt there are good legal reasons for this structure), which would lead to too many false positives, in which the concepts would appear to be linked but actually are not.

5.5 Which Companies Fear Public Backlash?

the same sentence, whereas only 15.9 percent mentioned revenue or sales.

Yet because the language is complicated and nuanced, these keyword searches do not and cannot tell the whole story since people can use a variety of different words and phrases to convey the same ideas. It is helpful, therefore, to look at the texts themselves and see what the documents actually say. The documents provide compelling evidence that at least a subset of companies acknowledge the central claim of this chapter: that social media and negative publicity – whether they are called boycotts, protests, or something else – can damage a company's reputation and thus its bottom line.

Ascena Retail Group, which is responsible for the retail brands Ann Taylor, LOFT, Justice, and Lane Bryant, among others, focused primarily on the damage to the company's reputation and brands. They linked these ideas in three separate sentences, noting that "the use of social media by the Company and consumers has also increased the risk that the Company's image and reputation could be negatively impacted." They went on to explain that the damage can be swift ("The availability of information, reviews and opinions on social media is immediate, as is its impact.") and difficult to fight ("Even if we react quickly and appropriately to negative social media about us or our brands, our reputation and customers' perception of our brands could be negatively impacted."). In other words, the risk is growing, the damage comes quickly, and it is hard to fight. Negative social media opinions are no small matter.

American Public Education, Inc. acknowledged both the reputation and revenue threats inherent in negative social media coverage and highlighted the chain of negative consequences that can stem from negative social media attention. They wrote, "Adverse media or social media coverage regarding others in our industry, or regarding us or our institutions directly, could damage our reputation, could result in lower enrollments at our institutions, lower revenue and increased expenses, and could have a negative impact on our stock price." In doing this, they highlighted that social media activism or negative attention affects reputation, but it can also have consequences for other aspects of the business, both linked to and independent from that reputational or brand damage.

Bloomin' Brands, which owns Outback Steakhouse, Carrabba's Italian Grill, and other restaurants, demonstrated in their 10-Ks how fragile brand value and reputation truly are and how their control over them is tenuous. "Brand value and reputation," they wrote, "is based in large part on consumer perceptions, which are driven by both our actions and by actions beyond our control, such as new brand strategies or their implementation, business incidents, ineffective advertising or marketing efforts, or unfavorable mainstream or social media publicity involving us, our industry, our franchisees, or our suppliers." In other words, the brands are important – Bloomin', in particular, knows how many options people have for dining out – and that negative attention paid to any aspect of their business can damage them.

These companies, however, are consumer-facing – it makes sense that their brand value might be a concern as people may more clearly link their opinions about the company with their sales. Is this strictly a concern limited to companies that sell directly to consumers?

No, the evidence also clearly demonstrated that even companies that never sell directly to people – companies that many people have likely never heard of – are also concerned about the consequences of negative social media attention. Callon Petroleum (in the 10-Ks for Carrizo Oil & Gas, Inc., a company they acquired after the publication of the 10-Ks), an independent oil and natural gas company that focuses on acquisition and exploration and does not actually sell to individual consumers, is one of the companies that most succinctly linked social media with damage to brand and reputation, even in a situation where individual consumers talking about them on the internet will never be in the position of opting to buy or not buy from their company. They wrote that "the use of social media channels can be used to cause rapid, widespread reputational harm." Similarly, Cassava Sciences, a biopharmaceutical company working on Alzheimer's treatments that also does not sell to the mass public, cited concerns that "... negative, inappropriate or inaccurate posts or comments about us or our product candidates on social media internet sites could quickly and irreversibly damage our reputation, brand image and goodwill."

Are these companies necessarily talking about reactions to their political advocacy? No, as each of the aforementioned quotes indicates, the threats are broad. People can focus negative attention on any

5.5 Which Companies Fear Public Backlash? 147

aspect of the company – real or imagined – and cause damage. This is not a threat that is limited to companies taking political stances, yet it is a concern that companies need to think about when they make decisions about those political choices. Not all negative social media attention is generated by a company's political advocacy, and not all political advocacy will generate negative social media attention, but political advocacy can and does generate negative social media attention, and, as the 10-Ks demonstrate, that negative social media attention can be incredibly damaging to brand and reputation, leading to a chain of negative consequences for companies that may not be able to prevent or stop the onslaught.

Another way to establish that concerns about social media boycotts are linked more to reputation than to revenue – that is, it's more about fear of corporate character assassination than fear of consumer behavior changes – is to track the change in both over time. Social media has only been around since the mid-2000s, and it was not ubiquitous at first. The growth of social media should be, presumably, followed by increased corporate fear of the power of social media. The data can tell us whether this tracks with a fear of brand damage, a fear of decreases in revenue or sales, or both.

Figure 5.1 shows the percent of companies citing each of these things in their risk factors section for each year in the decade beginning in 2008. Although the fear of social media does grow over this time period – in 2008, only about one-quarter of 1 percent of 10-Ks mentioned social media, whereas 14.6 percent of 10-Ks mentioned it in 2018 – the really dramatic increase is in companies citing reputation or brand damage. In 2008, four years after Facebook was founded, three years after reddit, and two years after Twitter, 43 percent of 10-Ks mentioned reputation or brand. Ten years later, it was nearly all of them – 89.7 percent. Over that ten-year span, concerns about social media increased 55 percent whereas concerns about reputation and brand damage increased by 106 percent. At the same time, concerns about sales/revenue, protest, and boycott all increased slightly but remained mostly flat, as the figure illustrates. Noting that concerns about social media and concerns about reputation and brand damage both increased substantially over the same time period (and the tandem increases are correlated at $\rho = 0.95$), while concerns about sales/revenue were mostly stable across time is not conclusive evidence of causation by any means, but it is suggestive of

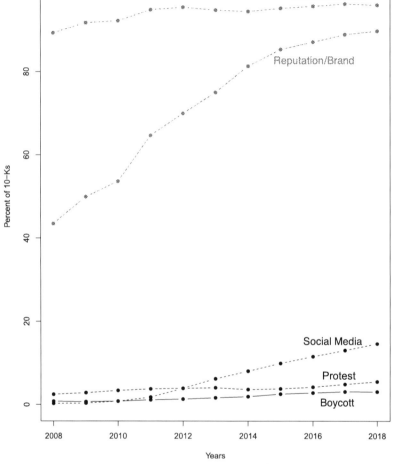

Figure 5.1 The percentage of 10-Ks in each year citing as a concern sales/revenue, reputation/brand, social media, protest, and boycott

a relationship.[12] Many other things also happened over this time period, but given the theoretical relationship between social media

---

[12] As the alt-text in the xkcd comic titled "Correlation" puts it: "Correlation doesn't imply causation, but it does waggle its eyebrows suggestively and gesture furtively 'look over there'" (https://xkcd.com/552/).

5.5 Which Companies Fear Public Backlash?

critiques of companies and concerns about damage to brand, it does seem likely the correlation is meaningful.

In addition to establishing the central claim that the concern is brand damage rather than direct hits to sales, the data can also give us an indication of which types of companies are more or less fearful of these dynamics. As the expectations in this chapter suggest, large companies and companies with especially valuable brands should be the most concerned since they are both more likely to be targeted and, presumably, will have their company damaged more severely by hits to their brand. Companies led by women should also be more concerned than companies led by men, all else being equal, given the harsh spotlight shone on women in positions of power.

To test these expectations, I merged the data on 10-Ks with data on company attributes from Orbis. Specifically, I used the number of employees in the US as a measure of size,[13] and I used their coding of the gender of the top manager or director in the company. Additionally, I coded for whether a company was in the Top 100 brands for 2019 from BrandFinance.[14] Using these data in conjunction with the 10-Ks data allowed me to statistically test whether larger companies, companies led by women, and companies with especially valuable brands are more likely to cite concerns about social media, boycotts, and reputation in their 10-Ks.[15] The first two – social media and boycotts – captured a company's likelihood of being targeted by that kind

---

[13] Number of employees correlates with operating revenue at $\rho = 0.75$, and I opted to use the number of employees because it cannot be negative and therefore can be logged to deal with outliers, whereas revenue can be negative and has to be dealt with using more complicated transformations. The substantive findings were mostly the same, and models with operating revenue instead of employees are given in Appendix C. There is one company in the data that is listed as having zero employees – American National Insurance Company – and I excluded it for ease of analysis.

[14] The BrandFinance data was originally accessed through Statista. I recoded each brand with the ticker symbol from the company that has majority ownership over the brand. Some companies have more than one brand in the top 100 (e.g., Facebook has Facebook and Instagram, Google has Google and YouTube, etc.).

[15] In unreported robustness checks, the findings all hold for mentions of the term "activist," but specifically excluding the term "activist investor," indicating that the intermediate theoretical step of activists triggering the backlash is also something companies are concerned with.

Table 5.2 *Results of a logistic regression predicting each of the three sets of terms – boycott, social media, and reputation/brand damage – in the 10-Ks as a function of company attributes plus sector random effects*

	Dependent variable:		
	Boycott	Social media	Reputation/ brand damage
	(1)	(2)	(3)
# Employees (logged)	0.217***	0.268***	0.214***
	(0.084)	(0.043)	(0.045)
Woman CEO	0.474	0.479	0.330
	(0.541)	(0.297)	(0.394)
Top 100 brand	0.264	−0.243	−1.608***
	(0.615)	(0.383)	(0.451)
Constant	−5.481***	−4.427***	0.705*
	(0.756)	(0.490)	(0.370)
Observations	1,449	1,449	1,449
Log likelihood	−190.449	−547.651	−439.167
Akaike inf. crit.	390.899	1,105.301	888.335
Bayesian inf. crit.	417.292	1,131.695	914.728

Note: $^*p < 0.1$; $^{**}p < 0.05$; $^{***}p < 0.01$

of mass action, whereas reputation/brand damage captured vulnerability to a brand-based attack. The theory predicts large companies and companies with valuable brands should be positive in all three, indicating that they are more likely to be targeted and more vulnerable if they do come under attack, whereas companies led by women should be more likely to be targeted but should not necessarily be more vulnerable to attack.

The results of three logistic regressions predicting any concern about boycott, social media, or reputation are shown in Table 5.2. These tables model *any* mention of the three concepts, without regard to how they come up in the text. For the sake of interpretation, it is helpful to remember what Figure 5.1 illustrated: that boycott and social media are mentioned relatively rarely in the data, whereas reputation and brand damage concerns are ubiquitous. Only 3 percent of companies mentioned boycott at all, whereas about 15 percent mentioned social media, which a reading of the 10-Ks suggests is where the commonly used term "internet boycott" shows up in the data. Reputation and

5.5 *Which Companies Fear Public Backlash?* 151

brand damage, on the other hand, appeared in 90 percent of the 10-Ks. This means the model that predicts mentioning boycott is predicting something that almost never happens, whereas the model predicting reputation is predicting something that almost always happens.

The results indicate that larger companies are more likely to be concerned about all three – boycott, social media, and reputation or brand damage – even after controlling for CEO gender, owning especially valuable brands, and the sector the company operates within. This supports the expectation that larger companies are more likely to be targeted and may also be more vulnerable to brand damage. However, the dummy variable indicating owning an especially valuable brand does not appear to have any particular relationship with either boycott or social media, suggesting such companies are no more or less concerned about those things than companies that own less valuable brands. Yet the results do suggest that companies that own a very valuable brand are less likely to mention concerns about reputation or brand damage, which goes against the theoretical expectations. This could possibly be a function of a mismatch between the concept and the measurement – in other words, maybe having a valuable brand and owning one of the 100 most valuable brands are far enough removed from each other that the latter does not fully capture the former. Since this only captures the top 100 brands, it may be the case that companies that own valuable brands that are not, however, *that* valuable are more concerned than companies that own brands with very little value, which this measurement could not capture. Similarly, it could be the case that there is a level of brand value above which companies feel more secure due to their status, and that a dichotomous measure – or even estimating a linear effect – will not fully capture that effect.

The results for having a woman as the top manager or director of the company are more straightforward. The theory predicts a positive coefficient in the first two and a null result for the third, indicating that companies led by women are more likely to be targeted by activists for a successful mass action, but there is no reason to believe they will sustain more damage than companies led by men if the mass action succeeds. In the results, all three coefficients were positive, although none was statistically significant at conventional levels. In the social media model, the coefficient on woman CEO just narrowly fell beneath the threshold for 90 percent confidence, with a p-value of 0.106. In robustness checks, when I estimated this model using a probit regression instead of a logistic regression,[16] the coefficient falls just below that threshold ($p = 0.09$), so it has a single star in the table.

What does this mean? It seems likely that companies led by women CEOs are, in fact, more likely to cite concerns about social media, but because they are relatively rare in the data, it is hard to gather enough evidence to say with statistical certainty. Of the 1,564 companies for which I have data on the gender of the top director or manager, only 94 are led by women, which is just over 6 percent. It is the relative rarity of women in these positions, of course, that contributes to the theoretical expectations that they ought to be monitored and scrutinized more than peer companies, of course, so seeing a greater representation of women would have brought into question an assumption of the theory. Yet, frustratingly, it makes statistically evaluating that claim difficult. There just aren't that many women in general from which we can discern patterns. With that in mind, I interpret this as a finding in support of the theory – women-led companies are more likely to cite social media as a concern, as predicted, but not more likely than companies led by men to cite boycott (not as predicted). We similarly see no evidence that they are any more or less likely to cite reputation or brand damage as a concern.

As a second test, I looked again to whether companies linked social media and reputation/brand damage within the same sentence at least once in the 10-Ks. This has the benefit of conceptual clarity – unlike just indicating whether a company mentions "social media" in any context in their document, which is as likely to identify companies concerned about social media movements as it is to identify companies concerned about their company's inability to successfully maintain a social media presence, looking for sentences linking these ideas more clearly means that I am comparing companies that are concerned about the effect of social media on their brand/reputation with those that are not. The drawback is these are even rarer. Only 6 percent of

---

[16] Probit regressions are based on the Bernoulli distribution, like the logistic regression, and are therefore suitable for dichotomous data, but they use a normal cumulative density to link, whereas logit models use a cumulative logistic. This means they are, in most circumstances, interchangeable without affecting the substantive interpretation, but they do behave differently in the tails of the distributions.

5.5 Which Companies Fear Public Backlash?

Table 5.3 *Logistic regression that models having at least one sentence linking social media with brand or reputation damage. Model contains sectoral random effects*

	Dependent variable:
	Links social media and brand reputation
# Employees (logged)	0.319***
	(0.065)
Woman CEO	0.373
	(0.423)
Top 100 brand	−0.079
	(0.488)
Constant	−5.775***
	(0.629)
Observations	1,449
Log likelihood	−303.952
Akaike inf. crit.	617.905
Bayesian inf. crit.	644.298

Note: $^*p < 0.1$; $^{**}p < 0.05$; $^{***}p < 0.01$

companies have a sentence linking social media with brand/reputation, and only 3.5 percent link it with revenue/sales. The theory predicts that each coefficient will have a positive effect since larger companies, companies that own valuable brands, and women-led companies are all predicted to be more vulnerable to these forces.

Once again, the data show that larger companies have a higher probability of linking social media with brand damage. The coefficient estimate is positive and highly statistically significant. Yet nothing else in the model approaches conventional levels of statistical significance. Given the small number of companies that pass this hurdle – mentioning the two concepts in the same sentence as opposed to in the same paragraph and using those particular words – this is promising in that it at least demonstrates that larger companies pass the hurdle. Yet this is also a place where the shortcoming of the statistical models becomes clear since it is not clear whether women-led companies are actually no different from other companies when it comes to these ideas or whether it is an issue with limited data on women and a high hurdle of the dependent variable. It is on that note that I

154 Why Do Companies Care About Public Opinion?

depart from the statistical data and turn instead to more qualitative evidence.

5.6 Do Companies Connect Political Advocacy with Public Backlash?

The 10-Ks are mostly valuable for their breadth – they allowed me to analyze patterns among large samples of companies – but the depth of the reports was variable. Many of them listed "boycott" or "social media" in a cursory fashion, without much explanation or context. In other words, the 10-Ks gave a good sense of which companies are most concerned about boycott or other negative social media attention – concerned enough that they might open themselves up to legal action if they don't disclose the risk to shareholders – and they hinted at whether companies made the connection between social media and concerns about their brand or reputation, but they could not provide in-depth specifics about how the company considers these factors. Interviews, in conjunction with the 10-Ks, can provide a much more in-depth look into *why* companies might be concerned about boycott and specifically whether they connect their political influence and the likelihood they'll be boycotted.

Overwhelmingly, my interviews and the more in-depth 10-Ks reinforced the ideas that (1) companies are very concerned about damage to their brand and reputation and (2) they understand that getting on the wrong side of the public can cause that damage. A former in-house government affairs employee at an agriculture company, for instance, emphasized that a key rule was to not get the company in trouble with customers, no matter what. Even though the company's customers were mostly other businesses, they expressed a concern that popular opposition could still have consequences. As an example, they mentioned a popular blog that often criticized the company, in large part due to its work on genetically modified organisms (GMOs). The problem wasn't that the blog's readers would stop buying the company's products – most of them really didn't have that option – but that the negative publicity and all the attention cast the brand in a bad light. Moreover, public backlash to GMOs could hurt the company politically – if an anti-GMO movement got enough momentum, it could lead to popular support for bans, which could hurt the company's business. To deal with this threat, the company's social media team

5.6 Do Companies Connect Political Advocacy   155

actively monitored this blog and the blogger's social media accounts and would also reach out to the blogger directly in an attempt to handle the negative publicity.[17]

The importance of being perceived as a "good company" (or, often, a "white hat") came up repeatedly in my interviews. A representative from a global technology company emphasized that their company was "purpose-driven" and that failing to maintain a popular image of being a good company – one that makes the right decision and does good within the community – could harm the company with the community, with customers, and with political stakeholders.[18] At an extreme, negative publicity could make potential customers – other businesses, governments – unwilling to work with a company due to fears that there might be a halo effect, in which the negative publicity might end up hurting the customer company as well.[19] Negative publicity could also hurt a company's ability to produce, noted a representative from a large regional oil and gas production company. It wasn't uncommon, they noted, for negative attention locally to be redirected at its employees, who would have their company-labeled vehicles vandalized.[20] A representative of an industry group told me that his segment of the industry is generally perceived as the "white hats" already but that he would advise companies in a less popular subset of the industry to be concerned about how the things they did might affect popular opinion.[21]

For all companies, social media serves as a threat amplifier. It's a truism in retail and food service that a happy customer tells one person and an unhappy customer tells ten. In the era of social media, an unhappy customer can tell the whole world. Information, misinformation, rumors, grudges, and stories spread quickly. The company Boot Barn (symbol: BOOT), a retail chain that sells cowboys boots and other western-themed apparel and gifts, makes this point in their 10-Ks:[22]

---

[17] Anonymous interview subject #2.
[18] Anonymous interview subject #12.
[19] Anonymous interview subject #12.
[20] Anonymous interview subject #6.
[21] Anonymous interview subject #3.
[22] Italics are mine.

> Consumers value readily available information concerning retailers and their goods and services and *often act on such information without further investigation and without regard to its accuracy.* The harm may be immediate without affording us an opportunity for redress or correction. In addition, social media platforms provide users with access to such a broad audience that collective action against our stores, such as boycotts, can be more easily organized. If such actions were organized, we could suffer reputational damage as well as physical damage to our stores and merchandise.

Many other 10-Ks emphasize this point: social media allows people to spread information – whether true or untrue – to a large audience, and companies often struggle with shutting down this information. This is what Darden Restaurants, parent company of Olive Garden, experienced when a rumor spread on Twitter that it had donated money to Donald Trump's reelection campaign.[23] Despite repeatedly responding that the company does not make political contributions, the company struggled to fully shut down the rumor and whatever damage it caused. A lobbyist I interviewed backed this up when asked about whether companies are concerned about public backlash to their lobbying and influence-seeking, noting that companies keep a close eye on social media since any kind of "public policy misstep" could end up on social media and have consequences for how people react to their business.[24]

A public policy misstep, in this context, refers to a company taking a stance or performing an action around a policy that ends up being unpopular or hurting them. Three companies use nearly identical language in their 10-Ks to explicitly link such "political considerations" with threats to their reputation and "various adverse consumer actions, including boycotts." Clothing company Abercrombie & Fitch, L Brands (owner of Victoria's Secret and Bath & Body Works), and Coty Inc. (owner of brands including Clairol, CoverGirl, and Sally Hansen) all cited the concern that failure to comply with various standards "or related political considerations" could "jeopardize

---

[23] Carman, Tim. "Olive Garden: Unlimited Breadsticks, Yes. Trump Campaign Donations, No." August 26, 2019. Washington Post. www.washingtonpost.com/news/voraciously/wp/2019/08/26/olive-garden-unlimited-breadsticks-yes-trump-campaign-donations-no/.

[24] Anonymous interview subject #10.

5.6 Do Companies Connect Political Advocacy 157

our reputation." L Brands, Abercrombie & Fitch, and clothing company Guess?, Inc. all went on to note that "damage to our reputation or loss of consumer confidence ... could have a material adverse effect on our results of operations and financial condition, as well as require addition resources to rebuild our reputation." Although it's hard to say where the language originated, the fact that this boilerplate language is so pervasive in the sample suggests that concerns about political considerations causing damage to companies is sufficiently widespread.

Although "political considerations" such as a "public policy misstep" is a bit vague and open to interpretation – for instance, are "political considerations" strictly about politics, or is it more akin to "political correctness," referring to taking an action that offends broader society? – it's also clear from the evidence that some companies clearly understand that their efforts to influence politics, and their policy positions more generally, may get them into hot water with consumers in a way that may be damaging. Target (symbol: TGT), the retail chain, explains this clearly in their 2019 10-Ks:

> Target's position or perceived lack of position on social, environmental, public policy or other sensitive issues, and any perceived lack of transparency about those matters, could harm our reputation with certain groups or guests. While reputations may take decades to build, negative incidents can quickly erode trust and confidence and can result in consumer boycotts, governmental investigations, or litigation.

In this passage, Target clearly states that stance-taking can be harmful for its reputation, although does not specify whether action on the stance or simply taking the stance is what matters. As a company that has been targeted by activists for boycott in the past over its political and social stances, Target certainly would know. The phrase "while reputations may take decades to build, negative incidents can quickly erode trust and confidence" – speaking to the dire consequences and how negative publicity can undo years or work and growth – is used verbatim in 10-Ks for Marriott International, the hotel chain, and emphasizes the importance to companies of their reputation and brand.

The Coca-Cola Company (symbol: KO) even more clearly links the company's political activities with the potential of adverse consequences for the company:

> In addition, from time to time, we and our executives engage in public policy endeavors that are either directly related to our products and packaging or to our business operations and the general economic climate affecting the Company. These engagements in public policy debates can occasionally be the subject of backlash from advocacy groups that have a differing point of view and could result in adverse media and consumer reaction, including product boycotts.

Monster Beverage Company (symbol: MNST) includes the same sentences, almost verbatim, although with more a passive voice, thus distancing the company from its actions, writing instead "there are public policy endeavors that are either directly related to our products and packaging or to our business. These public policy debates can occasionally be the subject of backlash from advocacy groups that have a differing point of view and could result in adverse media and consumer reaction, including product boycotts." In both cases, the companies make clear that the political actions and stances they may have to take to defend the company's interests in public policy might end up hurting them enough that it could be materially damaging. Starbucks (symbol: SBUX) doesn't go quite as far in making the connection, but in discussing the potential for boycott and other actions that might diminish brand value, they list "publicly [taking] controversial positions" as a potential trigger, acknowledging that stance-taking may be very dangerous for a company. Perhaps most tellingly, a journalist I spoke to explained to me that companies were so afraid of protests outside of their businesses that they didn't want to be interviewed about their opposition to a popular municipal ordinance.[25]

The lobbyists I interviewed were candid and clear-headed about how unpopular lobbying is and pointed out that it definitely had consequences for both the companies and the lobbyists themselves. (The popular distaste for lobbying – and, accordingly, of lobbyists – was a common thread throughout our conversations.) One lobbyist said that, in a previous position at a retail-oriented industry group, companies were especially mindful of their political actions, especially

---

[25] Anonymous interview subject #11.

5.7 Conclusion

when dealing with local politics, because the community was their customers, and angering their customers would have negative consequences.[26] Another lobbyist noted that negative public perceptions of lobbying was among the most difficult things they dealt with in their job, in large part because it actually made lobbying harder. Public opposition to lobbying was even trickling up to state lawmakers themselves, they told me, leading to new state legislators, policymakers, and staff who don't really understand lobbying but had a very negative view of it. This, in their estimation, made it harder to lobby because lawmakers did not want to meet with lobbyists.[27] Ironically, another lobbyist pointed out that broad public criticism of lobbyists that focused on lobbyists being too powerful actually drove up business – since, in many companies' estimations, if lobbyists were actually that powerful, it probably behooved them to hire one.[28]

Yet a fourth lobbyist clearly illustrated that the way a company chooses to influence politics can have negative consequences for the company, even if some companies didn't realize that. Part of the lobbyist's job, they argued, was to protect companies from their own bad political impulses. This included reminding companies that certain ways of obtaining political influence would be bad for public opinion and therefore bad for the company. To illustrate this, they cited an example of a company that wanted to donate money to a particular politician in order to encourage the politician to sponsor a bill. Yet the lobbyist was concerned that appearing on that particular politician's fundraising report might be detrimental to the company in the long term by linking them with an unpopular or controversial politician, a cost not worth any short-term political gain. They advised the company to pursue other tactics instead.[29]

5.7 Conclusion

It only matters that people will boycott companies for their political activities if the companies actually care about the boycott. In this chapter, I argue that companies do care about boycott and that

---

[26] Anonymous interview subject #10.
[27] Anonymous interview subject #9.
[28] Anonymous interview subject #7. The same subject pointed out that, as much as people dislike lobbyists, nearly everything someone buys is going to pay for a government affairs professional because nearly every industry hires lobbyists.
[29] Anonymous interview subject #7.

many of them understand that their political actions might make them vulnerable to boycott.

Yet I also argue that boycotts work in a different way than is typically assumed. Often boycotts, especially in the era of social media, are more about public discussions of perceived wrongdoing and aligning oneself with a particular group than about actual consumption decisions. Far from alleviating fears of boycott, the threat of people talking about boycott actually makes even more companies vulnerable. Although the revenue threats may be minimal, discussions of boycott – especially if they're large, public, and spawn negative media attention – can cause damage to a company's brand and reputation. For many companies, their brand is among their most valuable assets, and public discussions of boycott and wrongdoing open up interpretation of their brand to public scrutiny. From the perspective that boycotts concern companies because they get in the way of a company's control over brand identity, all companies that are concerned about their brand should express concern about boycotts. I argue that certain types of companies – large companies, companies with especially valuable brands, companies led by women, and companies that have been the target of boycotts in the past – are most likely to be targeted for these kinds of boycotts since they're under increased scrutiny. And a subset of those companies – large companies and those that own valuable brands – are uniquely vulnerable to the kind of brand damage these boycotts can generate.

To figure out if this is true, I assembled the risk factors section from Securities and Exchange Commission (SEC) reports for over 3,000 companies over time, for a total of 27,000 reports. The risk factor section is where companies explain the factors that might threaten their business to current and potential shareholders, providing those shareholders with information about the company's core risks so that they can make an informed decision. Often in these reports, risks are listed but not discussed in any depth, and so in these reports I studied mentions of boycott and social media. I demonstrate that concerns about social media are often linked with concerns about reputation, and I show that concerns about reputation and brand damage increased significantly after the rise of popular social media. Finally, I demonstrate that large companies and companies led by women appear to be more likely to be concerned about social media (and possibly about boycott) and that large companies are also more likely to be concerned about

5.7 Conclusion

brand damage. I found no evidence that companies that own strong brands perceive themselves as more vulnerable.

The concern that social media can spread information and misinformation and lead to boycotts and discussion thereof turns up in the more in-depth 10-Ks and also in interviews I conducted with in-house government affairs professionals, contract government affairs professionals (lobbyists, strategists, and PAC employees), and journalists. All of these people, who experience corporate political influence in different ways, both from within and from the outside, emphasized that companies are indeed concerned with boycott, and many companies explicitly connect their political actions with the possibility of consumer backlash.

In summary, this chapter provides strong evidence that companies do indeed care about boycott, and many companies understand and are concerned that their political and policy activities – lobbying, taking stances on public policy, and so forth – can open them to potentially damaging consumer response through damage to their reputation and brand. Yet expressing concern and acting on that concern are different things. Whether this concern actually changes behavior – whether companies take strategic action to avoid consumer backlash when they try to do politics – is the subject of the next chapter.

6 Do Companies Try to Avoid Public Backlash?

6.1 Introduction

Nearly every company will, at some point, find itself facing a situation in which a policy stands to potentially harm its business. At that point, the company has to decide what to do. Since politics is the process by which policy comes to pass, the question is whether to engage in politics. If they want to assert themselves in a policy debate, the act of doing so – of trying to influence politics and policy – can bring them into conflict with the public. Whether it's because people don't like that the company is trying to have political influence at all, or whether people specifically dislike the stance they perceive the company as taking, corporate efforts to influence politics can be unpopular and can open companies up to the potential for negative backlash (Chapter 4).

These boycotts, even though they mainly remain within the realm of political discussion and may never or rarely directly influence consumer behavior, can hurt companies, and companies know it (Chapter 5). Although internet "boycotts" are often criticized for the lack of consumer follow-through, even if people only talk about boycotting, if they talk loudly enough and in public – for instance, on social media – boycotts can still damage companies by imperiling their brand. For many companies, intangible assets such as their brand – how people see the company and the associations they have with it – and their reputation are among the most valuable assets they own. Public discussions of proposed boycotts and a company's wrongdoing can damage a company's brand. Boycotts, and public backlash more generally, whether real or part of the public imagination, can be a serious concern to companies.

Does this concern about public backlash, and the knowledge that it might arise from a company entering the political fray, shape how companies choose to engage with politics?

6.2 The Claim 163

On one hand, it might seem like the easy answer is for companies to just stay out of politics. Getting involved can prompt public backlash, and public backlash can hurt the brand and the company's revenues, so the risk-averse conclusion is that companies should just hold their metaphorical noses, deal with the policies they don't like, and not engage. And, indeed, this is what some companies do. Some companies certainly weigh the risks of a political "loss" – whatever negative consequences might arise from a policy that isn't in their favor – against the costs of trying to engage to shape the policy and come to the conclusion that it just isn't worth it.

Yet if you've gotten this far in the book, you know that my answer to this question is yes, the fear of popular backlash does change how companies engage politically. The central claim of this chapter – and of this book – is that the fear of consumer backlash changes the shape of their political influence. In particular, I argue, it can lead companies to pursue strategies that limit this threat. Specifically, I argue that companies that worry about the link between political advocacy and public backlash are more likely to opt to hide their advocacy or defuse the public's negative reaction to it. In this chapter, I explain more about why that's likely to be true, explain the strategies in more detail, and assess the evidence to support this claim. In service of that, first I look at lobbying in cities and test whether companies with demonstrated opposition to a popular ordinance (minimum wage increases), as well as demonstrated concern about boycotts, are less likely to lobby. Then I move to evidence from interviews, from which I assess the alternative strategies that companies pursue when they're concerned that lobbying or campaign contributions might end up hurting them.

6.2 The Claim

Companies condition their political influence strategies on their fear of public backlash.

Although the previous two chapters tested components of the theoretical mechanism – that people boycott companies as a form of political speech and positioning and that companies (and, in particular, certain types of companies) are concerned about boycott for fear of brand and reputation damage – this chapter's claim is the overarching claim of the theory: that concern about boycott actually influences how companies influence politics and policy. We've already established that consumers don't like political influence-seeking, especially when they disagree with the politics of it (Chapter 4), and that companies are concerned about consumer backlash, even if the boycotts are only talk (Chapter 5), and both of those are fundamental to the mechanisms in the theory. If consumers don't actually know or care or respond negatively to corporate political influence-seeking, then there's no reason for companies to fear it. If companies don't actually fear it, then there's no reason to believe that they'd actually change their strategies based on that fear. But just because there's evidence that people boycott for political reasons and that companies fear boycott for reasons of their reputation, and the implication follows from those assumptions, it doesn't actually mean fear of boycott shapes corporate influence-seeking strategy. The point of this chapter is to test that claim. Does concern about public backlash actually shape corporate strategy?

As outlined in Chapter 3, concerns about boycott should, in theory, prompt companies to advocate for their interests in ways that decrease the probability of a boycott actually occurring. There are two primary methods companies can use to do this: they can hide their activity or they can aim to defuse the anger and, therefore, the damaging potential of the boycott. In other words, in a situation in which they might make people angry, they should either aim to make it less likely anyone will know they did something or endeavor to reduce the amount of anger people might feel. The overarching idea is this: companies that are concerned about boycott should avoid creating visible associations between the company and highly partisan actors and issues. To avoid this, companies can operate on two different parts of that sentence: "creating visible associations between the company" and "highly partisan actors and issues." This maps onto four different strategies open to companies that want to influence politics but don't want to become the target of a boycott: hidden advocacy, distanced advocacy, creative advocacy, and careful advocacy.

The first two strategies, hidden advocacy and distanced advocacy, are what I term "hiding" strategies. These are strategies that allow companies to approach their political advocacy how they wish to – using conventional and straightforward methods, such as lobbying and campaign contributions, and being associated with whoever or whatever they want or need – but reduce the probability that the activity will be noticed and criticized, at least in a way that is linked to the

6.2 The Claim

company. The core idea is that, if people don't know about it, they can't get mad.

The two strategies approach this in different ways. Hidden advocacy entails a company engaging in advocacy that may lead to backlash but doing it in a way that keeps it from being publicly reported. Distanced advocacy is when a company works through a third party, such as a trade association, such that the advocacy occurs and is reported but is not reported in the company's name. Both strategies allow companies to engage in advocacy that may cause trouble for them, but they reduce the probability that it's noticed and linked to the company, thus reducing the chance that anyone calls for a boycott. In the case of hidden advocacy, the goal is to have the activity go unnoticed entirely, whereas distanced advocacy permits the activity itself to be noticed but breaks the link between the advocacy and the company.

Hiding Expectation #1: Companies that are concerned about political boycotts should be more likely to try to evade reporting requirements.

Hiding Expectation #2: Companies that are concerned about political boycotts should be more likely to engage in political influence-seeking through third parties.

The last two strategies, creative advocacy and careful advocacy, are defusing strategies. These are strategies that companies undertake not to reduce the probability that their activity is noticed and criticized but rather to reduce the public anger that could turn the criticism into a full-blown boycott. To understand how these strategies work, it helps to recall why the public backlash typically occurs in the first place. People are angered by companies behaving in partisan ways and use criticism of those companies as a way to signal their own political positions. In other words, if it becomes known that a company donated to a prominent Republican politician, people who conceive of their partisanship as being in opposition to that politician and people like him can signal that to those in their social networks by publicly criticizing the company. The idea here is not to avoid detection but to approach advocacy in a way that doesn't make people angry and doesn't provide that easy signal.

Yet again, creative advocacy and careful advocacy approach defusing in different ways. Creative advocacy approaches influence-seeking and advocacy as giving politicians things they need and value, as discussed in Chapter 2, but in unconventional ways that don't *look* like influence-seeking and don't give the illusion of taking a political "side." They meet politicians' needs – for money, information, and various aspects of doing their jobs – but not in ways that people typically associate with political advocacy (i.e., campaign contributions and lobbying). Philanthropy and community development are two activities companies frequently engage in that might be useful for political advocacy but are not immediately obvious as being political advocacy. From the perspective of someone who might be apt to criticize, it is not obvious that companies are engaging in advocacy, and it's not obvious which politicians or issues they may be contending with. This makes it difficult to criticize the action, first of all, and second, it makes it hard to rally people around opposition.

Defusion Expectation #1: Companies that are concerned about political boycotts should be less likely to pursue campaign contributions and lobbying and more likely to pursue strategies such as community development and philanthropy.

Careful advocacy is more straightforward. The idea behind careful advocacy is that, if companies are going to engage in conventional and obvious political advocacy and influence-seeking, they should be careful about which politicians and issues they end up associating themselves with, such that they do not provide such ripe opportunities for people to oppose them as a form of political speech. This means that companies that are concerned with boycott or backlash should be more apt to donate to politicians who are less politically divisive or less well known, less apt to donate to politicians who are well known and especially partisan, and more likely to avoid publicly lobbying on very partisan-linked issues. Restricting their public advocacy to associations with politicians and issues that are less obvious targets for political signaling can allow companies to advocate on issues while reducing the probability of a large, negative public reaction by acknowledging and circumventing why it is that people join these public boycotts in the first place.

Defusion Expectation #2: Companies that are concerned about political boycott should be less likely to associate themselves with partisan-linked political issues, even if those issues concern the company.

6.3 Why and How This Might Be Wrong 167

Defusion Expectation #3: Companies that are concerned about political boycott should be less likely to associate themselves with very partisan and/or divisive politicians.

These strategies are, of course, not mutually exclusive. Companies don't have to lock into one and only one strategy that they use exclusively forever.[1] These strategies hinge on a company's concern about boycott – companies that do not fear boycott should have no reason to jump through these hoops and are likely to prefer the efficiency of doing direct advocacy to whichever politician or on whatever issue they wish – but they also depend a lot on the situation. If a company needs to advocate many politicians on an issue, creative advocacy might be very expensive and inefficient because it depends on addressing a politician's specific needs, so a company might opt to work through a third party, if possible, or practice careful advocacy. If a third party isn't available and if a company can't avoid associations with partisan leaders and issues, then it might opt to try to hide its advocacy efforts. There is no "best" answer for trying to avoid backlash nor a cohesive and consistent preference ordering. Instead, the overarching argument is simply that companies should use specific strategies to avoid creating visible associations with partisan leaders in order to either reduce the probability of being noticed or reduce the probability of a backlash occurring.

6.3 Why and How This Might Be Wrong

There are also several reasons to doubt that companies actually let concerns about boycott shape their influence-seeking, even if they are concerned about boycott more generally. In this section, I'll explain three reasons why it might not be the case that concerns about boycott influence how companies do politics.

1 Companies Just Don't Think About It: The first and most obvious reason why this claim could be wrong is that companies just don't think about it. This doesn't require any complex explanation about

---

[1] Notably, there are good reasons to believe these strategies should change over time – as companies become higher profile they may be more likely to hide their activity, for instance, or as they become lower profile they may be less likely to change their strategies – but data availability and quality preclude me from testing this. I leave this to future research.

costs and benefits, but, rather, it's just not on their radar. Whatever fear of boycott exists just isn't connected to any thinking about political influence-seeking. This could easily happen if, for instance, a company is especially large and different divisions of the company are so distant organizationally that the people worried about boycotts and the people who consider government affairs are different and don't interact. If this is true, we wouldn't expect to see any perceivable relationship between boycott vulnerability and the strategies companies engage in.

2 **The Threat of Boycott is Too Small to Influence Strategy:** On the other hand, it could be that companies know that boycott is a potential consequence of their influence-seeking and advocacy and are worried about boycott in the abstract, but they just don't think the costs are substantial enough to warrant taking into consideration. In other words, companies might have too much to gain from engaging in politics that whatever is lost by potential boycotts pales in comparison. This is slightly different from the argument that they don't think about it – in this explanation, they think about it and know it's a threat, but it's not enough of a threat to change their behavior.

3 **Influence Strategies are a Signal to Attract Consumers:** The opposite of a boycott is a "buycott," where people intentionally buy from companies that mirror their values, and the same companies that are vulnerable to boycotts should also be "vulnerable to" buycotts. It is possible that companies use the very same influence-seeking strategies that might deter consumers as a signal to attract consumers who agree with their stance. This is a partisanship, rather than a negative partisanship, argument: people will be attracted to companies that take political stances they approve of and then make deliberate efforts to buy their products.

In this version of the story, retail companies should be more likely than other companies to take highly visible political stances because they have consumers to attract. Although this doesn't mean they should only take these stances when they're trying to influence politics – this explanation suggests they should take highly visible political stances with some frequency, not only when they also want something from politicians – they should definitely take highly visible public stances when they want to influence politics as it kills two birds with one stone.

6.4 Sources of Evidence

The challenge with assessing this theory is that the core of the theory is about what companies do not do or what they should not be seen doing. It is fundamentally a theory that predicts what we should not see, but the things it predicts will happen – companies hiding behavior, companies acting through third parties unassociated with their name, companies taking tailored and less visible strategies – are, by intention, harder to track. Were the activities easy to track – if we could easily know who was hiding their activity, for instance, or specifically which companies worked through which interest groups and were active in discussions at which times – they wouldn't be effective in side-stepping public anger. Not being noticed is the point. By its very nature, then, the overall theory is hard to test. That is why testing the mechanisms within the theory in the previous two chapters was so important, but it also felt somewhat unfulfilling. How, then, to try to understand when companies are *not* doing something we'd otherwise expect them to do but for the fear of backlash?

To deal with this, I approached the evidence in two ways. The first way looked at lobbying and campaign finance data in a large-N quantitative framework and compared companies that ought to be concerned about boycott with companies that ought not. If the theory is correct, these companies should have different patterns in their observable advocacy activity. Companies that should, theoretically, be concerned with boycott should be less likely than their peer companies to donate to highly partisan politicians or have their names associated with lobbying on highly partisan issues. It also suggests that, if they do contribute to campaigns, they should strategically target less partisan, lower-profile politicians. These data allow me to answer the question of whether it appears companies are trying to avoid transparent, obvious advocacy that seem partisan and might land them in hot water with the public, but the data do not allow me to answer the question of what they might be doing instead.

The second source of data relied, as in the previous chapter, on interviews, which give me a good lens into what companies do instead. I interviewed, under promise of anonymity, several representatives from companies, lobbyists, representatives of PACs, journalists, local and state politicians, and representatives from municipal ethics boards. This got around the issue of observable behavior and allowed me to more thoroughly probe the logic of the theory. These interviews provided useful insight into both whether fear of boycott does, indeed, change the way companies approach engaging in policy and what companies might do instead of lobbying or campaign finance if they opt not to delve into those. Talking with people who have experienced corporate political influence from all angles – engaging in it, reporting on it, being the target of it, and monitoring and tracking it – provides unique insight into how the process works, one that quantitative testing simply can't provide. I analyze these interviews to demonstrate the alternative ways that companies influence politics and why.

In the next two sections, I discuss the sources of data themselves in more detail.

6.4.1 Evidence from Federal Lobbying and Campaign Contributions

Although the theory predicts a variety of actions companies can take in lieu of donating to campaigns or lobbying, one commonality – and, in fact, the central unifying prediction – is that it predicts that companies that are likely to be concerned about boycott should avoid donating to campaigns or lobbying. This implies that, all else being equal, companies that are in categories that indicate they might be vulnerable to backlash should be less likely to make campaign contributions and lobby (at least in their own name and at least on the public record) than other companies. These are expectations that can be tested using statistical data. In other words, the statistical data allow us to answer the question: Are big companies or companies led by women (the two categories that the data suggest are most fearful of social media backlash) actually less likely to donate to campaigns through PACs or lobby in their own name?

To answer this question, I used two sources of data. The first was the LobbyView data set (Kim 2018). The LobbyView data provide unique insight into which companies are lobbying at the federal government level, how much money they are spending, and what issue(s) they are lobbying on. The second was campaign finance data from the Federal Election Commission, and, in particular, data on contributions by committees, a group that includes corporate PACs. I use these two data sets to code every company from a data set on publicly traded companies operating in the United States, from the database

6.4 Sources of Evidence

Orbis as to whether they lobbied[2] or made a contribution through a PAC in their own name.[3] This means that for every company, for years from 2012 to 2019, I could know whether (and how much) they lobbied, how much they spent on lobbying, and which issues they lobbied about, along with whether (and how many times) they donated through their own PAC, how much they spent doing that, and which politicians their PACs donated to.

Although the point of this analysis was not to establish causality, there were several clear hurdles to causality that needed to be addressed. The first was that the theory suggests large companies should be less likely to lobby or donate to political campaigns, but large companies also have more resources than smaller companies and are therefore more able to engage in these forms of advocacy. This makes the counterfactual reasoning difficult because large companies that fear public backlash may be less likely to lobby and donate than they otherwise might be in the absence of those fears but not necessarily less likely than smaller companies. This made the regression results relatively less useful since any term that measured company size would by necessity involve comparing large companies with small companies. Even truncating the sample to only large companies – such that large companies were only being compared with other large companies and then measured by the degree of their largeness – was not sufficient since it did not address the underlying problem that larger

---

[2] The data from Kim (2018) very helpfully contains unique company IDs that allow these data to be merged with the Orbis data.

[3] Matching these up was harder than matching the lobbying data since the FEC does not provide a company name, let alone a unique ID, for each corporate PAC. That said, corporate PACs are required to follow specific naming conventions, including containing the company's full name. Although in some cases the name the company uses for their PAC is an official name that would be unrecognizable to most people – I learned while coding these that GEICO, the insurance company with the popular gecko mascot, is actually the Government Employee Insurance Company, for instance – for the most part it allowed me to use partial string matching to merge the data sets. I matched two different ways: once matching the company's full name in Orbis against the PAC name and once matching the name minus the word "Corporation" and words indicating business type (i.e., Inc, Corp). The first method was prone to false negatives, meaning I falsely concluded a company hadn't contributed when it really had, and the second was prone to false positives (especially because so many company names are acronyms that might also be a part of other words). For every analysis, I ran it with both of these methods, assuming that the "true answer" was somewhere in between.

companies have more resources alongside their theoretical fear. As a result, although I present and discuss regression results in Appendix D for the sake of transparency, I opt to discuss the results primarily by looking at distributions and thinking through counterfactuals rather than statistically testing them. In lieu of looking directly at size, I also tested the hypothesis by looking directly at whether companies cite a concern about social media or brand damage and reputation in their 10-Ks, as described in Chapter 5.

The second hurdle was the demand side. In other words, understanding how often companies try to advocate for themselves politically, and how they do that, requires some understanding of how much they need to do that. What are the concerns they face? How often do they face them? Some companies will not lobby or donate to campaigns because nothing comes up that requires them to advocate for themselves in that way. Other companies might lobby or donate to campaigns because they perceive themselves as frequently embattled on the political stage, but, for instance, they might advocate less in these ways than they might otherwise. This means that comparing companies that do and do not lobby or do and do not donate to political campaigns is itself fraught without some underlying measure of their need to advocate. In these models, I used a company's industry[4] to try to understand a company's need to advocate, in the sense that I assume companies in similar industries face similar pressures federally and therefore are comparable from the perspective of political necessity.

6.4.2 Evidence from Interviews

The theory is most clear about what companies should *not* do when they fear public backlash: they shouldn't be seen influencing politics and they shouldn't take political stances, and, if they do, they should be donating to the least prominent, least partisan politicians and lobbying on the least politicized issues. Those two aspects are testable using statistical methods because the data collection is more straightforward. Instead of those activities that pose more risk of public backlash, the theory predicts companies should pursue a variety

---

[4] Since I am using data from ORBIS, these are the European Union NACE Rev 2 codes.

6.5 Are Some Companies Less Likely to Lobby 173

of substitution strategies – strategies that will allow the company to advocate for its political interests while lowering the probability of public backlash. Yet because those strategies are intentionally opaque and highly variable, they do not lend themselves to statistical analysis. For that reason, I supplemented the evidence from quantitative data with interviews to test the expectation that companies do actually pursue alternative strategies and that those strategies do map onto the theoretical expectations (e.g., they are either less visible, more popular, or both).

The sample of interviews in this chapter is the same as in Chapter 5 – I solicited interviews from corporate representatives, lobbyists, journalists, representatives from interest groups and PACs, local and state politicians, and representatives from municipal ethics boards. Each person spoke with me on condition of anonymity, and we discussed at length their experience with corporate political influence, whether as someone engaged in crafting it (the in-house and contract government affairs professionals), someone at whom it had been directed (politicians), someone reporting on it (journalists), or someone engaged in observing, tracking, and regulating it (representatives from municipal ethics boards). Interviewing people with experience with the subject from different angles gave me an especially three-dimensional perspective of the topic.

With most of my interview subjects, the conversation typically turned to the ways that companies try to influence politics when they are concerned about public opinion. In this chapter, I gather all of these and analyze them to draw out the common themes focusing on why companies might not want to engage in traditional, higher-visibility, stance-taking methods of political influence – the kinds that tend to get them in trouble – and what they do instead.

6.5 Are Some Companies Less Likely to Lobby in Their Own Name?

The theory predicts a few things about what should be observable in the public record about companies political donations and lobbying. First, it predicts that, on average, companies that are concerned about backlash should be less likely to donate through PACs[5] or lobbying in

---

[5] Technically, a PAC with the company's name may not always be a company donating, but I counted any PAC that contained a company's name as their

their own name. This might mean that they do not donate or lobby, that they hide their donations or lobbying activity, or that they donate or lobby through some third party, but all three are observationally equivalent in the data as companies not showing up in publicly available data on lobbying or campaign contributions.

Despite popular perceptions of the ubiquity of lobbying and campaign contributions, the data suggest that, overall, the practice is relatively rare. Of the 16,825 companies in the data, fewer than 4 percent filed at least one lobbying report at the federal level, indicating they engaged in lobbying activity independently (that is, not through a third party) and in their own name.[6] Figure 6.1 shows the percentage of companies in the sample that filed at least one lobbying report for every year between 1999 and 2020 and illustrates that more companies lobby as time goes on, but the number never exceeds 4 percent.

Campaign contributions through corporate PACs are even rarer. As illustrated in Figure 6.2, about 0.2 percent (yes, percent![7]) of the sample, about thirty companies per election year on average, actually donated to federal candidates through their own PACs.[8] Although

---

name is associated with the contribution, which should be fodder enough for backlash.

[6] These data are specifically about lobbying or donating to campaigns at the federal level. At the state level, I used a slightly different metric to estimate prevalence: a company having a lobbyist registered with the state. Drawing inferences from a random sample of 400 publicly traded companies in 2019, I found numbers that were slightly higher that the federal estimates in some states, but about the same in other states. I estimated that (95 percent confidence intervals are in parentheses): 7.5 percent (4.9 percent, 10 percent) of companies have a registered lobbyist in Texas, 6 percent (3.7 percent, 8.3 percent) in Pennsylvania, 6.25 percent (3.9 percent, 8.6 percent) in New York, 3.5 percent (1.7 percent, 5.3 percent) in Ohio, 3.8 percent (1.9 percent, 5.6 percent) in Georgia, and 2.3 percent (0.80 percent, 3.7 percent) in North Carolina. 15.5 percent of companies (12 percent, 19 percent) have a registered lobbyist in at least one of those states. Using the same method of inferring from a random sample of 400 for the federal government and looking at whether a company filed a single lobbying report in 2019 provided an estimate of 2.75 percent of companies (1.1 percent, 4.4 percent).

[7] This is true regardless of how I did the string matching between company and PAC names.

[8] Of this small group of companies, some companies donated every year, whereas others donated less frequently. Tyson Foods Inc., for instance, donated every year in this sample, but most companies only donated one year or a couple of years.

6.5 Are Some Companies Less Likely to Lobby

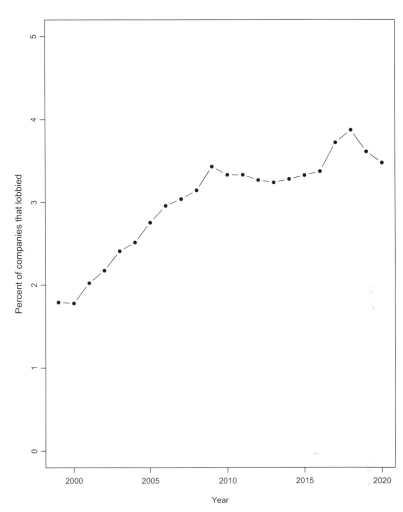

Figure 6.1 The percent of companies in the sample that filed at least one federal lobbying report in each year between 1999 and 2020. Note that 2020 data are through October and are therefore incomplete

the numbers are slightly higher when matching in a way that likely overcounts contributions, the numbers are still consistently low. This is consistent with the spirit of the theory in this book since campaign contributions are maligned by the public at a much higher rate – at least anecdotally – than lobbying is. Following the logic of Kono (2006) – the simpler a thing is, the easier it is for the public

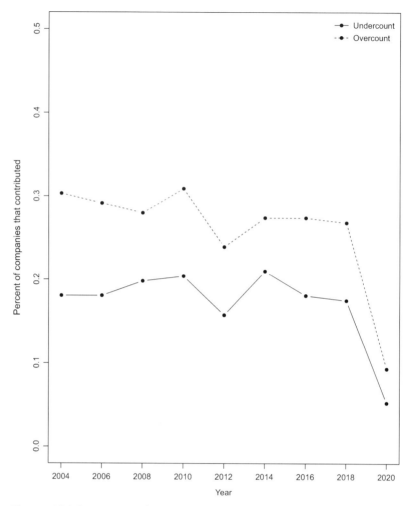

Figure 6.2 The percent of companies in the sample that donated at least once through a PAC to a candidate for federal office in their own name for every election year between 2004 and 2020. Note that 2020 data are through October and are therefore incomplete. The solid line represents matching of companies to PACs based on full company name (an undercount), whereas the dashed line represents matching of companies to PACs based on company name minus corporate type identifiers (an overcount)

to get riled up about it – campaign contributions are simple and easy for the public to understand and get angry about, whereas lobbying is

6.5 Are Some Companies Less Likely to Lobby 177

complicated and more nuanced. It doesn't easily fit in a tweet. Thus, the theory would expect that campaign contributions would be quite rare, whereas lobbying would be rare but more common. Both might get companies in trouble with the public, but campaign contributions are a much clearer path to that outcome.

Yet it is clear from the data that, although overall conventional corporate advocacy is uncommon, it is relatively more common among some groups of companies than others. As Figure 6.3 illustrates, although only just over 3 percent of companies in the sample lobbied in 2018 (according to Figure 6.1), over 40 percent of companies in the top decile by employee size lobbied in that year, compared with less than 10 percent of companies in each of the lowest six deciles.[9] Similarly, although only a fraction of a percent of the total number of companies in the sample donated to at least one political candidate, the results reveal that only three companies below the 70th percentile donated (according to the overcounting measure – according to the undercounting one, it's zero), whereas 2–3 percent of companies above the 70th percentile did. In other words, the low numbers are driven largely by the absence of smaller companies, which masks the (relative) prevalence of the activities – especially lobbying – among the largest companies. When using the number of employees as a measure of a company's size, there seems to be a breakpoint at the 70th percentile. The deciles below that do fairly little lobbying and do not donate to political campaigns through PACs in their name. These forms of advocacy appear reserved for the largest corporations.

It makes sense that larger companies would be more likely to advocate in these ways, in part because doing so is expensive and many companies are likely to not have enough resources to do so. Even among the largest companies, however, this isn't exactly common behavior. Even among the biggest of the big companies – companies that have more employees than 90 percent of companies in the sample, which dominate all other companies in their advocacy – less than half filed at least one lobbying report in 2018, and less than 5 percent contributed to a political campaign through an identifiable PAC. This means that less than half of the biggest companies advocated

---

[9] I use 2018 because it is the most recent year for which I have complete data for both outcomes since the data for 2020 was incomplete at the time of the analysis and 2019 was not an election year.

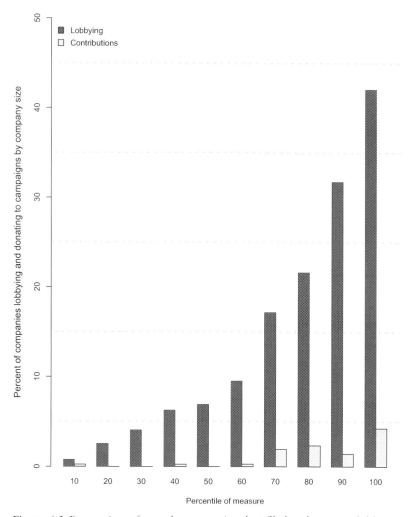

Figure 6.3 Proportion of sample companies that filed at least one lobbying report in 2018 (dark bars) or donated to at least one political candidate through a corporate PAC, broken down by percentile of size as measured by the number of employees. The conclusions of the graph are unchanged if operating revenue is substituted for number of employees

through conventional means in 2018. In some ways, this can be read as evidence against the theory at hand since I have argued that larger

6.5 Are Some Companies Less Likely to Lobby 179

companies should be more worried about backlash and therefore less likely to engage in advocacy. On the other hand, larger companies have more resources and therefore more ability to engage in these ways. If advocacy through conventional channels is simply an issue of resources, we would expect to see many more companies, especially among the largest companies with the most resources, lobbying and donating to campaigns. Even if there is no immediate, pressing policy need, in the absence of any downside beyond cost, there is a clear benefit to having access to a sympathetic politician's (or staffer's) ear. The data do not suggest that this is true. Most companies do not lobby, even those with the most resources. Very few companies donate to political campaigns through their own PACs. Although it is certainly true that some of these companies may opt not to engage in political advocacy and influence-seeking at all, it seems very unlikely that most companies opt to not engage. This indicates they are probably doing something else instead, which is consistent with the theory.

There are two other things that were fairly clear from the data. First, there were so few women CEOs in this sample that it was difficult to draw firm statistical conclusions about them.[10] Of the 17,149 companies for which I had data in 2018, 15,264 had data on the gender of the CEO or top manager, and only 1,360 of those had a woman in that position. That's just under 9 percent of companies.

Despite their small numbers, it was clear from the data that women-led companies are significantly less likely to lobby or donate to political campaigns through PACs that share the company's name, at least at the federal level. Figure 6.4 shows the percentage of companies that lobbied or donated through a PAC at least once in 2018, broken down by the gender of its top manager. In keeping with previous findings, the number of companies that lobbied and donated through identifiable PACs was low. About 4.5 percent of companies led by men filed at least one lobbying report, whereas about 2.9 percent of companies led by women did. A t-test, testing against the null hypothesis that the true difference in the means of these groups was

---

[10] This is a bit inside baseball, but I tried to simulate confidence intervals around an estimate of the percent of companies led by women v men that were engaging in lobbying and campaign contributions, but most of the samples redrawn from the sample contained zero women CEOs, and therefore I could not calculate the quantity of interest for the majority of iterations.

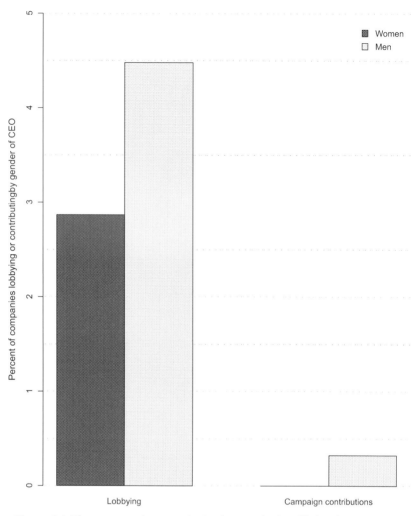

Figure 6.4 The percent of companies in the sample that filed at least one lobbying report or donated to at least one campaign through a PAC that shares the company name in 2018, broken down by gender of CEO or top manager. For this plot, I use the "overcounting" method of matching company name to PAC, and even using that, there was not a single woman-led company donating through corporate PACs

actually zero, rejected the null hypothesis at greater than 99 percent confidence, suggesting that the difference in lobbying prevalence by

6.5 Are Some Companies Less Likely to Lobby 181

companies led by men and those led by women is significant, even if neither group engages much.[11] For campaign contributions, the difference is starker: although only about one-third of a percent of companies in the sample (0.32 percent) that were led by men donated through identifiable corporate PACs in 2018, not a single woman-led company did. The difference in means between these two groups is also statistically significant at at least the 99 percent confidence level, indicating a high level of certainty that the groups are not actually the same, with differences introduced by random noise.[12] Here, the support for the expectation is much clearer: companies led by women are far less likely than companies led by men to donate to political campaigns through PACs that share their company name or to lobby at the federal level, suggesting that many of these companies, too, pursue alternative strategies to cultivate influence and advocate for their political interests.

Although analyzing the effect of size was problematic, assessing the effect of a stated fear of social media or concerns about damage to their brand or reputation was more straightforward. To do this, I used the data on 10-Ks from the previous chapter – mandatory reports filed by publicly traded companies with the Securities and Exchange Commission (SEC) that include a section on risks to the company – to test

---

[11] In a logistic regression predicting at least one lobbying report in 2018 that included industry random effects, the coefficient on the dummy variable "man" CEO was 0.1905, with a p-value of 0.289, suggesting that companies led by men are still more likely to donate than companies led by women, but the effect was no longer statistically significant, suggesting that the different distributions of men and woman across industries might also account for some of the difference. There was only one NACE industry code that was disproportionately women – "Trusts, funds and similar financial entities" – a category that 51.7 percent of women CEOs belonged to, as compared with 42.8 percent of men, but there were 248 NACE industry codes that had not a single woman leader within them, which is about 64 percent of the sample. This suggests that any findings related to industry are driven by the lack of women leadership, not any categories with an abundance of women in leadership.

[12] In a logistic regression predicting a PAC contribution but including industry random effects, the effect of gender was large and statistically significant. The coefficient on men was 37.56, with a z-value of 7.276, and an extremely small p-value. This indicates that, unlike with lobbying, the differences between men- and women-led businesses in PAC campaign contributions remains statistically significant after accounting for the different ways men and women CEOs are distributed across industries.

whether companies that state social media or damage to their brand as a concern are less likely to lobby or donate through branded PACs. In both cases, I found evidence that they are less likely to advocate using these methods, even after accounting for size (for campaign contributions) and for size, leadership, and industry (for lobbying).[13] As Table 6.1 illustrates, in the case of lobbying, a stated concern about social media reduced the probability of lobbying, even after controlling for other relevant variables, although it was not statistically significant at conventional levels ($p = 0.250$). A stated fear of reputation or brand damage, however, did reduce the probability of lobbying in a way that was statistically distinguishable from zero. Similarly, fears of both social media and reputation damage reduced the probability that a company would contribute through a PAC that shares its name, although neither coefficient was statistically significant (social media was $p = 0.427$, whereas reputation was a more believable $p = 0.181$).

In sum, both lobbying and donating in a company's own name are fairly rare activities, much rarer than conventional wisdom about corporate influence over politics would suggest. Although larger companies are more likely than smaller companies to engage in both forms of conventional, tracked advocacy in their own names, even among the best-resourced companies in the sample, over half do not lobby, and the vast majority do not donate to candidates through their own PAC. There is also evidence that companies led by women are less likely to engage in either form of advocacy, and companies that have stated their concern about social media or reputation damage publicly are also less likely to advocate in these ways, strongly suggesting an understanding that engaging in politics in such a way might lead to public backlash. Yet that does not – and should not – imply that these companies are not advocating for their interests or are not cultivating political influence, just that they are pursuing alternative channels. In the next section, I explore what they are doing instead.

6.6 What Do Companies Do to Influence Politics?

As illustrated in Chapter 5, at least some companies express an understanding that their efforts to influence politics and policy in their favor

---

[13] Contributing through PACs is so rare that the statistical models were finicky and often would not estimate properly with too many covariates.

6.6 What Do Companies Do to Influence Politics?

Table 6.1 *Logistic regressions predicting filing at least one lobbying report or donating to at least one campaign through a PAC in the company name in 2018*

	Dependent variable:			
	Lobbied generalized linear mixed-effects		Contributed logistic	
	(1)	(2)	(3)	(4)
Social media	−0.246		−0.498	
	(0.214)		(0.627)	
Reputation		−0.408*		−0.752
		(0.240)		(0.562)
2nd Quartile: revenue	0.300	0.298	16.329	16.321
	(0.269)	(0.269)	(932.445)	(928.321)
3rd Quartile: revenue	1.499***	1.507***	16.752	16.756
	(0.245)	(0.245)	(932.445)	(928.321)
4th Quartile: revenue	2.351***	2.347***	17.386	17.371
	(0.247)	(0.246)	(932.445)	(928.321)
Male CEO	0.185	0.198		
	(0.326)	(0.326)		
Constant	−2.683***	−2.375***	−20.538	−19.948
	(0.376)	(0.421)	(932.445)	(928.321)
Industry REs	Yes	Yes	No	No
Observations	1,375	1,375	1,378	1,378
Log likelihood	−631.390	−630.665	−111.223	−110.811
Akaike inf. crit.	1,276.780	1,275.330	232.446	231.621
Bayesian inf. crit.	1,313.363	1,311.914		

Note: *$p < 0.1$; **$p < 0.05$; ***$p < 0.01$

can lead to consumer backlash, and many are concerned about it. Yet being concerned and actually changing strategy are different things. In other words, companies can express concern that their political influence tactics might get them into hot water and still think it's worth it and do it anyway. The quantitative evidence suggests that the forms of advocacy most likely to get companies in trouble – lobbying and campaign contributions – are relatively rare and systematically avoided by companies that ought to be worried about a backlash, but that doesn't tell us what, if anything, they do instead. Interview evidence, on the other hand, suggests many companies opt to change their strategies in order to avoid public backlash. The strategies they pursue instead tend to fit into the categories predicted by the theory. Either companies try to "hide" their political activity – avoiding high-visibility strategies and opting instead for methods that allow them to evade public scrutiny – or they aim to defuse the anger, choosing methods of influencing politics that might be less unpopular.

6.6.1 Evading Attention

Hiding is, by far, the most common category of strategy alternatives that showed up in my interviews. A company "hides" by distancing its name and brand from its political influence. This allows the company to take the high-visibility, stance-taking actions that it wants but with decreased concern that the public will find out and link the company with its actions. This allows companies to have their cake and eat it too – using the same tried-and-true, broadly applicable influence strategies while typically avoiding public backlash. My interviews suggest two clear ways that companies hide their political influence efforts: flying beneath the radar and enlisting third parties.

6.6.1.1 Hidden Advocacy

Flying beneath the radar refers to companies influencing policy using traditional tactics and in their own name but in a way that allows them to evade scrutiny. My interviewees described this, variously, as companies working "behind the scenes" or being "less public."[14] One way of doing this is to bypass lobbyists and have representatives of companies contact elected officials directly. Two local elected officials I spoke to, one a county commissioner and the other a city commissioner, both relayed to me that the accessibility of their elected office made it easy for an aggrieved party to get in touch with them directly, either over the phone, by email, or in person.[15] Depending on the jurisdiction, this may not be tracked or "count" as lobbying. In some places, only officially registered lobbyists are required to disclose their

---

[14] Interview #18 and interview #3, respectively.
[15] Anonymous interviews #18 and #14.

6.6 What Do Companies Do to Influence Politics? 185

contacts. Even if that isn't true, if the direct lobbying is relatively minimal, it might not meet a threshold that requires it to be disclosed. In most places, lobbying disclosure ordinances have either a minimum amount of time or minimum amount of money that must be spent before disclosure is required.[16]

Companies can also fly beneath the radar by keeping their activities minimal enough to either not meet disclosure thresholds or to just not attract a lot of attention. For instance, if a company properly parcels out its money and time, it may be able to avoid disclosing its activity by virtue of being beneath these disclosure thresholds. A municipal official that I interviewed pointed out that, under their city's rules, an interested group can spend a lot of money, but as long as no individual person necessarily meets the minimum time threshold, the activity doesn't need to be disclosed.[17] As a lobbyist explained it to me, it might be better for a company to "spread out" its funds rather than donating as a lump sum if they're making campaign donations that might be politically unpopular. This might not evade detection, and it still may be tracked, but, as the lobbyist explained, it might not capture as much attention or look quite as bad.[18]

6.6.1.2 Distanced Advocacy

More common in my interviews than flying beneath the radar, however, is companies using third parties to intervene politically on their behalf. A former in-house government affairs professional I interviewed succinctly described this strategy as "let someone else be your henchman."[19] Another in-house government affairs professional echoed this with less evocative imagery, pointing out that the company working as itself – or having its hat on, as they phrased it – made influence harder. The idea is that companies will work through other people or groups who are not directly affiliated with the company and have those people do the work that might receive negative attention. This way, the company's name is not attached to its activity, but the activity is still going on.

Trade associations are a common way that companies use third parties to influence politics. One lobbyist I spoke to explicitly said

---

[16] Ethics board interviews #1, #2, and #3.
[17] Anonymous interview #21.
[18] Anonymous interview #7.
[19] Anonymous interview #6.

that many of their corporate clients belong to trade associations that are primarily responsible for their more controversial lobbying, and the lobbyist said they believed it was an intentional strategy to avoid public backlash.[20] A former in-house government affairs professional echoed this, noting that his company – a large regional independent oil and gas production company – would "play both sides of the street." In public, in its own name, the company was upfront about the necessity to work on climate-related issues while simultaneously sitting on their hands and allowing the trade group to be the "400 lb gorilla pounding their chest" about resisting the changes necessary to confront climate change.[21] Yet another lobbyist pointed out that working through trade associations or chambers of commerce was mostly beneficial because of the strength in numbers, but the lobbyist also noted that companies don't want an issue to be "all about them when it isn't all about them." Working through a trade association not only lets companies outsource their more unpopular activity to a third party that doesn't bear their name, it also allows them to, in some ways, make the issue not "about them" at all, avoiding the issue and allowing the political advocacy around the issue to be unlinked from their brand.

Companies can also form new groups or nonprofits to avoid associating their name with the political influence they're seeking. A former state legislative associate I interviewed gave an example of several companies forming a new group – purportedly a citizens' group opposing the expansion of their industry – to lobby the state legislature to disallow new licenses to other companies in their industry. What looked like a group of people against a sometimes controversial business activity was actually a group of companies in that industry lobbying to prevent competition while making sure no one knew it was them.[22] This isn't unique, however – in many places, it is perfectly legal for companies or groups of companies to form nonprofits for the purposes of lobbying. In some places, for instance, if a company forms a nonprofit – specifically a 501(c)(3) – they can "teach"

---

[20] Anonymous interview #9.
[21] Anonymous interview #6.
[22] Anonymous interview #5. It's worth noting that I wasn't able to confirm their claims about the group – which is anonymized here to prevent identification – but I trusted the interviewee and also understood that the point of this group was to hide its primary funders.

6.6 What Do Companies Do to Influence Politics? 187

politicians about their cause without it legally counting as lobbying and needing to be disclosed.[23]

Short of forming new groups, companies can also use third-party influencers to help make their point without putting their name on it. An in-house lobbyist at a global technology company spoke at length about this, pointing out that using contract lobbyists is much more "obvious" and that they prefer, in many cases, to instead make use of the networks of the politicians they're trying to influence. The key, they emphasized, is to find someone who shares the company's view on an issue and has a preexisting relationship with the official. That person, as a trusted resource outside the company, can relay the company's message to the official more genuinely and effectively than the company itself can.[24]

Finally, companies can use the public – or "grassroots lobbying" – to influence politicians. Instead of paying a lobbyist or writing a check to a politician, companies spend their money on billboards, ads, social media campaigns, and other forms of advertising that aim to convince the public to hold the company's view and to agitate their politicians about it.[25] New technologies, such as "geo-fencing," make this even easier by allowing companies to target ads and messages by a user's geographic location, down to the zip code or block.[26] In some cases, companies will also pay people to show up at a public meeting.[27] In some places this is publicly disclosed – San Francisco, for instance, tracks it and calls it "expenditure lobbying" – but in other places it isn't. Two municipal ethics board officials noted that this kind of thing is especially hard to track because it's informal and need not necessarily even go through traditional bank accounts, meaning it may create no paper trail at all.[28]

Grassroots lobbying can be a tactic to change the hearts and minds of the public, but under certain circumstances it need not even convince people to actually change their views. On the former point, one official gave me the example of people wearing t-shirts supporting a

---

[23] Anonymous interview #23.
[24] Anonymous interview #12.
[25] Anonymous interviews #21, #22, #23, and #10.
[26] Anonymous interview #12.
[27] Anonymous interviews #21 and #22.
[28] Anonymous interviews #22 and #23.

political issue. When asked about their position, they just said they were given $20 to be there in a t-shirt.[29] A municipal elected official from a large Midwestern city, similarly, gave me a few examples of opponents of municipal ordinances providing misleading or sometimes incorrect information to the public in an effort to stir up public discontent and kill the measures, an organization effort that they termed "artful."[30] In some cases, companies or other interest groups simply provide resources to already like-minded groups of people so that those groups can make their case more effectively and the company can benefit as a result.[31] Because the people are not being paid, in some places this does not meet the definition of lobbying.[32]

6.6.2 Defusing the Public Response

Instead of hiding their influence by flying beneath the radar or enlisting third parties, companies may instead choose to perform their advocacy in full view of the public but in forms that are less likely to fuel partisan signaling and political speech. Within this category, there are two types: creative advocacy and careful advocacy. My interviews turned up little evidence of careful advocacy – it appeared to be the case that the companies I spoke to were rarely in situations in which they felt they had to lobby or donate but didn't have an option to hide or distance. I did, however, find limited evidence of two strategies within creative advocacy: public services and philanthropic donations.

Providing public services as a form of political influence and advocacy is a circumscribed strategy. In contrast with companies aiming to mobilize the public to advocate for issues on their behalf, providing public services is a strategy deployed when the public needs to be *de*mobilized, such that they don't advocate for issues counter to the company's interests. It emerged organically in two interviews, both with in-house government affairs representatives. One former government affairs representative from a large regional independent oil and gas production company explained to me that their company frequently dealt with political problems

---

[29] Anonymous interview #22.
[30] Anonymous interview #13.
[31] Anonymous interview #22.
[32] Anonymous interview #22.

6.6 What Do Companies Do to Influence Politics? 189

resulting from tense relationships with local residents. These community members, who worried about the local environmental and quality-of-life consequences (e.g., noise, light pollution, air emissions) of sharing their community with oil and gas production, often agitated their local representatives to impose harsh regulations or even shut down the companies. In addition, the community members also sometimes took matters in their own hands – protesting and periodically vandalizing company property.

Because these political issues originated within the community, the response was to engage proactively with the community. This took two forms. The first was independently responding to the community's concerns in an attempt to alleviate their concerns without needing to get the government involved. For instance, the company was proactive in setting limits on which roads the company's trucks can be on and at what times and at what speeds. They also took the initiative in trying to proactively address environmental, safety, and health concerns. Second, the company provided the community with improved infrastructure. The company in particular took the lead in fixing, resurfacing, and repaving many county roads, in part because its trucks were responsible for some of the damage. Community engagement was an extremely important strategy for the company because, as the representative explained it, there are so many ways the community can shut down the company's production if the company doesn't engage with the community.[33] A representative from another company was less expansive about their company's efforts but explained that reminding people of the company's investment in communities – through advertising, especially – was part of their targeted influence strategy.[34]

Philanthropic donations are another way that companies try to influence politics, according to my interviews, echoing findings in Bertrand et al. (2018). Similar to how companies can form nonprofits as a way to evade public scrutiny, companies can also donate to nonprofits that are associated with officials they want to influence. A former mayor explained that another former mayor, when he was campaigning, set up a charitable foundation that included his name. Companies and others could donate money to that foundation, which

---

[33] Anonymous interview #6.
[34] Anonymous interview #12.

they did not need to divulge, and then the foundation could sponsor public events and could itself make donations. As they explained it to me, "It's not electioneering. It's a perfectly legitimate charitable enterprise ..." that has the benefit of putting the mayor's name in front of the community, without it counting as electioneering.[35] Even when it's not linked to philanthropy, companies providing politicians a platform – by inviting them to speak to employees, giving them awards, or inviting them to ribbon-cuttings – also came up as a way that companies can help politicians without directly giving to their campaigns or lobbying.[36]

6.7 Conclusion

Previous chapters have provided evidence that consumers care and respond badly to companies' political activities and that companies know and are concerned about the potential for that consumer backlash. The overarching argument in this book is that this potential for boycott and public backlash shapes how companies try to influence politics. If companies worry about public backlash, they should eschew the influence strategies most likely to provoke it. Lobbying and campaign contributions, as the most well-recognized, high-visibility, and inherently stance-taking forms of political influence, should be the most likely influence strategies to lead to a large public backlash, and so, I argue, companies should avoid them, and instead should pursue lower-profile, less unpopular tactics.

In this chapter, I used two forms of evidence to assess whether that's true. First I tackled the question of whether certain types of companies – large companies, companies led by women, and companies that are explicitly concerned about social media and the possibility of reputation damage – are less likely to engage in lobbying and campaign contributions in their own name. To do this, I used data on lobbying reports filed with the federal government [from Kim (2018)] and contributions from corporate PACs to candidates for federal office from the Federal Election Commission (FEC). I found evidence that both lobbying and campaign contributions in this format –

---

[35] Anonymous interview #17.
[36] Anonymous interviews #2, a former in-house government affairs professional, and interview #13, a city council member.

6.7 Conclusion

in the open, in the company's name – are far more rare than conventional understanding of corporate influence on politics would suggest. I found that less than half of the largest companies in my sample lobbied, despite being the best able to do so financially, and that the vast majority of companies overall do not donate to political campaigns. I also found that companies led by women are less likely to engage in both, as are companies that state concerns about social media or reputation and brand damage in their 10-Ks. Taken together, this evidence suggests that many companies that we might expect to engage in these strategies are not. It shows that many companies are not lobbying or donating through branded PACs.

Yet knowing what companies are *not* doing tells us little about what they *are* doing. The lack of activity either points to companies actually not acting or to companies using other strategies. To answer the question of what companies are doing instead, I supplement the quantitative tests with interview evidence with government affairs professionals, both in-house and contract, as well as journalists, municipal ethics boards representatives, and others with direct experience of corporate political influence. In those data, I found strong evidence of two categories of alternative strategies that companies pursue in lieu of lobbying and campaign finance: hiding and taking pro-social actions. Most of the strategies fall under the category of hiding, which permits companies to do the same lobbying and campaign contributions they'd have done otherwise but in ways that make it harder to attribute the action to them. Mostly this involves either a deliberate action to evade reporting or the use of third parties.

In total, in this chapter, I've provided evidence that companies do condition their political influence strategies based on their fear of boycott and consumer backlash more generally. Companies that are worried about boycott are more likely to try to take political behavior that's untracked or less politically unpopular, but they aren't less likely to seek out political influence. Boycott, and concerns about it, mostly push political behavior underground, into new forms and harder-to-track strategies because boycott doesn't solve the fundamental problem that companies have – policy influences them, and they want a hand in shaping it – it just makes them worried about doing it in the open. In the next, and concluding, chapter, I talk about this implication and other implications of the book in more detail.

7 So What and Now What?
Summaries and Concluding Thoughts

7.1 Summary of Book

Politics permeates everyone's life. This is true of both individual people and groups. Companies, too, are often in situations in which politics influences their core interests. Political decisions at the federal, state, and municipal levels of government have consequences for corporate operations. Political decisions meant to help people in low-wage jobs also increase the cost of labor for companies. Political decisions meant to curb the use of single-use plastics, intended to help the environment, can also increase operating costs for businesses. These are just two examples – all manner of political decisions and public policies affect companies, sometimes in negative ways. Under those circumstances, companies have to decide whether to try to intervene to voice their opposition and shape the policies they're subject to and, if so, how to do that.

In this book, I address these questions. In short, I argue that, because public opinion is often against corporate influence, the potential for public backlash in the form of boycott chastens companies and causes them to choose strategies that are least likely to provoke public ire. In particular, I argue that the potential for public backlash leads some companies to avoid publicly engaging in forms of political influence that are highly visible and widely maligned – the tried-and-true methods of lobbying and campaign donations – in favor of either stealthily engaging in the same strategies or using other tactics that are less politically unpopular. Public opinion increases the costs of doing politics, but it doesn't make companies stop caring. Therefore, it doesn't stop companies from trying to influence politics – it mostly just makes them hide.

To understand why and how this happens, Chapter 2 explains how political influence works. Political influence, in the popular imagination, is typically limited to two things: campaign donations and lobbying. Both of these strategies are often viewed as a quid pro quo, in which interest groups write checks and politicians "sell" their votes. Yet this is a very limited, and perhaps incorrect, understanding of political influence. In Chapter 2, I explain how political influence is really about relationships. Companies can either develop and maintain relationships on their own or they can co-opt existing relationships by third parties, but in either case, it's the presence of a relationship that allows companies to relay their information and opinions to policymakers.

When companies decide to cultivate their own relationships, rather than using someone else's, they often do it by providing solutions to policymakers' problems. This can then be "rewarded," in a sense, by access to the politician. Campaign contributions and lobbying are so prominent and widely accepted as forms of influence-seeking because they address two common problems politicians have: a lack of funds for campaigns and a lack of information (or the time and resources to collect that information) about the matters they have to weigh in on. Yet this is an incomplete list of politicians' problems, and therefore campaign contributions and lobbying are an incomplete list of political influence strategies. In Chapter 2, I provide a more thorough discussion of the kinds of problems politicians face – informed especially by the experience of municipal politicians, whose experiences can be useful in understanding politicians' problems more broadly – and the strategies that emerge as a result of companies trying to solve those problems.

In Chapter 3, I argue that political influence fundamentally shapes how companies engage in politics and try to shape policy. In other words, how companies decide to advocate for their perceived political interests in any given policy situation is shaped by their fear of public backlash. This is because any political step or stance a company takes is scrutinized by the public, and individuals can use their disapproval of a company's political stances as a form of political speech, intended to both reaffirm to themselves the kind of person they are and to signal to others what their politics are, two things that are increasingly important in an era of strong political, ideological, and social partisanship. In other words, people are, in some ways, actively looking for ways to signal their politics, and if companies give them an opportunity, they will seize on it. This is bad for the company because, if the firestorm grows large enough, it can damage the company's brand and reputation, which can, in turn, hurt the company's bottom line. Yet not all companies are equally vulnerable to this. I argue that larger companies, companies led by women, and companies with strong brands are more highly scrutinized and also possibly more likely to be concerned about brand damage. This pushes those kinds of companies to take steps to either hide their political behavior or approach it in a way that makes it a less useful tool for people aiming to demonstrate their partisanship.

In Chapter 4, I test the implications about public opinion and individual motivations using two experiments and social media data. In the experiments, I find strong evidence that people disapprove and are more willing to boycott companies that make political donations that oppose the individual's own political views (in other words, Democrats punish companies for donating to Republicans and vice versa). In the social media data, I find that partisan language is strongly predictive of it being retweeted, creating the dangerous firestorm that companies are worried about. Taken together, the suite of evidence suggests support for the key individual mechanism: that public backlash is a form of political speech and partisan signaling.

Chapter 5 asks whether companies know and care about the potential for public backlash, and why. Using data from corporate reports and interviews, I demonstrate that companies do understand that their political influence-seeking might cause public backlash, and they do care. Moreover, I argue – and find – that larger companies and companies led by women express more concern about social media and reputation damage in their official documentation. My interviews reflected the same themes. Especially in the era of social media, in which discussions of boycott can become extremely prominent and actually become newsworthy on their own, boycotts are dangerous to a wide range of companies because they threaten the company's ability to control its own brand. Brands – how a company is known and perceived by the public and whatever reputation and value comes along with that – are among the most valuable assets for many companies. When the company becomes the subject of broad popular scrutiny, and especially when that scrutiny is politicized, companies can lose control over their brand, damage that can be very difficult to recover from. As a result, I demonstrate evidence that not only do companies care about the potential for politically motivated boycotts but also that the types of companies that are concerned are broader than expected.

7.1 Summary of Book

The overarching theory of the book – that companies change their strategies based on their fear of boycott – is tested in Chapter 6. First, I test the expectation that companies that are concerned with boycott should be unlikely to lobby or donate to political campaigns in their own names – that is, not through an industry group or other third party. Using data from federal corporate PAC contributions and federal lobbying, I demonstrate that this kind of political advocacy is particularly rare, consistent with the theoretical expectation that companies know it gets them in trouble and, accordingly, aim to avoid it. I show that companies led by women and companies with a stated concern about social media and reputation damage are even less likely than other companies to engage in this kind of advocacy in their own name. Although the quantitative data helped me understand what isn't happening, my interviews pointed me toward what companies are doing instead. I use data from interviews with a variety of different types of people with experience of corporate political influence-seeking from different angles. I talked to in-house government affairs personnel (people who handle a company's affairs with the government from inside the company), contract lobbyists, representatives from political action committees, municipal and state politicians, journalists, and representatives from municipal ethics boards. These are the people who make decisions about corporate political influence strategy, who observe and track it, and at whom it is aimed. I document and analyze the variety of alternative strategies they described for when companies are concerned about consumer backlash. I find strong evidence that companies frequently aim to distance themselves from their political actions, typically by using third parties with pre existing relationships with politicians (including the public and politicians' own social networks) or by structuring their behavior in such a way that it evades tracking, and I find slightly weaker evidence that they also aim to pursue more palatable influence strategies.

In sum, the suite of evidence collectively supports the key claim of the book: companies know about and are worried about public backlash to their political activities, and so they change their strategies to try to avoid the backlash. Most often this means they pursue the same conventional strategies they always have – lobbying and campaign donations – but they try to do so in a way that puts distance between the company's actions and its name in the hope that people won't connect the two and won't punish them. The strongest evidence suggests that when companies are worried about public backlash, they just try to make sure the public doesn't know what they're doing. The effect of people using disapproval of corporate politics to define themselves politically has been to force political influence underground.

7.2 Big Takeaways

1 Boycotts in Response to Corporate Political Behavior Probably Work Better Than Many People Think, Just Not in the Way They Think: A common refrain surrounding political boycotts and the people that engage in them is that the boycotts don't work – and might even help the company in question! – because the people who are boycotting would never buy that company's products anyway. Yet I find evidence that these criticisms are rooted in a misunderstanding of the social function of online boycotts and how they work to hurt companies. That is, it might not even matter if, under other circumstances, people would have purchased the product they're proclaiming they'll never buy again.

It also might be partially right: it may be true that many of the people who discuss and threaten boycotts might not regularly buy products from the company they're claiming to boycott. Even the people who *do* buy products from the company might not actually stop buying from the company. Yet a key finding of this book is that it probably doesn't even matter, and the people publicly leveling that criticism of the boycotters may inadvertently be exacerbating the boycott.

The reason that's true is because one big finding in this book is that boycotts are as much about brand management, if not more, than they are about revenue. In other words, companies don't necessarily worry about boycotts because they think people will follow through and stop buying their products. Instead, a much bigger concern is that boycotts – and especially people talking about boycotts – can cause a company to lose control of its popular image. Brands are extremely important assets for companies, and they invest significant time and money into maintaining them. When people discuss boycotting a company, its image becomes politicized and what the company is and what it stands for become a matter of public debate and imagination. Although in some cases "brand hate" can redound

7.2 Big Takeaways

to the company's benefit, many companies express concern about the potential for losing control of their brand.

That's the first reason that boycotts work, but they don't work the way people think they do: they work by targeting a company's brand, not necessarily directly targeting its revenue. This means that politically induced boycotts can be damaging for companies even if the people discussing it don't or can't actually boycott. If they talk loudly enough and in a public enough space, like on social media, and if they spur a discussion, whether they actually buy Nike shoes or hammers from Home Depot is probably irrelevant.

The second reason that boycotts work but not how people think they do is that politically induced boycotts don't stop companies from trying to influence politics. It's unclear if this is exactly what people think happens, but the logic behind it is intuitive: if a company is "punished" by the public for trying to influence politics in a particular way, it'll think twice about doing that again. The logic is right, but the (possible) conclusion is wrong. Companies do think twice about doing that again, but "that" refers to "the exact thing that got them into trouble." Public backlash can damage companies, and it can cause them to change their behavior, but public backlash doesn't make companies care less about policy. Public backlash doesn't make policies that worry companies less damaging. So public backlash doesn't stop companies from trying to seek influence; it just stops them from trying to seek influence in ways that will get them in trouble with the public.

In practice, what this means is that companies that worry about public backlash will often opt to not take high-visibility political influence strategies in situations in which doing so might be politically unpopular. Instead, they'll either choose a way to influence politics that they think will go unnoticed – the idea being that people can't respond badly to something they don't know is happening – or they'll choose a method that's less likely to cause public backlash. In the former case, it means companies might, for instance, still donate money to a candidate or still lobby, but maybe they'll do it through some third party that's not directly linked to the company. In the latter case, companies might engage in philanthropy or take some type of pro-social behavior, still in the hopes of influencing policy but without getting in trouble.

So, boycotts do work, it just doesn't necessarily matter if people actually boycott, and they work by changing the shape of a company's influence-seeking rather than determining whether or not companies seek influence at all.

2 Consumer Response to Corporate Political Activity Mostly Just Pushes It Underground: When I started this project, I had a suspicion that companies might turn to more pro-social behavior to influence politics without provoking public backlash. In other words, I thought companies might do good things for the community to influence politics if they were concerned that their conventional strategies might hurt them. Instead, the bulk of the evidence suggests that, when people respond to corporate political activity by boycotting, or even talking about boycotting, it doesn't result in public service provision, and it doesn't result in less lobbying or fewer campaign contributions. It just creates incentives for companies to hide their political behavior, mostly by enlisting third parties – influencers, the public, and so on – to agitate on their behalf and by structuring their political activity to make it less easy to track, and, therefore, less easy to understand and scrutinize. In some ways, this represents no meaningful change from the status quo. Companies are still seeking influence; they're just doing it in less formalized and harder-to-track ways.

The key question that emerges from these findings is whether this state of affairs – companies trying to influence politics through channels less likely to provoke consumer ire – is an improvement over companies seeking influence openly. Is the kind of informal lobbying, untracked and through third parties, better than formal lobbying?

I think the answer is no, for a few reasons. The first reason is that lobbyists – actual, professional lobbyists – serve an important function in our political system, a theme that emerged repeatedly throughout my interviews, not only with lobbyists (obviously) but also with elected officials. Lobbyists are important because elected officials are busy and they aren't experts on everything. Although, to be sure, there are other ways to find out about issues facing their jurisdictions – some elected officials explained to me how they use national groups to find information or how they use their staff to do research – lobbyists, and companies providing information about issues more generally, are an important way that elected officials learn about the issues they have to

7.2 Big Takeaways

make decisions about. Stopping formal, tracked lobbying may not be a worthwhile goal.

More to the point, though, transparency seems better for democracy than the lack of transparency. In other words, it's probably better if everyone knows what's going on – even if they don't like it – because then, at least, they know that things they don't like are going on. They can hold their politicians accountable. They can protest. Not knowing what's going on might make people feel better, but it impedes accountability.

3 Corporate Political Influence Probably Can't Be Eliminated (Except Through Large-Scale Electoral Reform), But It Can Be Better Understood, Tracked, and Scrutinized: If you're reading this and you're someone who thinks companies have too much influence over politics, the obvious question is: now what? If public pressure and consumer tactics – among the few tools actually available to concerned people – doesn't reduce political influence-seeking, then what can people do to reduce the influence companies have on politics?

The answer is that, short of large-scale electoral reform that removes the problems politicians have that companies can try to solve (see Chapter 2), it's really unlikely that corporate political influence can be significantly reduced, and it's probably impossible to eliminate it. As long as politicians have problems – as long as they need so much money to run for office, as long as they need information and don't have the time and resources to acquire it, and as long as there are impediments to job performance – companies will have tools to influence politics. And as long as there are policy issues that matter to companies, they're probably going to use those tools. In other words, as long as there is demand, powerful interests will be there to supply.

Perhaps even less encouragingly, any changes to the system are going to be opposed by people who benefit from the system. In other words, there are good reasons to believe that companies and other interest groups benefit from elections being expensive, for instance, because that creates a tool for influence. As is often the case in politics, people who benefit from an existing system have no incentive to change that system and instead have incentives to try to keep the system intact. The problems politicians face that create tools for companies to influence politics are no different.

What people can, and should, do instead is to understand, track, and scrutinize political behavior. In this section, I will explain each in turn.

First, people need to have a broader and more comprehensive understanding of what corporate political influence is, how it arises, and what it looks like. That is the motivation behind Chapter 2 of this book. An understanding that political influence comprises campaign finance and lobbying is a minimal working understanding, and it misses a lot of other behaviors that function equally well as political influence but don't get the same top billing. As explained in Chapter 2, companies seek political influence by building relationships, and they build relationships in part by solving problems for politicians. Understanding this helps to give a broader perspective on what political influence might look like in any given situation. If you live in a municipality with terrible roads or underfunded schools, companies might try to seek influence by helping out with those things. If you have an elected official who has an associated charity, companies might seek influence by donating to that charity. Understanding the different forms that political influence can take and how it can vary by context is a crucial first step. If you don't know where to look for influence, you're going to miss a lot of it. That's what makes those unconventional strategies, discussed in Chapters 3 and 6, so effective: no one's looking, and if no one's looking, no one's going to get angry.

A second step is better tracking. A municipal ethics board representative I interviewed told me that they keep trying to increase the reporting requirements – meaning that anyone who lobbies would have to provide more information about what they're doing – but their proposals stall out and aren't implemented. Fittingly, it is probable that there is lobbying against the increased lobbying reporting requirements, but the existing requirements aren't robust enough to know who that might be or how it's happening. One thing concerned citizens can do is research the ethics requirements in their municipalities and state and at the federal level and agitate for more reporting, more tracking, and more transparency. Moreover, people can agitate for tracking of more things. There should be centralized systems to track politicians' philanthropies and corporate philanthropic donations, for instance. The funding of public services within municipalities is devastatingly difficult to figure out in most places, especially where

7.2 Big Takeaways

corporate grants might be concerned. The more tracking that can surround politicians, as well as companies and interest groups, the better we can understand the entire political environment.

The third step is scrutiny. Companies can do things to cultivate political influence, but it doesn't mean politicians have to grant that influence. Understanding what's going on, publicizing it, discussing it, and addressing it with elected officials is a crucial step. One of the municipal city council members I interviewed for this book told me they return any campaign contributions from developers or from anyone who might represent a conflict of interest. They do that in part because of their own moral compass but also because their constituents care. Be a constituent who cares. Hold elected officials accountable.

A fourth thing that people can do is to support high-quality journalism, especially at the local level. All the ethics board representatives I spoke to told me that their online databases and other resources are mostly used by journalists, trying to follow the money and trace out influence. The media is and remains the primary forum for democratic checks on the role of corporations in politics, but increasingly local news outlets are being bought up by national conglomerates who often have their own partisan leanings and fewer incentives to do quality state and local journalism. These media outlets rely upon financing from ads and from subscriptions, and without that money, there isn't funding for the kinds of journalists who do the painstaking work of tracking political influence. If you want checks on corporate influence – or, indeed, to even know what's happening – you should support high-quality journalism with strong local reporting.

In sum, this book lays out an argument for how public backlash forces corporate influence-seeking to take forms that are harder to identify and track. I didn't set out to find ways to limit corporate political influence, and I didn't accidentally find any along the way. What I did learn is that people actually do have a very strong influence on companies, even if perhaps not to the end some of them would want, and I also found many ways that companies can shape political influence without anyone necessarily being any the wiser. My hope is that by illuminating this corner of the political world, it will spur greater data collection and research and help people who seek to answer more normative questions.

7.3 Areas for Future Research

As is often the case in science, there are many more questions that I did not or could not answer, for reasons of space, data, or coherence. Other questions arose as a result of the answers that I found. In this section, I discuss a few lingering and new questions that may be promising areas for future research in this area.[1] Many of these questions involve developing theories that speak more to differences between types of companies and trying to understand which companies might be particularly vulnerable, or perhaps more insulated, from public opinion.

First, does it matter if the company is primarily consumer-facing when it comes to understanding how public opinion shapes a company's political influence strategies? In other words, if a company primarily sells products to consumers, rather than selling intermediary goods to other companies or governments, are they more vulnerable to negative public opinion? There are good reasons to believe this should be true. These companies can be hurt by consumer behavior, they can be hurt by public opinion, and they can be hurt by public opinion *leading to* consumer behavior. Further, if they also sell non-durable goods, as many consumer-facing companies do (e.g., food, clothing, etc.), they are also likely to have narrower profit margins, so we might expect that they are also more vulnerable to public opinion simply because they have less of a financial buffer against negative events.

Second, are firms more vulnerable to public pressure if they are publicly held? In Chapter 3, I point out that publicly traded companies may be different from companies that are privately held because boycotts and public opinion can influence the company's reputation directly and indirectly by influencing the behavior of shareholders. Yet because of data constraints, I focused on publicly traded companies in this book, because there is more data available about them. If it is true that publicly traded companies are more responsive to public opinion and therefore pursue seeking influence in different ways, this could be normatively interesting because it could imply that listing on a stock exchange might serve to make companies more accountable to the public than is popularly recognized.

---

[1] I thank an anonymous reviewer for these excellent suggestions.

7.3 Areas for Future Research

Third, do a company's global reach and investment patterns matter? Do companies that operate in many markets fear backlash in any individual market less than companies that are more reliant on that individual market? Put more simply, if a company is based in the United States but does most of its business abroad, does it care less about US public opinion? On one hand, the social media platforms that enable the kind of backlash I discuss in this book do not respect national boundaries per se, so a campaign against a company in the United States can, in principle, easily be seen and then spread in other countries, such that the reputation damage will not be confined to the country or region in which it originates. If anything, companies that are globally active might actually be more vulnerable because, if the backlash picks up in other countries, the politicians of those countries and the media in those countries might join in, exacerbating the backlash. On the other hand, the role of social media and the laws surrounding it are not stagnant, backlash is not confined to social media, and not all issues are interesting enough outside the domestic market to fuel backlash. What this suggests is that some kinds of investment patterns should be associated with companies being insulated from political pressure about their political activities, whereas other investment patterns should not be.

Since I began writing this book, the world has changed in significant and meaningful ways, which raises question about how the role of companies in politics – and how they respond to public opinion – might shift over time. For instance, as I write this final section, in January 2021, in the immediate aftermath of an insurrection[2] in Washington, D.C., many companies are announcing their intentions to stop or change their political donation strategies, in part in response to public opinion about the role that Republicans in Congress played in said insurrection. Social media, traditional media, and some activists are praising companies for these steps. Some companies have taken other actions in response to the insurrection and threats of political violence, such as the short-term rental company Airbnb canceling all reservations in D.C. around the inauguration of Joe Biden in anticipation of political violence, and companies such as Airbnb are being similarly praised for their actions. This raises the question of whether

---

[2] See Ritter and Davenport (2021) for a discussion of terminology surrounding this event.

companies' strategies might also respond to the potential for praise rather than strictly backlash. Might activists highlight companies that take stances they agree on, drawing positive attention to those actions, and therefore create incentives for companies to proactively behave in ways that attract positive attention? Many of the representatives of firms I spoke with implied that being linked to any political stance or group – whether positive or negative – was something they wanted to avoid. Yet it seems likely that, under some circumstances, some subset of firms probably would benefit from this, especially if doing so reinforced aspects of their brand, and it would behoove researchers to understand these dynamics better.

Finally, the COVID-19 global pandemic has led many companies to shift significant portions of their workforce from centralized offices to working from home. One of the key arguments for why companies engage in politics at all, as discussed in Chapter 2, is that the relative immobility of companies means they cannot easily "run away from" policies that they do not like. Yet, if certain industries shift to working from home in the long run, such that perhaps they terminate their leases and cease to exist in a physical space as much as they used to or primarily exist in a decentralized way in the basements and guest rooms of their employees, does that mean that those companies are now more mobile and therefore can more easily evade regulation? If so, will companies be less compelled to engage in politics, if they can instead just avoid regulations? Will this make it harder for governments to regulate companies? On the other hand, if jobs are not centralized, then perhaps politicians cannot easily claim credit for creating jobs or be held accountable for losing them, which might deprive companies of some of their leverage.

In this book, I highlight how the ease of viral backlash against companies that has been enabled by the internet in general and social media in particular has made them responsive to public opinion, shifting their political engagement into less easily detectable forms as companies aim to avoid that public backlash. Prior to the internet and social media, generating such a large and visible public response to a company's actions was much more difficult. Social media enables people to easily take stances and increase the visibility of a movement, and the growth of polarization has created incentives for people to take those stances in order to signal and broadcast their own values and political leanings. Yet companies adapt to their circumstances, and, as such, the relationship between companies, the governments that regulate them, and the public will continue to evolve. Companies will always seek to develop and exert influence over politics and policy because politics and policy will always shape how companies can operate. What changes is how they do that and how much it matters. Political influence that is poorly understood or invisible cannot be kept in check, and therefore understanding and tracking corporate political influence as it evolves is crucial to a functioning democracy.

Appendix A
Interview Methods

Sampling Frame, Response Rate, and Response Type

The first wave of interviews for this book included corporate representatives, lobbyists, representatives from interest groups and political action committees, local and state politicians, representatives from municipal ethics boards, and one journalist, and were all recruited in the summer of 2019.[1] All initial contacts were made over email and all interviews were conducted over the phone except for two, which were conducted in person. I learned two very important things in conducting these interviews. The first is that it is difficult to recruit for interviews when you are aiming to test a theory that specifies people will not want to speak about something and may actively try to obscure it (e.g., their companies' political influence tactics). The second thing I learned is that recruiting for elite interviews without being able to first build rapport with potential subjects and without initial contacts within the population is extremely challenging. While recruiting for these interviews, I frequently thought of a quote I once read about how to breathe while running, which, and I am paraphrasing, told new runners to take in air through any part of their body that would take it in, down to their fingernails. I often felt like I was trying to recruit for interviews in all possible ways, even ways that were implausible, impossible, or doomed to fail.

To construct the sampling frame for corporate representatives, I solicited interviews for the top three to five largest companies from several industries that had an email address available for a government affairs department (or similar department), with a focus on oversampling companies that were consumer-facing (i.e., food service, hotels). I also included the largest companies based in Minnesota, as I expected

---

[1] The formatting and information included in this appendix draws heavily from the excellent guide by Bleich and Pekkanen (2013).

Appendix A Interview Methods 207

a higher probability of response from them given my university affiliation. (Incidentally, that ended up not being true.) I also recruited based on personal contacts, in particular after my more representative strategy yielded few responses. I recruited for all interviews over email. Our (fantastic) coordinator of undergraduate advising, Becky Mooney, also included a request for interviews in the alumni newsletter sent out on behalf of the University of Minnesota Political Science Department, and several friends and colleagues aimed to recruit their contacts for me.

For lobbyists, I contacted the largest lobbying firms in the United States that had a focus on state and local government lobbying, and I also relied on snowball sampling. Interest group and PAC representatives were based strictly on personal referrals. I initially constructed a sampling frame of local politicians by contacting city council members in major cities. This yielded no interviews, and so I turned instead to using referrals from personal contacts. To interview representatives from municipal ethics boards, I contacted each municipal ethics board that published comprehensive data. (There are not many of those, which is bad for research in general but good for recruiting for interviews.) I spoke with one journalist, who I reached out to specifically because they had extensively covered a political issue that had been central to a previous version of the book. Although that political issue is no longer central to the book, the content of the interview still proved useful. As before, I sent all interview requests over email.

In total, I personally requested sixty interviews, and I cannot quantify the reach of requests sent out on my behalf, which makes it difficult to accurately report the denominator. I ended up with four interviews with current or former government affairs staff, one small business owner ("Mary," from the introduction), eight people who currently or formerly worked in or adjacent to lobbying and campaign finance, one journalist, four representatives of municipal ethics boards (two were from the same board), and seven current or former city, county, or state politicians, three of whom had held prior positions at different levels of local/state government and were therefore able to speak about different types of elected positions.

For the second wave, I only interviewed corporate representatives. Given the difficulty I'd previously had with recruiting interviews, I took a different approach in 2020, accounting for all that I had learned the first time. For the second wave, my sampling frame was a random sample of 400 companies from my data on publicly traded companies. Each was recruited by email, and I sent the majority of emails to public relations department accounts or shareholder information department accounts,[2] and all interviews were conducted either on video chat or phone.[3] (It is worth noting that both my recruitment and my interviews for the second wave happened during the global pandemic, which likely affected my response rate and greatly increased people's familiarity with video chat platforms, which were not as widely used during the first wave.) Of the 400 companies, 370 had publicly available and functioning email addresses; 31 of those companies responded, and 8 of the companies that responded agreed to have a representative be interviewed (that is, 25.8 percent of companies that responded and 2.16 percent of those contacted).

Format, Length, and Recording

All interviews were semi-structured, by which I mean I began each interview with a core set of questions (which varied by type of interviewee, see below) but allowed for interviewees to make additional comments, and I periodically asked follow-up questions based on the responses. The interviews averaged 30 minutes long but ranged between about 10 minutes and 60 minutes. Interviews were not recorded; instead, I took running dictation throughout.[4] As a result, I relied primarily on paraphrasing. All interviewees were promised both anonymity and strict confidentiality.

---

[2] Between the first and second waves, I learned how to use mail merge software, which accounts for why I was able to send so many more requests the second time.

[3] There was also an experimental treatment embedded in the recruitment emails. The difficulty I had with recruiting for my first wave piqued my interest in interview recruitment as a methodological issue. The experiment sought to evaluate whether certain aspects of a recruitment email increased response rate and the probability of agreeing to be interviewed. We found no statistically significant differences between groups.

[4] I'd like to thank the attorneys at the firm formerly known as Eby, Conner, Smillie, and Bourque, PLLC in Ann Arbor, Michigan for requiring me to learn how to take dictation, back before I went to grad school.

Appendix A Interview Methods   209

Interview Questions

For the first wave, each company representative was asked some or all of the following questions, although not always phrased in exactly this way. Lobbyists and those adjacent to lobbying were asked the same set of questions, but they were generalized to be about their clients in general rather than any particular company.

- How would you like your company described/what do you do?
- Who would you say are [Company Name's] core customers?
- What are the biggest policy/political/governmental challenges facing your company right now?
- What are the biggest challenges historically?
- What are the primary strategies that your company uses to deal with these challenges?
- Which levels of government are responsible for these challenges?
- What are the different factors your company considers when you choose a strategy?
- How much, if at all, are you ever worried about negative consequences arising from these strategies? What might the negative consequences entail?
- Is your company concerned about the threat of consumer boycott? Have you ever experienced a boycott before?

Politicians were asked:

- What are your primary concerns as a politician? Do you think these concerns are different than for politicians at other levels of government?
- How do you gauge constituent support for issues?
- How do you typically deal with [making decisions on] issues you're not an expert on?
- Can you speak to any experience you've had with companies supporting/opposing local ordinances/issues?

In the second wave, company representatives were asked the following questions, although not always phrased in exactly this way:

- What are the political issues of most interest to your company, and which levels of government are responsible for them?
- How does your company handle advocacy surrounding these issues?
- Does your company have any concern about social media or boycotts?

Appendix B
Chapter 4 Study Methodology and Full Results

Situations

There were three situations in total, as outlined in the list below. The stories were all written in a parallel format, and each described a company that operated in a city that announced a policy proposal. The policy proposal may hurt the company in a specific way, which was described in the story. Each story had one of five different ending sentences, tying up the story by explaining some action the company took. For each story, one of the possible endings had the company donating money to city council members who opposed the policy, one had the company lobbying city council members in opposition to the policy, and one had the company considering relocating to a nearby city. The first two endings modeled explicit political influence-seeking, as discussed in the previous section – since most people agree that campaign contributions and lobbying are used for political purposes and the plurality agree they're highly effective and because they're widely disliked without political context – this allowed me to see if they were actually favored less when loaded with political context and not presented in the abstract. The third ending – threatening to leave – modeled the situation in which a company aimed to influence politics by threatening to leave, as discussed in Chapter 2. The other two possible endings varied by situation but followed a pattern: one was the company taking an action that might be used for political influence-seeking but also might not be (sponsoring a youth soccer team, volunteering employees to tutor, and funding redevelopment of a city park), which mapped onto some of the corporate activities that belong in that "murky middle" ground. The last ending was an irrelevant, nonpolitical action (releasing a quarterly profit report, announcing an update of a popular product, and raising its own workers' wages[1]). Which ending each survey-taker

---

[1] Preemptively raising wages might be seen as a form of political influence in the case of the minimum wage increase proposal, on the grounds that it sends the

saw was assigned at random, meaning that the five groups should be roughly similar along all relevant (and irrelevant) demographic variables.

The stories differed in a few ways. First, each one featured a different type of company. Situation 1 had a retail food chain, Situation 2 featured a retail company, and Situation 3 was a manufacturing company. The purpose of varying this was that it allowed for realistically exposing survey-takers to different local policy proposals. In other words, because policies affect different types of companies, analyzing different policies necessitated varying the type of company in order for the threat to be realistic. I chose three policies – a sugary drinks tax, a minimum wage increase, and a policy targeting undocumented immigrants – in the hopes of getting approval from different types of people to see how approving of a policy changes how a person responds to a company trying to influence politics to fight it. Specifically, because minimum wage increases are often favored by progressives, I expected most people who identified as Democrats to approve of it, and because policies that are tough on undocumented immigration tend to be favored by conservatives, I expected most people who identified as Republicans to approve of it. Sugary drinks taxes are not explicitly partisan. This should give me sufficient variation in policy approval to see whether approval of corporate political influence-seeking varies by an individual's policy approval and by partisanship more generally.

- Situation 1: Company A is a retail food chain. It has a retail operation in Oak City. Oak City has recently announced a proposal to institute a tax on sugary drinks, which will slightly increase the cost of buying sweetened beverages. This tax may reduce sales for Company A, as people may buy fewer sugary drinks.
    – Company A donated money to city council members who oppose the tax.
    – Company A lobbied city council members in opposition to the tax.

message that the policy is irrelevant and does not need to be passed because the company is doing it anyway. In this way, this ending is not really explicitly nonpolitical.

Appendix B Chapter 4 Study Methodology and Full Results 213

- Company A recently sponsored a youth soccer team in Oak City.
- Company A is considering relocating its store to nearby Birch City.
- Company A released a quarterly profit report last month.
- Situation 2: Company B is a retail company with an operation in Maple City. Maple City has recently announced a proposal to raise its minimum wage from $9.50 to $15 by 2022, which will gradually increase the minimum wage for workers in the city each year until it reaches $15. This tax may increase costs for Company B, as it will have to pay its workers more per hour.
  - Company B donated money to city council members who oppose the increase.
  - Company B lobbied city council members in opposition to the increase.
  - Company B recently organized its employees to mentor local schoolchildren.
  - Company B is considering relocating its store to nearby Birch City.
  - Company B recently announced it will raise the wages of its lowest-paid workers to $15.
- Situation 3: Company C is a manufacturing company in Cedar City. Cedar City has recently announced a proposal to prohibit landlords from renting to undocumented tenants, which will impose a fine on any landlord that cannot provide documentation that their tenants are legal US residents. This proposal may slow production at Company C, which sometimes hires undocumented immigrants to fill large local labor shortages.
  - Company C donated money to city council members who oppose the ordinance.
  - Company C lobbied city council members in opposition to the ordinance.
  - Company C recently announced it will be funding a complete renovation of a popular local park.
  - Company C is considering relocating its manufacturing facility to nearby Birch City.

Table B1 *Results of ordered logistic regressions predicting a survey-taker's approval of Walmart on a five-point scale, ranging from strong disapproval (1) to strong approval (5). The omitted category for partisanship is "Neither Democrat nor Republican" and for "Woman" is "non-Woman" and includes both those who identify as men as well as those who identify as non-binary or neither man nor woman. HHI stands for household income. White includes anyone who identifies as white, including those who identify with multiple races including white. DNCC, Democratic National Campaign Committee; NRCC, National Republican Congressional Committee*

	Dependent variable: Approval of PAC donation			
	(1)	(2)	(3)	(4)
Treatment: NRCC	−0.043 (0.121)	0.117 (0.301)	−1.405*** (0.188)	
Treatment: DNCC				−1.706*** (0.224)
Republican	0.507*** (0.185)	−0.410 (0.268)		
Democrat	0.289* (0.173)	1.036*** (0.245)		
Frequent Walmart shopper	1.122*** (0.148)	1.161*** (0.149)	1.289*** (0.216)	0.911*** (0.261)
Age	−0.017*** (0.004)	−0.015*** (0.004)	−0.018*** (0.006)	−0.011* (0.006)
Disapprove of donations	−0.660*** (0.138)	−0.737*** (0.140)	−0.838*** (0.205)	−0.889*** (0.228)
Woman	−0.167 (0.122)	−0.196 (0.124)	−0.123 (0.179)	−0.285 (0.211)
Education: attended college	0.087 (0.139)	0.030 (0.141)	0.032 (0.203)	0.180 (0.248)
Education: attended graduate school	0.554** (0.232)	0.392* (0.235)	0.983*** (0.339)	0.264 (0.390)
HHI: 20,000–34,999	−0.231 (0.183)	−0.157 (0.185)	−0.544** (0.260)	0.328 (0.347)

Appendix B Chapter 4 Study Methodology and Full Results 215

Table B1 *(cont.)*

	\multicolumn{4}{c}{Dependent variable:}
	\multicolumn{4}{c}{Approval of PAC donation}
	(1)	(2)	(3)	(4)
HHI: 35,000–49,999	−0.260 (0.197)	−0.288 (0.200)	−0.430 (0.285)	−0.097 (0.351)
HHI: 50,000–74,999	−0.313 (0.194)	−0.417** (0.197)	−0.811*** (0.276)	−0.120 (0.354)
HHI: 75,000–99,999	−0.355 (0.243)	−0.217 (0.245)	−0.017 (0.409)	0.065 (0.386)
HHI: 100,000+	0.010 (0.234)	0.107 (0.238)	−0.054 (0.361)	0.447 (0.371)
White	−0.493*** (0.144)	−0.480*** (0.147)	−0.634*** (0.195)	−0.223 (0.312)
NRCC × Republican		1.624*** (0.370)		
NRCC × Democrat		−1.493*** (0.350)		
Observations	901	901	439	324

Note: $^*p < 0.1$; $^{**}p < 0.05$; $^{***}p < 0.01$

- Company C recently announced it will be releasing an updated version of its best-known product in 2021.

After each situation, survey-takers were asked to rate their approval of the policy, to rate their approval of the city, and to rate their approval of the company. The theory predicts that people should, on average, have lower levels of approval of the company when it engages in campaign donations or lobbying (and perhaps threatening to leave, although this is less clear) than when it engages in the other two activities. Yet it may also be the case that this effect is conditional on approval – in other words, as mentioned before, that people dislike political influence-seeking more when it's in the service of fighting a policy they like, and they are willing to forgive it when it aligns with their own politics.

Table B2 *Results of an ordered logistic model predicting professed changes in consumer behavior by party. Dependent variable is a five-category response to the question "Does this information make you more likely, less likely, or equally likely to shop at Walmart?" The omitted category for partisanship is "Neither Democrat nor Republican" and for "Woman" is "non-Woman" and includes both those who identify as men as well as those who identify as non-binary or neither man nor woman. HHI stands for household income. White includes anyone who identifies as white, including those who identify with multiple races including white. NRCC stands for National Republican Congressional Committee. DNCC stands for Democratic National Campaign Committee.*

	Dependent variable:		
	Less likely to shop at Walmart (five categories, increasing in likelihood of "boycott")		
	(1)	(2)	(3)
Treatment: NRCC	−0.159 (0.330)	1.147*** (0.200)	
Treatment: DNCC			1.102*** (0.229)
Republican	−0.031 (0.293)		
Democrat	−1.226*** (0.268)		
Frequent Walmart shopper	−1.390*** (0.165)	−1.748*** (0.246)	−1.032*** (0.278)
Age	0.020*** (0.004)	0.025*** (0.006)	0.016** (0.007)
Disapprove of donations	0.694*** (0.150)	0.719*** (0.217)	0.876*** (0.244)
Woman	0.378*** (0.133)	0.510*** (0.191)	0.258 (0.224)
Education: attended college	0.034 (0.151)	0.064 (0.216)	−0.112 (0.265)
Education: attended graduate school	−0.160 (0.243)	−0.484 (0.347)	−0.133 (0.401)

Table B2 *(cont.)*

	Dependent variable:		
	Less likely to shop at Walmart (five categories, increasing in likelihood of "boycott")		
	(1)	(2)	(3)
HHI: 20,000–34,999	0.432**	0.654**	0.441
	(0.201)	(0.281)	(0.376)
HHI: 35,000–49,999	0.557***	0.713**	0.384
	(0.210)	(0.296)	(0.373)
HHI: 50,000–74,999	0.463**	0.736**	0.104
	(0.211)	(0.296)	(0.370)
HHI: 75,000–99,999	0.150	−0.409	0.189
	(0.261)	(0.430)	(0.409)
HHI: 100,000+	0.133	0.484	−0.286
	(0.249)	(0.378)	(0.388)
White	0.166	0.337	−0.268
	(0.156)	(0.205)	(0.328)
NRCC × Republican	−1.032***		
	(0.400)		
NRCC × Democrat	1.333***		
	(0.382)		
Observations	900	439	323
Sample	Full	Democrats	Republicans

Note: $^*p < 0.1$; $^{**}p < 0.05$; $^{***}p < 0.01$

Full Results

The complete results, including controls, from the models in the chapter are in this section (Tables B1–B4). When interpreting these results, it is important to understand that each of the control variables is the effect of that variable on company approval compared with those in some reference group (e.g., women are compared with people who did not identify as women, education variables are compared with those who did not attend high school).

Table B3 *Dependent variable is a five-category response to the question "Does this information make you more likely, less likely, or equally likely to shop at Walmart?" The omitted category for "Woman" is "non-Woman" and includes both those who identify as men as well as those who identify as non-binary or neither man nor woman. White includes anyone who identifies as white, including those who identify with multiple races including white. DNCC, Democratic National Campaign Committee; HHI, household income; NRCC, National Republican Congressional Committee*

	Dependent variable:	
	Less likely to shop at Walmart (five categories, increasing in likelihood of "boycott")	
	(1)	(2)
Treatment: NRCC	0.861*** (0.225)	
Treatment: DNCC		1.082*** (0.253)
Infrequent Walmart Shopper	1.175*** (0.324)	0.993*** (0.350)
Age	0.025*** (0.006)	0.016** (0.007)
Disapprove of donations	0.727*** (0.219)	0.876*** (0.244)
Woman	0.516*** (0.191)	0.255 (0.224)
Education: attended college	0.043 (0.217)	−0.111 (0.265)
Education: attended graduate school	−0.543 (0.349)	−0.128 (0.402)
HHI: 20,000–34,999	0.699** (0.282)	0.445 (0.377)
HHI: 35,000–49,999	0.693** (0.296)	0.385 (0.373)
HHI: 50,000–74,999	0.828*** (0.298)	0.100 (0.371)
HHI: 75,000–99,999	−0.381 (0.426)	0.189 (0.409)

Appendix B Chapter 4 Study Methodology and Full Results

Table B3 *(cont.)*

	\multicolumn{2}{c}{Dependent variable:}
	\multicolumn{2}{c}{Less likely to shop at Walmart (five categories, increasing in likelihood of "boycott")}
	(1)	(2)
HHI: 100,000+	0.494 (0.380)	−0.289 (0.389)
White	0.329 (0.205)	−0.271 (0.328)
NRCC × Infrequent Shopper	1.185*** (0.448)	
DNCC × Infrequent Shopper		0.101 (0.557)
Observations	439	323
Sample	Democrats	Republicans

Note: $^*p < 0.1$; $^{**}p < 0.05$; $^{***}p < 0.01$

Table B4 *The effect of a company's actions on respondent approval. Each coefficient is compared with the group of people presented with a "nonresponse" action. Models are ordered logistic regressions with five categories and control for gender (woman vs. non-woman), education, household income, and race (white, including bi-/multi-racial vs. non-white).*

	\multicolumn{3}{c}{Dependent variable:}
	\multicolumn{3}{c}{Approval of:}
	Company A (Sugary drinks tax)	Company B (Minimum wage)	Company C (Undocumented immigration)
	(1)	(2)	(3)
Donated money	−0.730*** (0.194)	−1.267*** (0.199)	0.085 (0.187)

Table B4 *(cont.)*

	Dependent variable: Approval of:		
	Company A (Sugary drinks tax) (1)	Company B (Minimum wage) (2)	Company C (Undocumented immigration) (3)
Lobbied	0.058 (0.184)	−1.110*** (0.191)	−0.006 (0.185)
Pro-social	0.759*** (0.193)	0.151 (0.187)	0.257 (0.181)
Considering relocation	0.0003 (0.186)	−1.342*** (0.193)	−0.022 (0.191)
Age	−0.008** (0.004)	−0.002 (0.004)	−0.015*** (0.004)
Woman	−0.342*** (0.124)	−0.100 (0.123)	0.069 (0.121)
Education: attended college	−0.068 (0.141)	−0.127 (0.141)	−0.110 (0.138)
Education: attended graduate school	0.220 (0.223)	0.271 (0.230)	0.345 (0.224)
HHI: 20,000–34,999	0.154 (0.189)	0.031 (0.187)	0.131 (0.184)
HHI: 35,000–49,999	0.327 (0.199)	−0.096 (0.196)	0.010 (0.194)
HHI: 50,000–74,999	−0.062 (0.195)	−0.188 (0.196)	0.008 (0.191)
HHI: 75,000–99,999	−0.021 (0.238)	−0.048 (0.240)	−0.424* (0.241)
HHI: 100,000+	0.729*** (0.239)	0.236 (0.234)	0.418* (0.233)
White	0.065 (0.139)	−0.390*** (0.141)	−0.314** (0.137)
Observations	896	900	900

Note: $^*p < 0.1$; $^{**}p < 0.05$; $^{***}p < 0.01$

Appendix B Chapter 4 Study Methodology and Full Results   221

Table B5 *The effect of a company's actions on respondent approval among respondents who support the policy the company opposes. Each coefficient is compared with the group of people presented with a "nonresponse" action. Models are ordered logit with five categories and control for gender, education, household income, and race.*

	Dependent variable:		
		Approval of:	
	Company A (Sugary drinks tax)	Company B (Minimum wage)	Company C (Undocumented immigration)
	(1)	(2)	(3)
Donated money	−0.385 (0.295)	−1.552*** (0.242)	−0.123 (0.262)
Lobbied	−0.101 (0.269)	−1.538*** (0.239)	−0.282 (0.254)
Pro-social	0.958*** (0.268)	0.135 (0.227)	0.047 (0.249)
Considering relocation	−0.106 (0.299)	−1.785*** (0.243)	−0.323 (0.261)
Republican	0.534 (0.331)	0.527** (0.239)	0.449* (0.245)
Democrat	−0.057 (0.309)	0.007 (0.222)	0.732*** (0.252)
Age	−0.006 (0.006)	−0.001 (0.005)	−0.021*** (0.005)
Woman	−0.347* (0.185)	−0.030 (0.152)	0.159 (0.169)
Education: attended college	−0.425** (0.212)	−0.367** (0.180)	−0.131 (0.194)
Education: attended graduate school	−0.449 (0.326)	−0.026 (0.284)	0.304 (0.311)
HHI: 20,000–34,999	0.552* (0.294)	0.114 (0.225)	−0.124 (0.252)
HHI: 35,000–49,999	0.367 (0.289)	0.056 (0.240)	−0.298 (0.273)
HHI: 50,000–74,999	−0.065 (0.287)	−0.166 (0.241)	−0.304 (0.275)

Table B5 *(cont.)*

	Dependent variable:		
HHI: 75,000–99,999	−0.082 (0.379)	−0.026 (0.296)	−0.745** (0.313)
HHI: 100,000+	0.733** (0.347)	0.447 (0.290)	0.334 (0.319)
White	−0.211 (0.208)	−0.690*** (0.182)	−0.327 (0.203)
Observations	422	630	500

Note: $^*p < 0.1$; $^{**}p < 0.05$; $^{***}p < 0.01$

Table B6 *The effect of a company's actions on respondent approval among respondents who belong to the party associated with support for the policy the company opposes. Each coefficient is compared with the group of people presented with a "nonresponse" action. Models control for policy approval. Models are ordered logit with five categories and control for gender (women vs. non-women), education (omitted category: no college), household income (omitted category: less than $20,000), and race (white, including multiracial white vs. non-white)*

	Dependent variable:	
	Approval of:	
	Company B (Minimum wage) (1)	Company C (Undocumented immigration) (2)
Donated money	−1.464*** (0.294)	−0.216 (0.335)
Lobbied	−1.812*** (0.295)	−0.595* (0.321)
Considering relocation	−1.523*** (0.280)	−0.391 (0.323)
Pro-social	0.042 (0.267)	−0.189 (0.306)
Policy approval: Good	1.062*** (0.380)	0.693** (0.329)

Table B6 *(cont.)*

	Dependent variable: Approval of:	
	Company B (Minimum wage) (1)	Company C (Undocumented immigration) (2)
Policy approval: Neutral	0.250 (0.416)	0.319 (0.378)
Age	0.010 (0.006)	−0.016*** (0.006)
Woman	−0.055 (0.180)	0.248 (0.214)
Education: attended college	−0.432** (0.209)	−0.157 (0.246)
Education: attended graduate school	−0.102 (0.336)	−0.114 (0.373)
HHI: 20,000–34,999	−0.259 (0.265)	0.220 (0.348)
HHI: 35,000–49,999	−0.036 (0.281)	−0.214 (0.342)
HHI: 50,000–74,999	−0.277 (0.280)	−0.045 (0.342)
HHI: 75,000–99,999	−0.241 (0.397)	−1.049*** (0.391)
HHI: 100,000+	0.299 (0.356)	0.502 (0.373)
White	−0.518*** (0.192)	−0.083 (0.311)
Observations	439	324

Note: $^*p < 0.1$; $^{**}p < 0.05$; $^{***}p < 0.01$

Appendix C
Chapter 5 Robustness Checks

Table C1 recreates the models in Tables 5.2 and 5.3 but substitutes a company's operating revenue for the log of the number of employees as a measure of company size in an attempt to assess whether the underlying concept of size has a positive effect on the dependent variable rather than strictly the particular employee-based measure. Like number of employees, a company's operating revenue is also heavily skewed, but, unlike the number of employees, revenue can be negative or zero and therefore cannot be logged to put it on a more linear scale. Instead, I use the deciles of a company's revenue to indicate where it falls in the distribution relative to other companies.

With the exception of boycott, the results suggest that companies in higher deciles of operating revenue are more likely to cite these concerns (or, in the case of Model 4, contain at least one sentence linking social media with brand damage) as compared with very small companies. As described in Chapter 5, having a woman CEO is right on the threshold of conventional statistical significance for the social media model, again illustrating that it is quite likely companies led by women are systematically more likely to cite concerns about social media. The statistical significance of the finding that companies that own very valuable brands are less likely to cite concerns about reputation or brand damage also arises in this model, although it is slightly less statistically significant.

Appendix C Chapter 5 Robustness Checks

Table C1 *Logistic regressions predicting the occurrence of topics in the 10-Ks as a function of company attributes. Omitted category for operating revenue is 0–10th percentile*

	\multicolumn{4}{c}{Dependent variable:}
	Boycott (1)	Social media (2)	Reputation (3)	Social media + Rep. (4)
Revenue, 20th percentile	−0.321 (0.920)	−0.095 (0.501)	0.471 (0.368)	−13.796 (885.759)
Revenue, 30th percentile	−0.029 (0.837)	0.178 (0.472)	0.866** (0.395)	0.768 (1.188)
Revenue, 40th percentile	−0.557 (0.937)	0.376 (0.458)	0.810** (0.392)	0.948 (1.155)
Revenue, 50th percentile	0.439 (0.763)	1.188*** (0.431)	1.353*** (0.437)	2.319** (1.075)
Revenue, 60th percentile	0.149 (0.794)	0.980** (0.439)	0.900** (0.391)	2.431** (1.073)
Revenue, 70th percentile	1.005 (0.703)	0.733 (0.451)	0.604 (0.370)	2.278** (1.081)
Revenue, 80th percentile	0.639 (0.742)	1.244*** (0.434)	1.339*** (0.437)	2.520** (1.076)
Revenue, 90th percentile	0.099 (0.799)	1.325*** (0.431)	1.341*** (0.438)	2.581** (1.071)
Revenue, 100th percentile	0.616 (0.782)	1.873*** (0.436)	1.034** (0.449)	2.392** (1.093)
Woman CEO	0.415 (0.545)	0.517* (0.296)	0.261 (0.391)	0.374 (0.438)
Top 100 brand	0.741 (0.707)	−0.253 (0.417)	−0.995* (0.531)	0.596 (0.553)
Constant	−3.987*** (0.650)	−3.234*** (0.508)	1.453*** (0.308)	−5.146*** (1.063)

Table C1 *(cont.)*

	\multicolumn{4}{c}{*Dependent variable:*}
	Boycott (1)	Social media (2)	Reputation (3)	Social media + Rep. (4)
Observations	1,444	1,444	1,444	1,436
Log likelihood	−193.562	−542.999	−442.894	−293.140
Akaike inf. crit.	413.124	1,111.997	911.789	612.280
Bayesian inf. crit.	481.702	1,180.574	980.366	680.785

Note: $^{*}p < 0.1$; $^{**}p < 0.05$; $^{***}p < 0.01$

Appendix D
Chapter 6 Robustness Checks

In this section, I present the results of parametric tests (logistic regressions) for the lobbying and campaign contributions data. I present these for the sake of full transparency but with some notable caveats that will help explain why I preferred other methods of exploring the data in the main chapter. The main finding of these models, in both Tables D1 and D2, is that larger businesses – whether measured by revenue or number of employees (split into quartiles to handle outliers and scale of the measure) – are more likely to lobby or donate to campaigns through PACs than smaller businesses. Where possible, these models include industry random effects to deal with the particular regulatory/political pressures that individual industries are subject to. Yet, as discussed in Chapter 6, any regression by necessity will be comparing larger companies with smaller companies, which conflates their resources and ability to engage in advocacy with their concerns about doing so. In other words, although these can tell us if larger companies are more likely than smaller companies to lobby or contribute (they are), it cannot give us a sense of how many more companies might have engaged in the absence of a fear. We record only what actually happened, not the counterfactual. In that way, these findings are not especially useful.

The secondary issue has to do with missing data in statistical models. Missing data in the underlying Orbis data set means that adding variables to the model reduces the number of complete observations that I can use to estimate the model. This is problematic on its own, but it is primarily a concern because there are already so few women CEOs in the data, meaning that reducing that number any further hurts my ability to draw any conclusions about the effect of CEO gender. Models (3) and (4) in Table D2, for instance, include data on revenue and leadership on the gender of the top leadership position in the company. This results in only 5,455 complete observations but

Table D1 *Logistic regressions predicting lobbying or contributions through PACs as a function of company size*

	Dependent variable:			
	At least one lobbying report logistic		At least one PAC contribution logistic	
	(1)	(2)	(3)	(4)
2nd Quartile: revenue	0.391 (0.288)		0.631 (1.225)	
3rd Quartile: revenue	1.579*** (0.246)		0.923 (1.155)	
4th Quartile: revenue	3.516*** (0.238)		3.427*** (1.014)	
2nd Quartile: employees		1.456*** (0.280)		0.059 (1.415)
3rd Quartile: employees		2.592*** (0.270)		2.277** (1.055)
4th Quartile: employees		3.775*** (0.267)		3.459*** (1.018)
Constant	−4.558*** (0.240)	−4.426*** (0.263)	−7.186*** (1.000)	−6.884*** (1.000)
Industry REs	Yes	Yes	No	No
Observations	5,931	3,731	5,931	3,731
Log likelihood	−1,505.288	−1,249.482	−221.589	−195.016
Akaike inf. crit.	3,020.576	2,508.965	451.178	398.031

Note: $^*p < 0.1$; $^{**}p < 0.05$; $^{***}p < 0.01$

with only 337 women, about 6 percent of the sample. Combining this lack of data with the very strong effect of company size (I use revenue in these because it has less missingness than employees) makes it difficult to detect an effect of gender, although the coefficient is always

Appendix D Chapter 6 Robustness Checks

Table D2 *Logistic regressions predicting lobbying or contributions through PACs as a function of company size and CEO gender*

	\multicolumn{4}{c}{Dependent variable:}			
	Lobbying logistic (1)	Contributions logistic (2)	Lobbying logistic (3)	Contributions logistic (4)
2nd Quartile: revenue			0.403 (0.289)	0.620 (1.225)
3rd Quartile: revenue			1.525*** (0.247)	0.866 (1.155)
4th Quartile: revenue			3.376*** (0.239)	3.293*** (1.014)
Male CEO	0.190 (0.180)	37.561*** (5.162)	0.119 (0.209)	14.619 (540.671)
Constant	−2.614*** (0.194)	−43.658*** (5.162)	−4.516*** (0.314)	−21.601 (540.672)
Industry REs	Yes	Yes	Yes	No
Observations	15,192	15,192	5,455	5,455
Log likelihood	−2,198.366	−270.904	−1,486.905	−218.007
Akaike inf. crit.	4,402.731	547.808	2,985.810	446.013
Bayesian inf. crit.	4,425.617	570.693	3,025.436	

Note: *$p < 0.1$; **$p < 0.05$; ***$p < 0.01$

positive. Finally, because contributions are so rare in the data, those models often cannot run with the random effects because the fitted model is singular. As with any uncommon event, you can only stretch the data so many ways before the models break.

References

Aaker, Jennifer L. 1997. "Dimensions of Brand Personality." *Journal of Marketing Research* 34: 347–356.

Ansolabehere, Stephen, John M. de Figueiredo, and James M. Snyder Jr. 2003. "Why Is There so Little Money in U.S. Politics?" *Journal of Economic Perspectives* 17 (1): 105–130.

Baaij, Marc G., Tom J. M. Mom, Frans A. J. Van den Bosch, and Henk W. Volberda. 2015. "Why Do Multinational Corporations Relocate Core Parts of Their Corporate Headquarters Abroad?" *Long Range Planning* 48 (1): 46–58.

Baccini, Leonardo, Pablo M. Pinto, and Stephen Weymouth. 2017. "The Distributional Consequences of Preferential Trade Liberalization: Firm-Level Evidence." *International Organization* 71 (2): 373–395.

Barberá, Pablo. 2015. "Birds of the Same Feather Tweet Together: Bayesian Ideal Point Estimation using Twitter Data." *Political Analysis* 23 (1): 76–91.

Barnes, Tiffany D. and Emily Beaulieu. 2014. "Gender Stereotypes and Corruption: How Candidates Affect Perceptions of Election Fraud." *Politics & Gender* 10 (3): 365–391.

Baron, David P. 2001. "Private Politics, Corporate Social Responsibility, and Integrated Strategy." *Journal of Economics & Management Strategy* 10 (1): 7–45.

Baron, David P. and Daniel Diermeier. 2007. "Strategic Activism and Nonmarket Strategy." *Journal of Economics & Management Strategy* 16 (3): 599–634.

Bartley, Tim and Curtis Child. 2014. "Shaming the Corporation: The Social Production of Targets and the Anti-Sweatshop Movement." *American Sociological Review* 79 (4): 653–679.

Bauer, Raymond Augustine, Ithiel De Sola Pool, and Lewis Anthony Dexter. 1972. *American Business and Public Policy: The Politics of Foreign Trade*. 2nd ed. Transaction.

Bel, Germá, Robert Hebdon, and Mildred Warner. 2018. "Beyond Privatisation and Cost Savings: Alternatives for Local Government Reform." *Local Government Studies* 44 (2): 173–182.

Benedictis-Kessner, Justin de and Christopher Warshaw. 2020. "Politics in Forgotten Governments: The Partisan Composition of County Legislatures and County Fiscal Policies." *Journal of Politics* 82 (2): 460–475.

Benoit, Kenneth, Kohei Watanabe, Haiyan Wang, Paul Nulty, Adam Obeng, Stefan Müller, and Akitaka Matsuo. 2018. "Quanteda: An R Package for the Quantitative Analysis of Textual Data." *Journal of Open Source Software* 3 (30): 774. DOI: 10.21105/joss.00774.https://quanteda.io.

Berry, Christopher R. and William G. Howell. 2007. "Accountability and Local Elections: Rethinking Retrospective Voting." *Journal of Politics* 69 (3): 844–858.

Bertrand, Marianne, Matilde Bombardini, and Francesco Trebbi. 2014. "Is It Whom You Know or What You Know? An Empirical Assessment of the Lobbying Process." *American Economic Review* 104 (12): 3885–3920.

Bertrand, Marianne, Matilde Bombardini, Raymond Fisman, and Francesco Trebbi. 2018. "Tax-Exempt Lobbying: Corporate Philanthropy as a Tool for Political Influence." No. *w24451*. *National Bureau of Economic Research* 110 (7): 2065–2102.

Birkinshaw, Julian, Pontus Braunerhjelm, Ulf Holm, and Siri Terjesen. 2006. "Why Do Some Multinational Corporations Relocate their Headquarters Overseas?" *Strategic Management Journal* 27 (7): 681–700.

Bleich, Erik and Robert Pekkanen. 2013. "How to Report Interview Data." *Interview Research in Political Science* 1: 84–105.

Bloem, Jeffrey. 2019. "Good Intentions Gone Bad? The Dodd-Frank Act and Conflict in Africa's Great Lakes Region." *Households in Conflict Network Working Paper, No. 300*.

Brass, Jennifer N. 2016. *Allies or Adversaries: NGOs and the State in Africa*. Cambridge University Press.

2014. "The Politics of Non-state Social Welfare," ed. Melani Cammett and Lauren M. MacLean, 99–118. *Section: Blurring the Boundaries: NGOs, the State, and Service Provision in Kenya*. Cornell University Press.

Budac, Camelia and Lia Baltador. 2013. "The Value of Brand Equity." *Procedia Economics and Finance* 6: 444–448.

Burnett, Craig M. and Vladimir Kogan. 2016. "The Politics of Potholes: Service Quality and Retrospective Voting in Local Elections." *Journal of Politics* 79 (1): 302–314.

Busch, Marc L. and Eric Reinhardt. 2000. "Geography, International Trade, and Political Mobilization in U.S. Industries." *American Journal of Political Science*: 703–719.

Carlin, George. 1972. "Seven Words You Can Never Say on Television." On Album Class Clown (Side two). Santa Monica, CA: Little David/Atlantic. www.youtube.com/watch?v=kyBH5oNQOS0.

Christensen, Henrik Serup. 2011. "Political Activities on the Internet: Slacktivism or Political Participation by Other Means?" *First Monday* 16 (2).

Cohen, Elisha, Anna Gunderson, Kaylyn Jackson, Paul Zachary, Tom S. Clark, Adam N. Glynn, and Michael Leo Owens. 2019. "Do Officer-Involved Shootings Reduce Citizen Contact with Government?" *Journal of Politics* 81 (3): 1111–1123.

Cook, Alison and Christy Glass. 2014. "Above the Glass Ceiling: When are Women and Racial/Ethnic Minorities Promoted to CEO?" *Strategic Management Journal* 35 (7): 1080–1089.

2013. "Glass Cliffs and Organizational Saviors: Barriers to Minority Leadership in Work Organizations?" *Social Problems* 60 (2): 168–187.

Cooper-McCann, Patrick. 2016. "The Trap of Triage: Lessons from the 'Team Four Plan'." *Journal of Planning History* 15 (2): 149–169.

Cottom, Tressie McMillan. 2019. "Girl 6." In *Thick: and Other Essays* 195–223. New Press.
Crittenden, William F., Victoria L. Crittenden, and Allison Pierpont. 2015. "Trade Secrets: Managerial Guidance for Competitive Advantage." *Business Horizons* 58 (6): 607–613.
de Figueiredo, John M. and Brian Kelleher Richter. 2014. "Advancing the Empirical Research on Lobbying." *Annual Review of Political Science* 17: 163–185.
Delgado-Ballester, Elena, Inés López-López, and Alicia Bernal-Palazón. 2019. "How Harmful are Online Firestorms for Brands? An Approach to the Phenomenon from the Participant Level." *Spanish Journal of Marketing* 24 (1): 133–151.
DeSantis, Victor S. and Tari Renner. 2002. "City Government Structures: An Attempt at Classification." *State and Local Government Review* 34 (2): 95–104.
Diermeier, Daniel. 2011. *Reputation Rules: Strategies for Building Your Company's Most Valuable Asset*. McGraw Hill.
Eckhouse, Laurel. 2019. "Race, Party, and Representation in Criminal Justice Politics." *Journal of Politics* 81 (3): 1143–1152.
Einstein, Katherine Levine and Vladimir Kogan. 2016. "Pushing the City Limits: Policy Responsiveness in Municipal Government." *Urban Affairs Review* 52 (1): 3–32.
Endres, Kyle and Costas Panagopoulos. 2017. "Boycotts, Buycotts, and Political Consumerism in America." *Research and Politics* 4 (4): 1–9.
Esarey, Justin and Gina Chirillo. 2013. "'Fairer Sex' or Purity Myth? Corruption, Gender, and Institutional Context." *Politics & Gender* 9 (4): 361–389.
Ettenson, Richard and Jonathan Knowles. 2008. "Don't Confuse Reputation with Brand." *MIT Sloan Management Review* 49 (2): 19–21.
Federico, Christopher M. and Pierce D. Ekstrom. 2018. "The Political Self: How Identity Aligns Preferences with Epistemic Needs." *Psychological Science* 29 (6): 901–913.
Feng, Yilang, Andrew Kerner, and Jane L. Sumner. 2019. "Quitting Globalization: Trade-Related Job Losses, Nationalism, and Resistance to FDI in the United States." *Political Science Research and Methods* 9 (2): 292–311.
Fortunato, David and Tessa Provins. 2017. "Compensation, Opportunity, and Information: A Comparative Analysis of Legislative Nonresponse in the American States." *Political Research Quarterly* 70 (3): 644–656.
Fournier, Susan and Shuba Srinivasan. 2018. "Branding and the Risk Management Imperative." *GfK Marketing Intelligence Review* 10 (1): 10–17.
Franca, Valentina and Marko Pahor. 2012. "The Strength of the Employer Brand: Influences and Implications for Recruiting." *Journal of Marketing & Management* 3 (1): 78–122.

Gawande, Kishore and Usree Bandyopadhyay. 2000. "Is Protection for Sale? Evidence on the Grossman-Helpman Theory of Endogenous Protection." *Review of Economics and Statistics* 82 (1): 139–152.

Gazley, Beth. 2008. "Beyond the Contract: The Scope and Nature of Informal Government-Nonprofit Partnerships." *Public Administration Review* 68 (1): 141–154.

Goode, Erich and Nachman Ben-Yehuda. 1994. "Moral Panics: Culture, Politics, and Social Construction." *Annual Review of Sociology* 20: 149–171.

Grossman, Gene and Elhanan Helpman. 1992. "Protection for Sale." *American Economic Review* 84 (4): 833–850.

Grumbach, Jacob M. and Paul Pierson. 2019. "Are Large Corporations Politically Moderate? Using Money in Politics to Infer the Preferences of Business." *Working Paper*.

Guisinger, Alexandra. 2009. "Determining Trade Policy: Do Voters hold Politicians Accountable?" *International Organization* 63 (3): 533–557.

Hall, Richard L. and Alan V. Deardorff. 2006. "Lobbying as Legislative Subsidy." *American Political Science Review* 100 (1): 69–84.

Hannah, David, Michael Parent, Leyland Pitt, and Pierre Berthon. 2014. "It's a Secret: Marketing Value and the Denial of Availability." *Business Horizons* 57 (1): 49–59.

Hansen, Nele, Ann-Kristin Kupfer, and Thorsten Hennig-Thurau. 2018. "Brand Crises in the Digital Age: The Short-and Long-Term Effects of Social Media Firestorms on Consumers and Brands." *International Journal of Research in Marketing* 35 (4): 557–574.

Heger, Lindsay, Danielle Jung, and Wendy H. Wong. 2012. "Organizing for Resistance: How Group Structure Impacts the Character of Violence." *Terrorism and Political Violence* 24 (5): 743–768.

Hertel-Fernandez, Alexander. 2019. *State Capture: How Conservative Activists, Big Businesses, and Wealthy Donors Reshaped the American States – and the Nation*. Oxford University Press.

2018. *Politics at Work: How Companies Turn Their Workers into Lobbyists*. Oxford University Press.

Hirschman, Albert O. 1972. *Exit, Voice, and Loyalty*. Harvard University Press.

Hiscox, Michael J. 2002. "Commerce, Coalitions, and Factor Mobility: Evidence from Congressional Votes on Trade Legislation." *American Political Science Review* 96 (3): 593–608.

Holman, Mirya R., J. Celeste Lay, Jill Greenlee, Zoe Oxley, and Angela Bos. 2019. "Partisanship on the Playground: Political Preferences and Negative Partisanship Among Children." *Working Paper*.

Hyde, Charles Cheney and Louis B. Wehle. 1933. "The Boycott in Foreign Affairs." *American Journal of International Law* 27 (1): 1–10.

Jensen, Nathan M. 2006. *Nation-States and the Multinational Corporation: A Political Economy of Foreign Direct Investment*. Princeton University Press.

Jensen, Nathan M. and Edmund J. Malesky. 2018. *Incentives to Pander: How Politicians Use Corporate Welfare for Political Gain*. Cambridge University Press.

Johnen, Marius, Marc Jungblut, and Marc Ziegele. 2018. "The Digital Outcry: What Incites Participation in an Online Firestorm." *New Media & Society* 20 (9): 3140–3160.

Johnston, Christopher D., Howard G. Lavine, and Christopher M. Federico. 2017. *Open versus Closed: Personality, Identity, and the Politics of Redistribution*. Cambridge University Press.

Kalla, Joshua L. and David E. Broockman. 2016. "Campaign Contributions Facilitate Access to Congressional Officials: A Randomized Field Experiment." *American Journal of Political Science* 60 (3): 545–558.

Keller, Franziska B., David Schoch, Sebastian Stier, and JungHwan Yang. 2020. "Political Astroturfing on Twitter: How to Coordinate a Disinformation Campaign." *Political Communication* 37 (2): 256–280.

Keller, Kevin Lane. 1993. "Conceptualizing, Measuring, and Managing Customer-Based Brand Equity." *Journal of Marketing* 57: 1–22.

Keller, Kevin Lane and Donald R. Lehmann. 2006. "Brands and Branding: Research Findings and Future Priorities." *Marketing Science* 25 (6): 740–759.

Keller, Kevin Lane and Keith Richey. 2006. "The Importance of Corporate Brand Personality Traits to a Successful 21st Century Business." *Journal of Brand Management* 14 (1–2): 74–81.

Kerner, Andrew. 2014. "What We Talk About When We Talk About Foreign Direct Investment." *International Studies Quarterly* 58 (4): 804–815.

Kerner, Andrew and Jane Lawrence. 2014. "What's the Risk? Bilateral Investment Treaties, Political Risk and Fixed Capital Accumulation." *British Journal of Political Science* 44: 107–121.

Kerner, Andrew and Jane Lawrence Sumner. 2019. "Salvation by Good Works? Offshoring, Corporate Philanthropy, and Public Attitudes Toward Trade Policy." *Economics & Politics* 32 (1): 1–10.

Kerner, Andrew, Jane Lawrence Sumner, and Brian Kelleher Richter. 2020. "Offshore Production's Effect on Americans' Attitudes Toward Trade." *Business & Politics* 22 (3): 539–571.

Kim, In Song. 2018. *Lobbyview: Firm-level Lobbying & Congressional Bills Database*. Technical report. Working Paper available from http://web.mit.edu/insong/www/pdf/lobbyview.pdf.

2017a. "Political Cleavages within Industry: Firm-level Lobbying for Trade Liberalization." *American Political Science Review* 111 (1): 1–20.

Kim, In Song and Iain Osgood. 2019. "Firms in Trade and Trade Politics." *Annual Review of Political Science* 22: 399–417.

Kim, Yunji. 2017b. "Limits of Property Taxes and Charges: City Revenue Structures after the Great Recession." *Urban Affairs Review* 55 (1): 185–209.

Kim, Yunji and Mildred E. Warner. 2016. "Pragmatic Municipalism: Local Government Service Delivery after the Great Recession." *Public Administration* 94 (3): 789–805.

King, Brayden G. and Sarah A. Soule. 2007. "Social Movements as Extra-Institutional Entrepreneurs: The Effect of Protests on Stock Price Returns." *Administrative Science Quarterly* 52 (3): 413–442.

Klein, Jill Gabrielle, N. Craig Smith, and Andrew John. 2004. "Why We Boycott: Consumer Motivations for Boycott Participation." *Journal of Marketing* 68 (3): 92–109.

Kogan, Vladimir, Stéphane Lavertu, and Zachary Peskowitz. 2018. "Election Timing, Electorate Composition, and Policy Outcomes: Evidence from School Districts." *American Journal of Political Science* 62 (3): 637–651.

2016. "Performance Federalism and Local Democracy: Theory and Evidence from School Tax Referenda." *American Journal of Political Science* 60 (2): 418–435.

Kono, Daniel Y. 2006. "Optimal Obfuscation: Democracy and Trade Policy Transparency." *American Political Science Review* 100 (3): 369–384.

Kristofferson, Kirk, Katherine White, and John Peloza. 2014. "The Nature of Slacktivism: How the Social Observability of an Initial Act of Token Support Affects Subsequent Prosocial action." *Journal of Consumer Research* 40 (6): 1149–1166.

Lenox, Michael J. and Charles E. Eesley. 2009. "Private Environmental Activism and the Selection and Response of Firm Targets." *Journal of Economics & Management Strategy* 18 (1): 45–73.

Malhotra, Neil, Benôit Monin, and Michael Tomz. 2019. "Does Private Regulation Preempt Public Regulation." *American Political Science Review* 113 (1): 19–37.

Mares, Isabela. 2003. *The Politics of Social Risk: Business and Welfare State Development*. Cambridge University Press.

Mason, Liliana. 2018. *Uncivil Agreement: How Politics Became Our Identity*. University of Chicago Press.

Milyo, Jeffrey, David Primo, and Timothy Groseclose. 2000. "Corporate PAC Campaign Contributions in Perspective." *Business and Politics* 2 (1): 75–88.

Morozov, Evgeny. 2009. "The Brave New World of Slacktivism." *Foreign Policy*. https://foreignpolicy.com/2009/05/19/the-brave-new-world-of-slacktivism/.

Motta, Matthew P. 2019. "Political Scientists: A Profile of the Congressional Candidates with STEM Backgrounds." *Working Paper*.

Mounk, Yascha. 2018. "America Is Not a Democracy." *The Atlantic*. www.theatlantic.com/magazine/archive/2018/03/america-is-not-a-democracy/550931/.
Nelson, Kimberly L. 2012. "Municipal Choices during a Recession: Bounded Rationality and Innovation." *State and Local Government Review* 44 (1): 44S–63S.
O'Connor, Amy. 2006. "Merchant of Mercy, Merchant of Death: How Values Advocacy Messages Influence Jury Deliberations." *Journal of Applied Communication Research* 34 (3): 263–284.
Osgood, Iain, Dustin Tingley, Thomas Bernauer, In Song Kim, Helen V. Milner, and Gabriele Spilker. 2017. "The Charmed Life of Superstar Exporters: Survey Evidence on Firms and Trade Policy." *The Journal of Politics* 79 (1): 133–152.
Osuna Ramírez, Sergio Andrés, Cleopatra Veloutsou, and Anna Morgan-Thomas. 2019. "I Hate What You Love: Brand Polarization and Negativity Towards Brands as an Opportunity for Brand Management." *Journal of Product & Brand Management* 28 (5): 614–632.
Owen, Erica. 2017. "Exposure to Offshoring and the Politics of Trade Liberalization: Debates and Votes on Free Trade Agreements in the U.S. House of Representatives, 2001–2006." *International Studies Quarterly* 61 (2): 297–311.
Owen, Erica, and Noel Johnston. 2017. "Occupation and the Political Economy of Trade: Job Routineness, Offshorability and Protectionist Sentiment." *International Organization* 71 (4): 665–699.
Pagano, Marco, Fabio Panetta, and Luigi Zingales. 1998. "Why Do Companies Go Public? An Empirical Analysis." *The Journal of Finance* 53 (1): 27–64.
Pandya, Sonal S. and Rajkumar Venkatesan. 2016. "French Roast: Consumer Response to International Conflict - Evidence from Supermarket Scanner Data." *Review of Economics & Statistics* 98 (1): 42–56.
Peterson, Paul E. 1981. *City Limits*. University of Chicago Press.
Pfeffer, Jürgen, Thomas Zorbach, and Kathleen M. Carley. 2014. "Understanding Online Firestorms: Negative Word-of-Mouth Dynamics in Social Media Networks." *Journal of Marketing Communication* 20 (1–2): 117–128.
Powell, Eleanor Neff and Justin Grimmer. 2016. "Money in Exile: Campaign Contributions and Committee Access." *Journal of Politics* 78 (4): 974–988.
Rauschnabel, Philipp A., Nadine Kammerlander, and Björn S. Ivens. 2016. "Collaborative Brand Attacks in Social Media: Exploring the Antecedents, Characteristics, and Consequences of a New Form of Brand Crises." *Journal of Marketing Theory and Practice* 24 (4): 381–410.
Riffkin, Rebecca. 2016. "Majority of Americans Dissatisfied with Corporate Influence." *Gallup* (January). https://news.gallup.com/poll/188747/majority-americans-dissatisfied-corporate-influence.aspx.

Ritter, Emily Hencken and Christian Davenport. 2021. "An Illustrated Glossary of Political Violence." *Political Violence at a Glance*. https://politicalviolenceataglance.org/2021/01/18/an-illustrated-glossary-of-political-violence/.

Romaniuk, Jenni and Magda Nenycz-Thiel. 2013. "Behavioral Brand Loyalty and Consumer Brand Associations." *Journal of Business Research* 66 (1): 67–72.

Rothkopf, David. 2012. *Power, Inc.* Farrar, Straus and Giroux.

Ryan, Michelle K., and S. Alexander Haslam. 2007. "The Glass Cliff: Exploring the Dynamics Surrounding the Appointment of Women to Precarious Leadership Positions." *Academy of Management Review* 32 (2): 549–572.

2005. "The Glass Cliff: Evidence that Women are Over-Represented in Precarious Leadership Positions." *British Journal of Management* 16 (2): 81–90.

Scholz, Joachim and Andrew N. Smith. 2019. "Branding in the Age of Social Media Firestorms: How to Create Brand Value by Fighting Back Online." *Journal of Marketing Management* 35 (11–12): 1100–1134.

Snyder, Jr., James M. 1992. "Long-Term Investing in Politicians; Or, Give Early, Given Often." *Journal of Law and Economics* 35 (1): 15–43.

Stolle, Dietlind and Michele Micheletti. 2013. *Political Consumerism*. Cambridge University Press.

Stone, Clarence N. 1989. *Regime Politics: Governing Atlanta, 1946–1988*. University Press of Kansas.

Stratmann, Thomas. 1998. "The Market for Congressional Votes: Is Timing of Contributions Everything?" *Journal of Law and Economics* 41 (1): 85–114.

Sumner, Jane L., Emily M. Farris, and Mirya R. Holman. 2019. "Crowdsourcing Reliable Local Data." *Political Analysis* 28 (2): 244–262.

Tiebout, Charles M. 1956. "A Pure Theory of Local Expenditures." *Journal of political economy* 64 (5): 416–424.

U.S. Bureau of Labor Statistics. 2019. "Characteristics of Minimum Wage Workers, 2018." *BLS Reports*. www.bls.gov/opub/reports/minimum-wage/2018/pdf/home.pdf.

Vernon, Raymond. 1971. *Sovereignty at Bay*. Longman.

Walker, Jack L. 1983. "The Origin and Maintenance of Interest Groups in America." *American Political Science Review* 77 (2): 390–406.

Index

10-Ks reports (SEC), 137–139, *143*, *148*, *150*, 154

Abercrombie & Fitch, 142
activism, *see also* public backlash; boycotts; firestorms, 65–66
activists, 54–56
adverse policies, 1–2, 7, 51–54
advocacy, political, *see also* influence-seeking, influence, political
  "careful", 81–82, 90, 93, 166
  "creative", 79–81, 90, 93, 165, 190
  "distanced", 77–79, 164–165, 185–188
  "hidden", 75–76, 164–165, 184–185, 191
  company size, *178*, 177–179
  future research, 202–203
  gender differences, *180*, 179–181
  strategies for, 21, 72–74, 79, 83, 164–165, 167, 184, 188, 192
  traditional methods of, 174–179, 190–191
advocacy, political
  "creative", 188
Affordable Care Act (2010), 42
Amazon, 64
"America Is Not a Democracy" (Mounk), 61
American Beverage Association, The, 77
American Public Education, Inc., 145
Ascena Retail Group, 145
assets
  corporate, 29–31, 69–70
  intangible, 69
astroturfing, 78

Bloomin' Brands (Outback Steakhouse, Carrabba's Italian Grill, etc.), 145
Boot Barn, 155
boycott tweets, *see also* Twitter; social media, *122*, 120–123
boycotts, *see also* public backlash;
  activism as statement of values, 66–68, 87–88
  corporate responses to, 135–137
  counterclaims, 90–93, 135–137, 167–168
  impact on companies, 3, 160, 66–160, 196–197
  role of partisanship, 86, 88–89, 106, 194
  traditional vs. online, 133–134
brand damage, 20–21, 132, 135, 143–145, 147–154, 194, 196–197
brand, corporate
  fragility of, 69–70, 131, 134, 147–149, 194, 196–197
  impact of social media on, 145, 144–147
  public perceptions of, 154–155, 160
business interests, *see also* interest groups; special interests, 10–11, 25
buycott, 168

Callon Petroleum, 146
campaign contributions, *see also* donations, political; philanthropy, 4, 41–42, 174, *176*
careful advocacy, 81–82, 90, 93, 166
carve-outs, 2
Cassava Sciences, 146
Chambers of Commerce, 77
Chick-fil-A, 62

238

Index

Citizens United v. FEC, 6
City Limits (Peterson), 27
Coca-Cola Company, 158
community service, *see also* public/municipal services; philanthropy, 80
consumerism, political, *see also* boycotts, 19–20, 62, 64, 66
consumption good, 6
contract lobbyists, *see also* lobbyists, 8, 31, 36, 187, 198
corporate assets, 29–31, 69–70
COVID-19, corporate response to, 204
creative advocacy, 79–81, 90, 93, 165, 188–190

Darden Restaurants (Olive Garden), 156
distanced advocacy, 77–79, 164–165, 185–188
Domino's, 142
donations, political, *see also* campaign contributions, 75
Dunkin' Donuts, 141

exchange theory, 4–6, 33–35
exit, voice, and loyalty framework, 25

Federal Election Commission (FEC), 32, 75
firestorms, *see also* public backlash; activism; boycotts, 70–72, 82–83
Ford Motor Company, 142

geo-fencing, 187
Google, 142
Goya Foods, 19, 84–85

hidden advocacy, 75–76, 164–165, 184–185, 191
Hirschman, Albert O., 25
Home Depot, 123, 126

identity, political, *see also* signaling, political, 85–86, 88
industry groups, *see also* trade associations, 77–78

influence strategies, 4, 23, 49–50, 164–165, 167, 187–188, 192, 195–197, 200
influence, political, *see also* influence-seeking, advocacy, political
 as problem-solving, 37, 38, 193
 definition of corporate, 17
 extent of, 12, 24
 in local government, 13–16
 methods of, 4
 negative perceptions of, 4, 11, 61–62
 theories regarding, 25–26
influence-seeking, *see also* advocacy, political, influence, political
 as a relationship, 8–9, 18, 22, 36–37, 48–49, 200
 as form of exchange, 4–6, 33
 as form of persuasion, 35–36
 definition of, 18
 impact of corporate mobility on, 26–27
 in exit, voice, and loyalty framework, 25
 informal, 78, 187–188, 198
 public backlash and, 3, 11–12, 19, 130, 193–194
 public perceptions of, 128
 traditional methods of, 31–33, 41–42, *175*
information gaps, legislative, 6–8, 38–40, 198
insurrection, corporate response to, 203
intangible assets, 69
interest groups, *see also* business interests, 10

job performance, political, 44–48
Johnson & Johnson, 69

King, Steve (Rep.), 19, 62

Land O'Lakes, 19, 62
legislative subsidy, 4, 7, 36, 49
lobbying, *see also* advocacy, political
 "grassroots", 187–188
 as form of persuasion, 6–7
 as legislative subsidy, 7, 36
 corporate use of, 174, *175*
 definition of, 4, 31, 33

negative perceptions of, 22, 33, 158–159
reporting requirements, 75–76, 200–201
lobbyists, *see also* contract lobbyists, 31, 35, 40, 198

mass public, 60–61, 89–90
mass recruitment, 65–66
Micheletti, Michele, 66
mobility, corporate, 26–31
Monster Beverage Company, 158
Mounk, Yascha, 61

National Restaurant Association, The, 77
negative partisanship, 63
Nike, 123, 126

obsolescing bargain, 26, 28
Ocasio-Cortez, Alexandria, 84
Olive Garden, 19
organized interests, *see also* business interests, 9, 22

PACs (political action committees), 4, 9, 32, 98–101, 174, *176*, 181–183
partisanship, 62–65, 68, 81–82, 86, 98–106, 121, 126–128, 194
Peterson, Paul E., 27
philanthropy, *see also* public/municipal services, 33, 80, 189–190
political action committees, *see* PACs
Political Consumerism, 66
private politics, 55–56
probability, role of, 52, 54, 55, 59, 68, 72–74, 82–83
public backlash, *see also* boycotts; activism, firestorms
 influence-seeking and, 3, 11–12, 19, 130, 193–194, 197
 internet and, 65–66, 204–205
 mass public and, 60–61, 89–90
 partisanship and, 62–65, 81–82, 194
 probability and, 52, 54, 55, 59, 68, 72–74, 82–83
public/municipal services, *see also* community service; philanthropy, 188–189

reporting requirements, 75–76, 200–201
risk factors, corporate
 brand damage, 150–152
 company size as, *57*, 153, 160–161
 gender differences as, 57–59
 social media and, 160–161
 study methodology, 142–144, 152–153
 types of, 135, 141–142, *150*, 149–150, 194
Rocky Mountain Chocolate Factory, 141

Securities and Exchange Commission (SEC), 20, 132, 137, 160
signaling, political, *see also* identity, political, 68, 123, 128, 193
social media, *see also* Twitter; boycott tweets, 145, 144–149, *153*, 155–156, 204–205
special interests, *see also* business interests, 10
Starbucks, 158
Stolle, Dietlind, 66
study methodology
 10-Ks reports (SEC), 137–139, *143*, *148*, *150*, 154
 local government, 16
 boycott tweets, 95, *122*, 120–123
 corporate risk factors, 142–144, 149–150, 152–153, 160–161
 influence strategies, 97–98, 111–112, *114*, 172–173, 195
 influence-seeking, 128
 interviews, 139–141, 154, 169, 172–173, 195
 lobbying and campaign finance data, 169–171
 Nike, Home Depot, 123–126
 PAC donations, 98–101
 partisan language, 121, *127*, 124–129
 partisanship, *101*, 102, *103*, *105*, *107*, *108*, *110*, 96–111, *116*, *117*, 114–118, *127*, 128
 political signaling, 128
 social media, 94–96, 128–129
 survey data, 93–94
 Twitter data, 119
 Walmart, 96, 98

Target, 157

Index

Tiebout model, 27, 28

trade associations, *see also* industry groups, 185

Twitter, *see also* social media; boycott tweets, 20, 95–96, 119

Walmart, 96, 98, *99–101, 103, 105, 107, 108, 110*

wants and needs, political
 campaign financing, 41
 definition of, 9, 18, 23–24, 193
 information gaps, 38–40
 job performance, 44

Books in the Series (continued from page ii)

CHRISTIAN R. THAUER *The Managerial Sources of Corporate Social Responsibility: The Spread of Global Standards*
MICHAEL P. VANDENBERG AND JONATHAN M. GILLIGAN *Beyond Politics: The Private Governance Response to Climate Change*
JEROEN VAN DER HEIJDEN *Innovations in Urban Climate Governance: Voluntary Programs for Low Carbon Buildings and Cities*
KIYOTERU TSUTSUI AND ALWYN LIM (EDITORS) *Corporate Social Responsibility in a Globalizing World*
LLEWELYN HUGHES *Globalizing Oil: Firms and Oil Market Governance in France, Japan, and the United States*
VICTOR MENALDO *The Institutions Curse: Natural Resources, Politics, and Development*
ASEEMA SINHA *Globalizing India: How Global Rules and Markets are Shaping India's Rise to Power*
HEVINA S. DASHWOOD *The Rise of Global Corporate Social Responsibility: Mining and the Spread of Global Norms*
EDWARD T. WALKER *Grassroots for Hire: Public Affairs Consultants in American Democracy*

Printed in the United States
by Baker & Taylor Publisher Services